CONGRESS

ITS CONTEMPORARY ROLE

FOURTH EDITION

ERNEST S. GRIFFITH

NEW YORK
UNIVERSITY
PRESS

$3.95

Congress

its contemporary role

Congress

its contemporary role

BY ERNEST S. GRIFFITH

FOURTH EDITION

New York • NEW YORK UNIVERSITY PRESS
London • UNIVERSITY OF LONDON PRESS LIMITED
1967

COPYRIGHT © 1951, 1956, 1961, 1967 BY NEW YORK UNIVERSITY
FIRST IMPRESSION, FOURTH EDITION
LIBRARY OF CONGRESS CATALOG CARD NUMBER: 67–11316
PRINTED IN THE UNITED STATES OF AMERICA

Preface

TO THE FOURTH EDITION

Since about 1958 there has appeared a veritable flood of new articles and books on Congress. These have greatly exceeded in number those during the same period on the Presidency. What this shift in interest signifies is difficult to say. In part, it is a reflection of the recent Congressional Intern Program of the American Political Science Association, many of whose participants have been among the most perceptive of the new generation of writers. In part, it is doubtless accounted for by the rich mine of empirical and quantitative material in congressional organization and behavior until recently largely unexploited. Members of Congress, themselves, have contributed a number of works, each reflecting a peculiar facet of that complex institution in which they have been participants. Textbooks have also appeared, setting out in systematic fashion the wealth of earlier writings and research, together with their authors' own insights. One of the most interesting and illuminating series is that by outstanding political scientists sponsored by the American Enterprise Institute, *Congress: The First Branch of Government*. In any event, we know much more in detail about Congress than before, and some of this is reflected (with due credit) in altered or additional material in the present book.

By contrast the actual changes in Congress itself have been relatively few. The Republican Minority in the House has played a more narrowly partisan role than in the immediately preceding years or than its Senate counterpart. Reapportionment on the basis of the 1960 census and Supreme Court decisions has altered the temper and quantity of domestic legislation. The increased importance of science has been made the subject of a new chapter. I owe much of the inspiration and information for this to Dr. Edward Wenk, Chief of the Science Policy Division of the Legislative Reference Service.

In general, most of the major themes of the original edition of 1951 seem to the author to remain valid today. What the present edition largely attempts is to enrich and bring up to date their exposition, adding, subtracting, and modifying as may be necessary.

ERNEST S. GRIFFITH
The American University

August 1966

Preface

THIS book in its original form and the second revised edition were written while the author was Director of the Legislative Reference Service of Congress. This position imposed certain necessary limitations as to scope. For example, overt recommendations were incompatible with the author's day-to-day work. The author owed a larger loyalty to the confidence which Congress was showing in the impartial character of the Service and in its renunciation of any attempt at direct influence on policy decisions. There were also obvious restraints as regards specific criticism of Congress. While within its defined scope the book represented an honest analysis and evaluation of Congress, this analysis was necessarily incomplete. These omissions did not, I believe, affect or distort the main strands as developed or the conclusions drawn therefrom as to the congressional role in the present age. The basic strands remain unaltered.

However, with retirement from the government, the permissible scope of treatment can be considerably widened; and it is this, rather than any change or outdating of the earlier material, which warrants a third edition. New material of this nature appears throughout the work, especially in the added chapters on "The Members and Their Leaders" and "Congressional Investigations." Also new is the chapter on "Legislative Responsibilities in National Defense."

E. S. G.

August 1960

Preface

THE rising tide of popular and scholarly interest in Congress shows no sign of receding. For the first time, at least in the present century, the number of new books on Congress exceeds those on the President. This interest would seem to justify a new edition of the present work, an edition which permits more up-to-date illustrative and statistical material. It also makes possible an incorporation into the text of an analysis of the sharpened controversy over the role of Congress in administration.

The basic approach of the first edition remains intact. This is to assess in broad outline the *function* of Congress today. This frame of reference is not hospitable to much in the way of detail of structure. Galloway's *The Legislative Process in Congress,* Gross's *The Legislative Struggle,* and Bailey and Simon's *Congress at Work* have all appeared within the past three years, and make even less necessary than before another study of structure as such or a detailed critique of the day-to-day operations of our legislative body.

Issues raised by the present work have been widely discussed since its first appearance in 1951. Certain themes pervading the book have gone counter to much of the prevailing opinion. May I therefore direct the reader's attention to the light shed herein upon certain of these questions. I am not arguing here for acceptance of my point of view on them, nor that the reader be critical of those scholars who differ. Rather am I suggesting that these questions are really pivotal ones, and the serious student in the field of the legislative process should secure all the light on them he can. Perhaps he himself will be led to the task of advancing the frontiers of knowledge by research of his own in one of these areas.

The most spectacular differences of opinion are in the roles that political scientists would assign to party. The lines are sharply drawn between the thesis herein expounded that party does and should fulfill principally the roles of organizer and critic, and the views of those who hold that party responsibility should extend to the formulation and enactment of a program, with the necessary organizational and other consequences.

The favorable view of Congress held by the author in legislative-executive relations goes counter to that held by a whole group of administrators and students of administration. These latter are sharply critical of much of congressional intervention in the administrative process and hold a sanguine view of the policy-forming function of the bureaucracy.

Those who find their inspiration in Bentley and his contemporary successors have found group activity extremely fruitful as a frame of reference. My difference with them is by no means as sharp as with the others, because I too have found Bentley's and, for example, Truman's approaches both stimulating and useful. My earlier study, *The Impasse of Democracy,* used this frame of reference. It is rather that I find it incomplete and even distorting as the basic approach to the congressional scene. The members of Congress themselves are so well aware of the power of organized groups that they take a much more objective view of them than surface impression would indicate.

Finally, the author may in many respects be more conservative than some. This reflects itself in my admiration for government by consensus as against government by majority rule; for parties that are cross sections rather than for parties on class lines; for state and local experiment and vitality rather than for great national programs.

In all these divergences I fully and freely recognize the strength of the case of those who differ. The fact that there are such sharp differences is itself witness to the need for more and more study of Congress in action, until enough is known to allow definitive answers. We do not differ greatly, I am sure, in our normative judgments of what would constitute the desirable end product in human terms. We do differ on the way of attainment.

What of Congress itself?

The factors entering into congressional attitudes and decisions are far too many, too complex, and some of them even too obscure to lend themselves to any simple formula. Increasingly it is apparent that each member is an individual, and not a counter in a party machine or a puppet whose strings are pulled by a special interest. He brings to his duties the environment of his home district and state and the pressures of his local party, and these must always be powerful factors or he will not be re-elected. Interest groups bombard him with their points of view. He also has a code, formulas, if you will, as to what is the nature of the public interest. He brings with him, and finds in Congress, the realization that party loyalty and party co-operation are factors in getting things done. Finally he has at hand in increasing measure a flood of information designed to illumine the background of any problem, the probable effects of any proposal. In this milieu five hundred and thirty-one congressmen make their decisions.

E. S. G.

July 1955

Preface

DURING many years of close association with Congress I came increasingly to be impressed with the gulf between the popular picture of our national legislative body and its reality. Nor had the insights presented in academic circles seemed to me by any means wholly accurate. Consequently, when New York University honored me with the invitation to give the Stokes Lectures on Politics and to make Congress the subject of these lectures, it came almost as a command. The approach which the University suggested did not call for a description of the minutiae of congressional organization and procedure, still less for a repetition of the detailed criticism that has been so frequently leveled at Congress in many of its aspects. Rather it pointed toward an analysis of Congress under the Constitution, of its place in the governmental setting, of the way in which it is responding to a changing age. It is in this frame of reference that the lectures have been written.

In the preparation, I have had the invaluable assistance and advice of many. Three of my colleagues in the Legislative Reference Service, Hugh L. Elsbree, George B. Galloway, and Meyer Jacobstein, have read the draft in its entirety. Three other colleagues, Edward S. Corwin, Halford L. Hoskins, and Howard S. Piquet, have read certain portions and offered helpful suggestions thereon. Within Congress itself, I would like especially to thank Senator Joseph O'Mahoney and Representatives James Dolliver and Sam Hobbs for their courtesy and counsel in connection with certain of the chapters. Wallace McClure of the State Department, Fritz Morstein Marx of the Bureau of the Budget, and George Harvey, Clerk of the House Appropriations Committee, have read portions of interest to them and have made valuable suggestions. My deep gratitude goes to all these who have helped me unstintedly with their insights and criticisms. The errors of judgment and fact that remain are mine and not theirs.

The writings and suggestions of others have influenced my thinking in ways too numerous to mention. However, three works have been so helpful by way of background that special acknowledgment is required. These are Arthur Holcombe's distinguished volume, *Our More Perfect Union,* Charles Hyneman's penetrating *Bureaucracy in a Democracy,* and the forthcoming edition of *The Constitution of the United States, Annotated,* edited and largely written by Edward S. Corwin.

My wife, Margaret Griffith, has given generously of her time in editing the manuscript, and in this she was assisted by our daughter, Margaret. My secretary, Miss Elsie M. Fetter, assisted by Mrs. Nora Caplan and Mrs. Elizabeth Miller, has assumed the taxing responsibility of transcribing my writing into a form legible to the printer and has earned my warm appreciation thereby.

E. S. G.

April 1951

Contents

Contents

Congress

its contemporary role

CHAPTER ONE

Introduction

THE Congress of the United States is the world's best hope of representative government. In its halls decisions are made which may make or break not only our own nation but also the whole free world. These decisions are major weapons in the struggle, not only for democratic survival, but for its advance.

Congress fights this battle for effective representative government against one major enemy and two fundamental dangers. First and foremost, it fights against communism, wherever found, against the view that man's significance lies in his being a part of an inexorable historical process, as defined by the self-appointed oligarchies of the various polit-bureaus. In the second place, it must deal with the dangers from self-centered special interests that would, if not curbed or integrated, tear apart our national unity and weaken our economic strength. Finally, and more subtly, it faces the problem of holding responsible the technically competent bureaucracy which in its growing strength unwittingly threatens to throw our representative government off balance.

One notes certain interrelations of these three dangers. The spread of communism has increased the tempo, magnified the complexity, and dramatized the urgency of American action in international affairs. It is in international affairs that the need for speed, the need for technical knowledge (often of confidential and secret material), the need for clear and even concentrated leadership, are pre-eminently factors tending in the direction of the ascendancy of the President and the supporting or derivative ascendancy of the bureaucracy. Similarly, the power of the special economic groups and their political insistences upon governmental in-

1

tervention largely determine the nature of governmental concern and activity on the domestic front. This activity more and more consists of the process of *adjustment* by an ever-expanding civil service of specialists or technicians.

The struggles between economic groups and interests ultimately must be and are resolved. In the scheme of *laissez faire* this resolution was, in theory (and also largely in practice), by means of a free, competitive market. In the contemporary age, adjustment is more and more likely to be a matter of administration, with government in the role of administrator. Agricultural controls, tariffs, insured mortgages, minimum wage, regulation of railroad rates, are examples of such adjustment. Each of these is the result of the insistences of one or more economic groups that government intervene in their behalf. Initially, the pressure may have been on Congress for legislation (or upon the President as party leader); ultimately, the highly intricate task of continuously intervening in the economic order has by virtue of legislative authorization and delegation of power become the task of a bureau or commission. Here is a transfer in the equilibrium of power and effectiveness, and the transfer is away from the operative significance of representative government and toward the bureaucratic ascendancy of the technically competent. Yet in the bureaucracy, too, the clientele of a particular bureau may so influence the adjustment process as to result in unintegrated effort!

Our Congress is a very human institution, part and parcel of our American culture. While it is itself untainted by any trace of communism, in its halls the issues precipitated by world communism echo and re-echo. These issues make up not so much its occupation as its preoccupation in foreign policy. The pleas and pressures of special interests furnish most of the background of domestic legislation; they are influential in much that is world-wide as well. Congressmen necessarily and properly reflect the attitudes and needs of their

2

individual districts, and many, if not most, of these are economic. It is perhaps the supreme task of Congress on the domestic front to create out of these individual, often very limited, local outlooks an amalgam that shall in some measure represent their fusion into the more general national interest and welfare.

Except for Brazil's, our Constitution, alone of the constitutions of major nations, gives to our legislature and executive positions legally independent of each other.[1] In this setting we shall study what is the central problem of executive-legislative relations, the way in which representative government affects and is affected by the sheer magnitude as well as by the specialized technical competence of the bureaucracy.

The fact that we are by all odds the most powerful of the units of the free world, without which the remainder might have difficulty in surviving, attaches to our Congress today a dignity and a responsibility at the same time inspiring and terrible, a responsibility unmatched in all its earlier history.

It is responding well to the challenge.

---

[1] Since 1964 the President of Brazil has been chosen by its Congress. This is regarded (1966) as probably temporary.

CHAPTER TWO

The Formal Constitutional Position of Congress

THE changing constitutional position of Congress today is not primarily the product of formal amendment. Nor is it primarily an outgrowth of changing judicial interpretation. Rather it lies squarely in the field of changing usage and custom—changes brought about on the one hand by the vast economic forces that reveal themselves in a transformed economy and on the other by the crisis in the clash of rival world cultures. The emerging outlines of this informal constitution will be the principal theme of this work. Nevertheless, it is appropriate at the beginning to note the much less formidable changes produced by formal amendment and judicial interpretation.

The principle of the formal separation of powers is one of the three great principles of our Constitution. It is fashionable these days in academic circles to be somewhat critical of this principle. Ordinarily this criticism is coupled with an admiration for the parliamentary system and suggestions of various devices by which our American government can be made more like the British model. It is usually, but not always, conceded that the installation of the parliamentary system by way of constitutional amendment is not practicable. Resort is therefore suggested to various devices, institutional and otherwise, centering around more integrated executive-legislative relations on the one hand and greater party responsibility on the other.[1]

---

[1] Cf. chaps. 6 and 17.

It is apparent that the line of reasoning that seemed most cogent to the architects of the Constitution in defense of separation of powers has today changed in its meaning. The labored reasoning that there was danger in the same man or body both making and executing the laws today means something other than was then urged, even though belief in the use of power to check power and hold it responsible is still valid. We have abandoned *laissez faire*. We need focal points of leadership within Congress and without. We need to see that this leadership is responsible. England with its formal union of the legislature and the cabinet executive is no more and no less in danger of a formal dictatorship than is the United States. The forces making for totalitarianism are not found primarily in the relationship between these two parts of the nation's government, except in so far as this relationship, when it assumes certain forms, may put a premium upon a virtual dictatorship of the technically competent.[2] The dangers lie rather in external forces, in the power of the special interests, in the menace of enemies, in national disunity. In so far as these factors are by-products of constitutions, they trace rather to multiparty systems fostered by proportional representation or to other divisive constitutional provisions which reflect the nation's disunities in its legislature.

The importance of separation of powers today lies in its relationship to the third menace to representative democracy already mentioned. This is the danger that the authority of technical competence as represented in the bureaucracy may transform an ostensibly democratic government into a dictatorship of the civil service behind the façade of its formal constitution. The great industrialized democracies of the world, including our own, have already gone some distance along this path. Yet close examination reveals that our Congress, perhaps alone among the legislative bodies of the world, has

---

[2] *Ibid.*

offered effective resistance to this trend.[3]   This it has done not merely in the negative sense of picking and choosing among the proposals of the executive but by revealing a capacity for developing the necessary leadership to share in policy formulation or even itself to devise and adopt independent policies.

Stated more precisely, this places the contemporary genius of our American Constitution not in the more negative emphasis upon its safeguards against arbitrary action but in an affirmative insistence upon responsibility.   Separation of powers has introduced a unique element into this relationship between Congress and the executive.   The heart of the matter is this: that, by and large, nowhere in our government can any agency operate irresponsibly for long in important matters.   Always it is required, and must expect, to justify its action and its proposals before its constitutional equal.   Irresponsible power is thus virtually unknown to our system. Even if power expresses itself in inaction rather than action, as is often alleged of Congress, the way lies open for the President to bring the popular will to bear upon the situation through press and radio.   But this is the less important aspect of the picture.   More important is the fact that, by and large, the Congress can hold the executive branch genuinely accountable for administration and need not follow its affirmative program unless it believes it justified.   Neither for that matter must the President follow Congress in this regard unless he in turn believes in a congressional measure, save only in the few instances in which a bill is passed over his veto.   This necessity on the part of each to justify its conduct and its proposals before its constitutional equal is one of the really great principles which determine the nature of our government.   Together with our federal system and the single-member constituency, it makes for a system of government

---

[3] Japan is moving in the same direction by strengthening the staff services available to its Diet.

in which progress takes place in an atmosphere of common consent or at least of widespread acceptance. It is unifying rather than divisive. To trace the workings of this principle in its relationship to contemporary social and economic forces is to come close to a real understanding of congressional behavior.

There never was a clear separation of function or even of powers as popularly understood. In the Constitution itself, checks and balances modified the pristine purity of the theory. In general, the facts are familiar and need not be elaborated. The legislative powers of the President and the power of Congress over the administration for the most part are well known, except perhaps as this latter power may find legislative expression in congressional insistence that the prescription of standards and procedures in administrative matters such as personnel, organization, purchasing, are legislative. The constitutional synthesis thus brought about deserves a better and more accurate title than either separation of powers or checks and balances. Institutionalized mutuality of responsibility of coequals more nearly expresses the real situation.

Historically, legislative-executive relations have been fluid in the extreme. They have varied with persons, with issues, with the tempo of the time. On the whole, however, it seemed as if certain inexorable forces had propelled our government, as they have other governments, more and more in the direction of the dominance of the executive. In his presidential message of May 1822, Monroe characterized the legislative branch, "from the nature of its powers, all laws proceeding from it, and the manner of its appointment, its members being elected by the people" as by far the most important. In this year the expenditure for Congress still exceeded that for the executive. Corwin put the situation as follows:

In short, the Constitution reflects the struggle between two conceptions of executive power: the conception that it ought always to be

7

subordinate to the supreme legislative power, and the conception that it ought to be, within generous limits, autonomous and self-directing; or, in other terms, the idea that the people are *re-presented* in the Legislative *versus* the idea that they are *embodied* in the Executive. Nor has this struggle ever entirely ceased, although on the whole it is the latter theory which has prospered. . . . Taken by and large, the history of the Presidency has been a history of aggrandizement.[4]

That such a development in the United States seems of late to have been arrested deserves most thoughtful examination. Whether this change is temporary remains to be seen. It may be only one of those cyclical changes in the locus of power as between Congress and the President which we have witnessed in the past. It may on the other hand represent something more fundamental, one of those major developments arising from the introduction of some new factor of the first magnitude in our governance.

The structure of Congress remains in formal terms substantially unaltered from early days, except for the direct election of the senators and the abolition of the Lame Duck Congress by the Twentieth Amendment. Both of these changes have had their principal effect in a sharpening of the accuracy of representation—important in an informal but positive fashion in the prestige and power of the body. The introduction of the direct primary into the structure of so many of the state governments has substantially affected the role of the parties in Congress—but, of this, more later.[5]

Judicial interpretation has registered and to some extent facilitated certain broad changes in the respective positions of Congress and the President. It is worth noting that the great historical constitutional studies have been of the position of the presidency rather than of Congress.[6] In part this may be

---

[4] Edward S. Corwin, *The President: Office and Powers* (4th ed., rev.; New York: New York University Press, 1957), p. 307.

[5] Cf. pp. 237 ff.

[6] Cf. Corwin, *The President: Office and Powers;* H. J. Laski, *The American Presidency* (London: Harper and Brothers [*ca.* 1940]); W. E. Binkley, *The Powers of the President* (Garden City: Doubleday, 1940); *President and Congress* (New York: Knopf, 1947); George F. Milton, *The Use of Presidential Power* (Boston: Little, Brown, 1944); Clinton Rossiter, *The*

because its story is more dramatic. The story of an up-building is more intriguing than the story of an erosion or decline. It would be an interesting and rewarding exercise to rewrite these same studies from the point of view of Congress.[7]

Most notable among constitutional changes as registering a transfer of function is the growth of delegated legislation within the extremely liberal metes and bounds set by the Supreme Court.[8] Let such delegation be according to defined limits; let it be essential for attaining the objective of the act; let it be recoverable; let it involve procedurally no violation of the "due process" and other clauses: there is then apparently no limit. The Schechter case[9] ruling has long since been conveniently interred. It should be noted in passing that such a growth in delegated legislation is inevitable in a setting in which more and more legislation consists essentially of the fixing of objectives (rather than the passing of laws) and the creation of an agency to carry them out. The characteristic process of the latter is the type of continuous intervention which we have termed "adjustment."

Over against this is the advantage taken by Congress of the ambiguity of the Constitution in regard to the congressional control over those matters which have come to be regarded as central in the administrative process. Thus Congress has come to prescribe in some detail the organization, personnel practices, methods of accounting, budgetary procedure, purchasing and disposal, and many other similar areas commonly associated with executive power.[10]

American Presidency (New York: Harcourt, Brace, 1956). Woodrow Wilson's Congressional Government (Boston, 1885) is perhaps an exception, though it is more descriptive than historical. See also James Burnham, Congress and the American Tradition (Chicago: Regnery, 1959).

[7] See Carl B. Swisher, Supreme Court in Modern Role rev. edit. (New York: New York University Press, 1965), chap. 2.

[8] Cf. Corwin, The President: Office and Powers, pp. 119–27. Note the possible use of the legislative veto and concurrent resolution in this regard. See also Swisher, op. cit.

[9] Schechter Poultry Corp. v. United States, 295 U.S. 495 (1935).

[10] Cf. chap. 10 for a fuller discussion.

The Supreme Court has seesawed a bit as regards the removal power of the President, but this has only indirectly involved Congress. However, Congress occasionally, as in the instances of the Comptroller General and members of the Tennessee Valley Authority, has made provision by statute to give itself the power of removal—other than by impeachment. At the same time Congress has by statute thrown certain limitations around presidential powers in this regard. The Humphrey case is more significant for its limitation upon the President than for any extension of congressional authority.[11] However, the examples of the General Accounting Office, the Government Printing Office, the Library of Congress, and the Botanic Garden reveal potential congressional administrative powers, despite skepticism about their existence; and in the so-called independent commissions there is obviously a twilight zone within which perhaps some congressional administrative power lurks. Apparently the full implications of congressional power to prescribe methods of removal have not been fully explored. On the other hand, in *United States v. Lovett*,[12] Congress is held subject to limitations in the use of the power of appropriations to force removals of individuals.

A succession of decisions (or the absence of ways to force a decision) has somewhat limited the investigating powers of Congress. The executive apparently may refuse papers and possibly may ignore subpoenas, though these steps are seldom taken. Within an expanding field it may decline to answer questions. Appearances are voluntary. The President apparently may transfer to his high officials something of his own immunities. Issues of this type in loyalty investigations are still unsolved, and their solutions are difficult to arrive

---

[11] *Humphrey's Executor* v. *United States,* 295 U.S. 602 (1935). In this case, the President was precluded from removing any member of a regulatory commission prior to the expiration of his term, except for cause as provided by law.

[12] 328 U.S. 303 (1946).

at through judicial processes. Perhaps a test case might be made through an arrest of the Attorney General by the sergeant at arms of one of the houses.[13] It is unlikely, however, that matters will ever reach such a pitch that extreme methods of this type will be used, and executive immunity in this regard will be determined or modified by political rather than judicial considerations.

Of more lasting significance is the long line of decisions expanding the independent sphere of the executive, especially in foreign relations, as commander in chief of the armed services, and as steward in an emergency because of the "nature of government." Such emergencies have included industrial disputes, crises in law enforcement, depressions, threats to national safety, and wars. Perhaps the most sharply defined and extreme expression of this doctrine was the demand by Franklin Roosevelt in connection with the repeal of part of the Price Control Act: [14]

I ask the Congress to take this action by the first of October. Inaction on your part by that date will leave me with an inescapable responsibility to the people of this country to see to it that the war effort is no longer imperiled by threat of economic chaos.

In the event that the Congress should fail to act, and act adequately, I shall accept the responsibility, and I will act.

At the same time that fair prices are stabilized, wages can and will be stabilized also. This I will do.

The President has the powers, under the Constitution and under Congressional acts, to take measures necessary to avert a disaster which would interfere with the winning of the war.

I have given the most thoughtful consideration to meeting this issue without further reference to the Congress. I have determined, however, on this vital matter to consult with the Congress. . . .

The American people can be sure that I will use my powers with a full sense of my responsibility to the Constitution and to my country. The American people can also be sure that I shall not hesitate to use every power vested in me to accomplish the defeat of our enemies in any part of the world where our own safety demands such defeat.

---

[13] Cf. p. 51 below.
[14] *The New York Times,* September 8, 1942. Cited in and discussed in Corwin, *The President: Office and Powers,* pp. 250–51.

11

When the war is won, the powers under which I act automatically revert to the people—to whom they belong.

The validity of the projected action was not brought to a test. Congress complied, and the crisis was averted. If under the guise of an emergency, with Congress in actual session, the President had in fact the power Roosevelt claimed of setting aside a law by unilateral action, then indeed the position of Congress would be seriously and perhaps critically impaired; for the nature of the world today is such that the claim of a national crisis can easily be advanced. Thus the presidency in the hands of a man temperamentally inclined toward dictatorship would be potentially a danger of the first magnitude.

In 1952, under guise that the strike constituted a national emergency, President Truman seized the steel mills. In the court actions that followed the government rested its case primarily on a President's inherent powers, with some support from his authority as commander in chief. The mills had extensive defense contracts. The Supreme Court ruled that the President had exceeded his powers, in that, not only had Congress not authorized such seizure, but had laid down other procedures.[15] Evidently there are limits even to the emergency powers.

Profoundly affecting Congress has been the intervention of the Supreme Court in reapportionment as regards both state legislatures and Congress itself. In *Wesberry* v. *Sanders*,[16] the Supreme Court laid down the principle of "equal representation for equal numbers of people." This has not yet been given full effect, but it is only a question of time before a very substantial number of hitherto rural seats will be transferred to urban and, even more, to suburban areas.

It should be emphasized again and again that it is by usage and not by formal amendment or judicial decision that the

---

[15] *Sawyer* v. *Youngstown Sheet and Tube Company*, 343 U.S. 937 (1952).
[16] 376 U.S. 1 (1964). See p. 220 below for its effect.

most far-reaching constitutional changes which involve Congress are taking place. These will be spelled out in greater detail later, but chiefly they lie within this area of legislative-executive relations. The role of Congress in international relations has changed. Treaties are less important. Appropriations are more so. Still more important are the actions of the executive which inexorably determine our future course. Agreements at Yalta, Potsdam, and Teheran, the decision to invade France and not the Balkans, the dispatching of troops to Korea and the Dominican Republic—these and scores of other actions reduce greatly the importance at one time attached to the roles of Congress in declaring war and ratifying treaties.

On the other hand, the weapon of congressional investigation is sharp and growing sharper—be it poniard or meat ax. Through its committees there has been set up an organ that not only largely assures executive responsibility to obey the intent of the law but also has a profound influence on the exercise of administrative power in the area of its discretion. A committee is a co-ordinate locus of power, and with the specialization thereby implied it has always presented a formidable rival to the department in the evolution of policy in its special area. Now that it has added to its arsenal the availability of permanent experts on its own staff and in the Legislative Reference Service, the observed decline in its effective oversight of the executive branch has been arrested.[17]

Neither the executive nor Congress, especially Congress, has been organized in such a fashion as to prepare and see through an integrated and harmonious national policy. The Joint Economic Committee may contain the seeds of such integration in Congress, just as agencies such as the Bureau of the Budget and the Council of Economic Advisers (and the Executive Office of the President generally) make possible in the executive branch such integrated planning as there is.

---

[17] Cf. chap. 10, for a study of the nature of this oversight.

Neither branch has as yet conspicuously succeeded in this task, but in a dispersive society and economy the need for integrating factors is obvious. Some would find a measure of integration in a party program.

We may conclude at this point by indicating that a large measure of the greatness of our Constitution lies in its fluidity and adaptability, in the fact that it allows so much that matters in relationships to be determined by custom and usage, as changing social forces play upon government. Yet some features are permanent, and of these none is more important than the separation of powers, which contains within it the deeper principle of the responsibility of power. This is the cornerstone of congressional-executive relations.[18]

---

[18] Attention should be called to the fact that the general problem of relationships between Congress and the judiciary, especially the Supreme Court, has not been considered. From time to time criticism of the former has risen almost to fever pitch in legislative halls. Yet never in recent decades has Congress taken any measures that would indicate that the majority of both houses shared this criticism. See Walter F. Murphy, *Congress and the Court* (Chicago: University of Chicago Press, 1962) and Herman F. Pritchett, *Congress Versus the Supreme Court* (Minneapolis: University of Minnesota Press, 1961) for standard works on the subject. Following such periods, both branches have tended to temper their actions.

CHAPTER THREE

The Members
and Their Leaders

CHARACTERIZATIONS of members of Congress have run the gamut from cartoons to statistics. The "typical" member has been pictured many times, but with somewhat more circumspection and respect of late. His average age is fifty. He is more often than not a lawyer, almost always a college graduate and a church member, native-born, a family man, extroverted, above average in height. In other words, he is not greatly dissimilar from the typical American of his years, albeit somewhat better educated, more likely to be religiously motivated, and naturally with far more interest in public affairs.

It is worthwhile to probe a bit more deeply at certain points, perhaps drawing some distinction between the man at the time of his first election and what the occupation itself subsequently does to him.

The post is a full-time job, but usually without the security that normally attaches itself in other walks of life to a post with comparable income and prestige. We live in a society of status, a society which puts a premium on security, public deference, and (it is to be hoped) character and ability. Being a congressman stands up well in all but the desire for security, and at this point it falls seriously short. So much is this true that we can say that those in certain occupations are effectively disqualified, for election so breaks the rhythm of their success that failure in re-election makes it almost impossible to take up where they left off. A small businessman cannot hope to do this. Neither can a small farmer, unless he has a son at exactly the right age to step into the breach.

A labor leader must be continuously at his job, or the infighting for promotion and preference that is characteristic of such a career will quickly seize upon his vacancy—and rarely if ever could he successfully re-enter after a lapse of years. Employees of firms, business or manufacturing, are not usually encouraged to take part in politics in the sense of running for office and, even if allowed to run, must usually resign their posts if elected. Most professions are similarly handicapped. Doctors and dentists become rusty, and others take over their practice. Teachers are expected to be nonpolitical, except possibly the college professors.

On the other hand, there are certain occupations in which security either is not a factor or is enhanced by service in Congress. Large-scale farmers can employ farm managers, at least temporarily. Housewives are not likely to be unoccupied even if eventually defeated for re-election. Retired businessmen, if they retire early enough to assume the vigor of a campaign, are obviously eligible. So are journalists, because service in Congress can be of subsequent assistance in return or alternative placement. College professors, especially in the social sciences, attain considerable glamour as well as experience through political success. Bankers may be granted leaves of absence, if they run on an approved conservative platform. Above all, lawyers find even candidacy for Congress an asset, and election usually brings a considerable measure of new business to their law firm. Add to this two facts: that the lawyer usually chooses his profession in the first place because of his interest in public affairs, and the further fact that analytic ability, the balancing of evidence, capacity for advocacy are all assets in the congressional setting as well as part of a lawyer's stock-in-trade. Finally there is a category of eligibility that cuts across all of the others, in the sense that it is usually a dimension of them. The candidates are for the most part also politicians. In other words, in any community, district, or state there is a certain nucleus of persons interested in party organization, campaigns, government, and the favors and powers involved therein. In this group are some that make a career of office-holding, elective or appointive. Hence the number of congressmen who list their earlier occupation as "public official." But whether the candidate is already an official or not, usually he belongs to this inner circle of the politically active. It should be noted in this connection that insecurity of tenure is often more apparent than real, inasmuch as the number of defeated congressmen that appear later among the presidential or gubernatorial or mayoralty appointees is not inconsiderable.

Certain personal qualities, while not universal, are so obviously assets that they may be largely presumed among members. The outgoing extrovert, genuinely interested in persons, able to project himself affirmatively into the thinking of groups (nationality, religious, occupational), gregarious, a "joiner," is usually the type successful. Of late, emphasis upon character and religion seems to be rising in the scale, as the seriousness and complexity of the nation's problems are borne in upon the electorate.

What happens to these men and women after they are elected, or, even more, after they are repeatedly re-elected? What does service in Congress do to a man's personality and character? It is a truism to say that it depends upon the man himself whether the good or the evil factors prevail in this occupational conditioning. Most likely it is something of both, for there are both occupational hazards and occupational constructs.

On the minus side, there is not the slightest doubt that the pace itself is terrific—too great, in fact, if there are inherent instabilities in a man's personality. Irritability in committee hearings is one very human reaction to this pace. Escapism of one sort or another is ever present as a temptation—escape from fatigue, escape from pressure. While a surprisingly small number are or become alcoholics, those who do are

17

symptomatic. A larger number undoubtedly drink too much for their own good, although whether these are a higher percentage than in the community at large is uncertain. Perhaps the principal "escape" is for the member simply to give up the fight for really serious accomplishment, to drift along with the party or committee leadership, and to cultivate his constituency.

In addition to the casualties of the hectic pace are the hazards of the virtual necessity of seeming to be understanding of all the individuals and groups who constantly seek special favors in the form of jobs, intervention with the administration, or support of or opposition to pending legislation. Probably much if not most of this is "front" only; and back of it all, the member will follow his judgment and his conscience, albeit frequently behind a smoke-screen of apparent sympathy with the point of view urged upon him. These pressures constantly tilt the scales in the direction of being all things to all men, and only the valiant and the thick-skinned can completely hold out. After all, the member is a *representative,* and "going along" on a minor matter may assure success on a major one, including his re-election to continue the fight for the right as he sees it. He is, after all, in Congress to get things done, and compromise is a necessary tactic in situations in which men honestly differ.

In the third place, there is the ever present danger of a dulling of the sharp ethical edge of a man. At what point does a gift become a bribe—when it is valued at five dollars or five hundred? Does a liberal honorarium to make a speech before an organization constitute a commitment to the organization's program? If not, does subconscious appreciation work in the same direction? What constitutes conflict of interest? Stock ownership that even preceded candidacy? The employment of a member of his family by a certain firm? What are legitimate expenses on travel accounts? What is a fair use of the congressional frank? Should a member's law firm take a fee in connection with a private immigration bill, or any other legislative matter? What obligations arise out of campaign contributions and testimonial dinners? The author has been present at many discussions of questions of this type among members, and has been impressed with the seriousness of many of these discussions. One member will accept a lunch but not a dinner! One will take gifts worth less than five dollars and return the others. Another returns all gifts. The problems involved are far from easy. Where does courtesy end and influence begin? Where is influence legitimate and where "undue"? All the wiles of the social lobby, all the devices of presents and subtle suggestions of favors to come, all the apparent friendships which are not friendships—these and a hundred other matters render impossible a sharp line between "mine and thine," between prerogatives of office and its exploitation, between the public interest and betrayal of the public trust. The daily life of a congressman is a constant round of temptations, not to overt malfeasance, but to blurred ethics.

Yet the other side of the ledger is even more impressive, especially after a frequent initial but superficial disillusionment. When a member becomes aware of the possibilities of accomplishment as well as of its limitations, then the channel of the public interest becomes clearer to him. He cannot accomplish everything; he can accomplish something; and team play is in large measure the means.

For one thing, the average member usually gains greatly in his appreciation of the nature of the public interest. More will be said concerning this later.[1] At this point it is enough to say that the transition is usually from an earlier identification of the public interest with the economic prosperity of the group or groups most strongly represented in his constituency; to a second stage in which he also sees the cogency of the "other side" in these economic struggles; to a third stage in which

---

[1] Cf. pp. 150 f.

19

larger considerations of general prosperity, human rights, the image of America overseas, and the strength of the free world become influential in decisions. His education as a congressman, because he has the experience of serving as a congressman, is well on its way when he senses that no *one* principle ever exhausts the meaning of a situation, that most decisions involve a conflict of principles, most of them good. He turns from principles to consequences as a basis for his decisions.

His experience as a member quickly teaches him the desirability of specializing. Even a first-term member is listened to, if he discusses a subject on which he is or has become an authority. The committee system advances this aspect of his education, especially in the House. The genius of this body lies in the conscientious and thorough nature of its committee work, not in glamour and drama of floor debate or in the emergence of great national figures. If a House member will limit the scope of his efforts, he will find himself with time to do well in his sector. He will be respected by his colleagues and his views will carry weight with them. After several terms of growth, his advocacy or opposition may be all but decisive within the limited, though important, sphere he has set for himself.

The genius of the Senate is of another character; its ethos affects a man in a somewhat different fashion. For one thing, he is much more visible than is a House member. Debating time is longer and divided among far fewer people. He is more likely to be a committee or subcommittee chairman, and much earlier in his career. He has a larger staff than a House member to take from him more of the burdensome detail. The very name by which he is called, "Senator," carries with it role-playing implications which are flattering, demanding, and sobering. He wants to belong to the "club" and inner circle, an expansible category limited only by the number of those of ability who are willing to play the game according to the on the whole excellent rules—rules of conscientious work, team play, mutual respect, an underlying integrity of purpose even though this latter is inevitably tinctured with ambition. In a sense he must take himself seriously, as seriously as the high office he holds demands—but with a certain lightness of touch which signifies a human being who gives credit to his colleagues for sincerity, even though they differ with him and must from time to time make compromises to ensure that their state will have experienced senators if and when they run for re-election. "The Senate has men who primarily investigate the executive branch, men who speak to the society at large, men who specialize in a wide variety of substantive areas, . . ." [2]

In other words, the House member thinks of himself as a "Representative," the senator as a statesman, and all the mores and the network of procedures, organization, and custom call upon him to play this role—and the great majority not only play it, but in the playing of it, become the role they play.[3]

One further factor should be noted, the Senator's constituency is likely to be more diversified than that of the House member. Because of this he is subjected to a broader set of experiences and pressures, and consequently he is more likely to search for an urban-rural consensus or a business-labor consensus. It is this factor, together with the time lag in House reapportionment, that in part accounts for the more "liberal" record of the upper body in recent decades.

No one can know scores and hundreds of these men intimately without coming to understand them, and out of this

---

[2] Nelson W. Polsby, *Congress and the Presidency* (Englewood Cliffs: Prentice-Hall, 1964), p. 40. Polsby also calls attention to the prevalence of home-state interest, politicking and coalition-building. See Donald R. Mathews, *U.S. Senators and Their World* (Chapel Hill: University of North Carolina Press, 1960) for a detailed analysis of the senators' backgrounds.

[3] If he has not already done so, the reader is urged to read Allen Drury's novel, *Advise and Consent* (Garden City: Doubleday, 1959). This is a skilled portrait of the Senate in action by one well acquainted and gifted with insight. See also William S. White's interesting and informal books: *Citadel* (New York: Harpers, 1956) and *Home Place: The Story of the House of Representatives* (Boston: Houghton Mifflin, 1965).

understanding coming to love and respect them. They are constantly on the firing line. The good they do is often obscured by committee procedures; the evil never wants for a reporter or critic. They are better, far better, persons—in ability and character—than the popular or even the academic view of them would hold. They wish to be better than they are, for the exigencies of the political scene, the importunities of the self-seeking, the group dispersiveness of the body politic set metes and bounds to the effectiveness and durability of the Utopian. The realist must be content to do what he can, and that is not inconsiderable.

The transition is a natural one from Congress as a collection of individuals to an analysis of the role played by its leadership. Where and whence are its leaders and its centers of power?

Consider first another aspect of the member as an individual. In one sense he is independent of leadership or of centers of power. Few are the sanctions that his colleagues or party leaders can impose on him in his own district or state. Within Congress as a body they can to a certain extent punish his insubordination, temerity, or maverick tendency—but, so long as he appears solicitous for his constituents, such punishment can rarely penetrate his re-election campaign. Then, too, in a sense the member is irresponsible nationally, but is responsible to his constituents.[4] This creates the setting for a leadership relatively decentralized and free.

Yet leadership there is. Basically this is because the individual is almost completely dependent upon others to get things done—whether for his district, state, or nation. Team play is necessary, and there must be a captain. Accommodation and compromise there must be, and these usually imply

---

[4] I use the word "responsible" in the sense of accountability. If the term "responsible" is used as a synonym of "self-disciplined, thoughtful, and conscientious," then, as a matter of conscience, he can be highly "responsible" nationally. Yet even this latter does not necessarily imply acceptance of leadership.

a broker. Carrying conviction there must be, and this very fact may well make each and every member in a sense a leader. In other words, a member must, to a very considerable extent, be an "organization man" starting at the bottom, and by accepted, though not completely binding, techniques, he must work his way up to a position in which he can attain more and more of his objectives.

Both houses place great store upon the customs and traditions which have been worked out over the years, and a member who wishes to exercise increasing influence would do well to observe them. These customs are definitely functional in the best sense of the word. They are designed to promote comity and to make accomplishments possible. In the House, the new member is closely watched in this regard. Without sacrifice of conscience or constituency, will he "go along" with the leadership where possible? Does he specialize? Does he refrain from brashness? If so, after a term or two, he will find himself entrusted with those as yet minor responsibilities which are nevertheless the sure mark of favor on the part of those in power. Gradually his influence will increase, even though he may have to wait a long time for a committee chairmanship, especially if recognition of his worth has taken the form of acceding to his desire for transfer to a more prestigious committee. In the Senate, recognition may come more quickly, for there are fewer to divide power. Here personal relationships may be as effective as ability, but playing according to the rules of the game is equally necessary. In both houses great store is placed upon willingness to make the necessary compromises to permit accomplishment, and upon mutual support between himself and his colleagues on matters which are important to certain ones but not to all.[5]

---

[5] For a sophisticated and thorough study of these customs as they affect the House, see Richard F. Fenno, Jr., "The Internal Distribution of Influence: The House," in David B. Truman, ed., *The Congress and America's Future* (Englewood Cliffs: Prentice-Hall, 1965), pp. 70–76.

Where then are leadership and power centered? [6] "Leadership on what type of question?" is the important consideration at this point.

On really major issues, leadership from within the government is found in an interplay of the President, the relevant cabinet member, the party leaderships in Congress, the responsible committees, and even isolated members with a strong stake in the results or an authoritative competence in the subject field. In other words, a major issue evokes the full panoply of the various centers of power and influence. The interplay is "political" in the best sense, often leading to an end result or decision which marks a large measure of consensus.

Regional or local issues on the other hand follow a somewhat different pattern. This is the sphere of "logrolling," as with the rivers and harbors, or "pork barrel" bills. Such measures are often collections of relatively minor items strung together with a specious unity; or they may be separate though still minor items, whose sponsors cash in on previously acquired or potential credit with their colleagues. Requests for help from a fellow-member are often very difficult to refuse, if the item in question is something involving his district. Some major regional issues, especially in agriculture, follow much the same pattern on a larger scale, though in such matters the President normally has a program toward which he works. Trades are in order as between commodity spokesmen or even with larger and implicitly alien groups such as labor or mining. In measures of these types, leadership is scattered and decentralized. Spokesmen in Congress and lobbyists outside provide the dynamics and engineer the tactics looking toward success in behalf of their respective constituents or clienteles. The interaction among the members of

---

[6] See George Galloway, "Leadership in the House of Representatives," *Western Political Quarterly*, June 1959, pp. 417–41.

a state delegation is often noticeable. Countervailing forces are of course present in all of the foregoing.[7]

Another group of issues are those of a specialized or technical nature. Leadership in such instances is usually the prerogative of the relevant committee and of individual members who are thorough in their mastery of the facts underlying the issues and of the probable consequences of the proposed change. The organizational or party leadership must naturally be enlisted in terms of granting the necessary priority in scheduling, but its active support is seldom needed.

Finally there are the issues of continuity. The extension of a previously approved social security program, the widening of foreign aid, the granting of additional powers to the Bureau of Narcotics, additions to the classified civil service, the tightening of the anti-trust laws, a raising of the ceiling on the national debt, authorization of new weapon systems, will serve as examples. This is the sphere in which the initiative usually rests with the executive departments and agencies. The role of Congress is usually to serve as a board of review of such proposals, seldom as their initiator. An exception to this latter may be found in situations in which a President of conservative bent may, in general, oppose most extensions of governmental activity, even along hitherto approved lines. However, in general, these represent proposals the major premises of which have been settled for many years past.

Leadership may thus be thought of as a series of interlocking systems with power fairly well distributed. Within Congress are three such "systems," the party hierarchy, the committee hierarchy, and the specialized and distributed power and prestige of those who are authorities in particular fields. External to Congress are the executive branch, the lobbyists, and the local party organizations.

Within Congress, what kind of *person* is the leader? Usu-

---

[7] See chap. 11 for a fuller discussion.

ally he is one who recognizes a measure of individuality, a zone of freedom as necessary to the rank and file of members. He is a man with a sense of the national interest, often an over-riding sense. He rarely behaves autocratically in little things, and only within limits in great things when the public interest dictates. He builds up a sizeable reserve of good will by assisting members when he can, and draws upon this reserve when the occasion warrants. He evokes admiration for his skill and sureness of touch, for his sense of fair play and his hard work.

He may become an autocrat, and this may bring rebellion, as with Speaker Cannon and more recently with certain committee chairmen. He may be inept, or even tired and old, in which event he is likely sooner or later to be replaced. Yet, in general, those chosen by their parties and those surviving election hazards until they attain committee seniority are far more likely than not to be *effective* and to exercise their undoubted power responsibly.

Provisionally, it is fair to say that the leadership and power structure of Congress are such that they offer ample opportunity for individual members to get things done, even if they belong to the minority party. In this latter case, the third leadership system, that of the technically competent specialists, is still open to them in a group in which national loyalty and considerations of the public interest transcend party lines. Such a structure is peculiarly adaptable to the needs of an age of multiplicity of issues of extremely varied character. Such an age demands a similar variation in the patterns of decision-making.[8]

---

[8] A perceptive study of the individual member and his experiences is found in Clem Miller, *Member of the House* (New York: Scribner, 1962).

CHAPTER FOUR

The Internal
Organization of Congress

ORGANIZATION and procedure have always been vital factors in the efficient operation of any legislative body. They are central in this day and age, for the business of legislatures has multiplied beyond all reckoning. The opportunities for service and betrayal of the public interest have correspondingly increased, with these formal matters at least influential in determining whether service or betrayal shall prevail. Books such as Galloway's *The Legislative Process*, Young's *This Is Congress* and *The American Congress*, Burns's *Congress on Trial*, Bailey and Samuel's *Congress at Work*, Keefe and Ogul's *The American Legislative Process*, Clapp's *The Congressman, His Work As He Sees It*, Berman's *In Congress Assembled*, or Bolling's *House Out of Order* contain such a wealth of illuminating detail on the internal organization of Congress that repetition is quite unwarranted. Moreover, a major study under the auspices of the American Political Science Association is in process. Therefore, at this point there are merely offered certain observations that may be helpful in understanding the broad spirit and purpose, rather than the details, of Congress in its corporate capacity.

There are certain determining factors that must preface any such over-all understanding. There are 435 members of the House and 100 of the Senate. Allowing for a session of 32 weeks, 5 hours a day, 5 days a week, this gives a total of about 800 hours in which floor business must be transacted.[1] Ob-

---

[1] The first session of the Eighty-sixth Congress showed the Senate in session 1,009 hours and the House 527; the first session of the Eighty-ninth,

27

viously the House at least must organize so as to limit debate. On the whole, it has done this well. The Senate, on the other hand, emphasizing other values, prides itself on unlimited debate. The larger body in practice is the more expeditious.

Both houses are engaged in a constant and, to a considerable extent, a losing struggle against the avalanche of business which the complexities, crises, and political insistences of the present day have produced. The quantitative aspect of the problem is the less acute. More serious is the qualitative. The quantitative has found a measure of solution in the floor rules, in additions to staff, and in division of labor among committees and subcommittees. However, it is the qualitative aspect that even more strikingly finds expression in the committee organization. The standing committee is the chief instrument with which Congress uses specialization to confront complexity.

It is interesting to note that the British House of Commons has faced a similar situation but has met the problem in a fundamentally different fashion. Its committees play a minor role, largely in examination of bills for soundness of detail. Legislation itself emanates from the "government"—in practice largely from the permanent officials of the civil service. These latter provide the element of specialization. Cabinet committees exist, but their role and influence are unclear.

Another generally operative factor in influencing congressional procedure is the natural desire on the part of most members for re-election. So much of American politics is made up of the activities of the various groups—economic, racial, religious, and others—that re-election often seems like a game in which a member avoids offending and caters to the desires of the maximum number of such groups as are represented in a given constituency. This reflects itself in procedures as well. On the positive side, it appears in the introduction of many

---

the Senate, 960 hours and the House, 798. In the House, probably twenty per cent of this time was in fact consumed by quorum and roll calls.

bills, in insertions in the *Congressional Record,* in speeches on (and off) the floor, in differential treatment of witnesses in committee hearings, and, of course, in numerous activities not directly related to either organization or procedure.

On the negative side, various devices are used to avoid offense. In a democratic, representative government in this day and age, it seems to be a practical necessity that ways and means be found whereby an elected representative, desirous of serving the broader public interest, can avoid taking positions publicly on issues strongly felt by minorities, if the positions thus urged are regarded by the representative as not in line with general welfare.

For many years the Rules Committee of the House has occasionally performed this particular role by refusing to allow a measure to reach the floor, at least in the form in which it was reported out by the standing committee. This it did when it felt the measure was not in the public interest and—this is the important aspect—when it had reason to suppose that the majority of the House felt as the Committee did concerning the measure. Yet because of the terrific organized pressure behind such a measure—pressure perhaps of veterans' organizations, of labor, of the Negro, of the aged (it matters not which)—many members would be faced with the alternatives of political suicide or a vote against their convictions if the measure ever reached the floor, and under such circumstances the measure would probably pass. Thus the Rules Committee saved them from having to go on record. The Committee itself normally consisted of members from districts in which re-election was virtually assured. It should be borne in mind that a discharge petition with 218 signatures could have brought the measure to the floor at any time if the Rules Committee had misjudged the temper of the House. On the other hand, the Committee had sanctions of its own against members with the temerity to sign such petitions. During almost fifty years only twenty-two such petitions succeeded in obtaining a sufficient number of signatures and only two of the bills so discharged subsequently became law.[2]

Between January 1949 and January 1951 the House Rules Committee no longer had this power. It could delay a measure but it could not block. At any time after twenty-one days the chairman of a committee for whose bill the Rules Committee had failed to grant a rule might call it up for House consideration. Yet other committee chairmen seldom [3] had the temerity to challenge this Committee, for it still had the power to punish members though it could not permanently block consideration of bills. With the opening of the Eighty-second Congress in January 1951 the power of the Rules Committee was restored, and since then it has functioned at least occasionally in the fashion described.[4] Criticism of this aspect of the Rules Committee was especially strong during the Eighty-seventh Congress (1961–62). Twenty-five bills failed to receive a rule without any further action being taken. Of these, 19 were from the Education and Labor Committee, indicating a basic ideological difference. Of nine others brought up in one fashion or another in spite of the denial of the rule, the House passed four.[5] In 1965 a further safeguard against action contrary to the real will of the House was added. The Speaker by majority vote may force a bill out of Committee after twenty-one days, if he so desires. Incidently this should somewhat strengthen party leadership and responsibility.

---

[2] Richard Bolling, *House Out of Order* (New York: Dutton, 1965), p. 199. Chapter 10 of this book contains the best insider's account of the struggle which led in 1961 to the enlargement and modest liberalization of the Committee.

[3] Eight times in the Eighty-first Congress.

[4] This is not to say that in its built-in conservatism it has not from time to time thwarted the will of the majority; while fear of reprisals has kept that majority from producing the necessary number of signatures on a discharge petition.

[5] Walter Kravitz, "The Influence of the House Rules Committee," in Joseph S. Clark, ed., *Congressional Reform* (New York: Crowell, 1965), pp. 127–37.

Congress is an institution in which power and position are highly valued. Seniority is not only a rule governing committee chairmanships, it is also a spirit pervading the total behavior. This is especially true between new members and the older ones. The latter want the former to seek their advice and have their own ways of clipping the wings of upstarts. This does not mean that a first-termer is not listened to in committee or even on the floor if he is really master of his subject, has something to say, and is not merely seeking prominence. After one or two years, during which his colleagues have taken his measure, he may be entrusted with a subcommittee chairmanship dealing with some problem close to his heart or even with the chairmanship of a special committee. By these devices many of the admitted disadvantages connected with rigid adherence to the seniority rule are overcome and its good side preserved.

Of all the criticisms of Congress from outside its own membership, that of the seniority rule is perhaps the most universal in educated circles.[6] The term "senility rule" is occasionally used, and those who know Congress intimately will find it not too difficult to think of appropriate examples. More fundamental are two other bases of criticism—the obstacle the rule presents to responsible party government, and its alleged overweighting in the direction of conservatism.

If one is an advocate of responsible and disciplined party government, the seniority rule is certainly an obstacle. It is not so much that the committee chairmen frequently and sharply diverge from "party line" votes. Goodwin has shown that such divergence, while present, is certainly not as great as is usually supposed.[7] What is more important is that the

---

[6] For a more extended discussion of the seniority rule as it appears to the members themselves, see Charles L. Clapp, *The Congressman: His Work as He Sees It* (Washington: Brookings Institution, 1963), pp. 221–34.

[7] See George Goodwin, Jr., "The Seniority System in Congress," *American Political Science Review,* June 1959, pp. 412–36 for this, and for many other interesting facts concerning the rule.

rule insures a rival network of power and leadership. Moreover, it tends to overlap a third center of leadership, that of the subject matter specialist. It will appear later that the author does not believe in the desirability of strengthening a party-enforced majority rule as against rule by shifting majorities, inasmuch as these are determined by members' individual views on specific issues. The latter would seem more suited to contemporary needs.[8]

The overweighting in the direction of conservatism is a more serious charge. To put the matter in concrete terms, if the Democrats are in control, about sixty per cent of the committee chairmen are from the South, which is in general its conservative sector. However, once the consequences of the Republican congressional victories of 1946 have run their course this imbalance will apparently be corrected, and the Northern Democrats will materially increase their percentage of ranking members.[9] If the Republicans control, about forty-five per cent of the chairmen are from the Middle West, which is usually more conservative than this party's second center of strength on the Eastern seaboard. If leadership is, as it should be, a reflection of the general will of the majority of a legislative body, then such overweighting is a serious matter, unless adaptations to circumvent or modify it have been forthcoming. Perhaps the discrepancy is more serious in the Senate than in the House. The latter seems normally to have a conservative majority in any event. In the Senate one must look, if at all, to adaptations for remedy. Yet a conservative mood is more characteristic of the Senate than would ordinarily be inferred.

Health and age considerations should also be subject to

---

[8] See chap. 17 for a fuller discussion of the issue.

[9] See Raymond E. Wolfinger and Joan Heifitz, "Safe Seats, Seniority, and Power in Congress," *American Political Science Review*, June 1965, pp. 337–49. The number of seats won by the Democrats in the urban north by sixty-five per cent or more increased from sixteen in 1946 to eighty-one in 1964.

remedy by adaptation, if criticism of the rule is to be blunted.

Have there been such adaptations? The answer is certainly "Yes," though in varying degree and not in every instance. If he will exercise it wisely, a chairman has great power. Chairmen usually call meetings apart from those which a committee may schedule at stated intervals. They usually name the staff and assign their duties. They have priority in questioning witnesses and assume floor leadership on reported bills. They are members of conference committees. They ordinarily name the subcommittees and strongly influence the selection and priority of agendas. As presiding officers, they may rule as to quorums, points of order, and other matters. They have very considerable opportunity to penalize individual committee members if they wish to use it. They can usually veto the assignment or transfer of a member to their committees, if they do not agree with his point of view. In the great majority of instances, these powers are exercised after consultation with the membership, and the decisions are often submitted to vote. In such cases, no adaptation is necessary other than that which the chairman himself voluntarily exercises.

Such adaptation was forthcoming in the House Foreign Affairs Committee when health factors stood in the way of full activity on the part of Representatives Eaton and Chiperfield, its two Republican chairmen in the last two decades. Both of them delegated major responsibility to colleagues junior to themselves. Senator Green voluntarily relinquished the chairmanship of the Senate Foreign Relations Committee when he was over ninety. In most committees with heavy agendas, the subcommittee device is freely used, and this gives to a number of other members the chance to exercise substantial leadership. In fact the growth of the subcommittee has itself been cited as a further evidence of fragmentation of congressional leadership. Furthermore, its role in mitigating the evils of the seniority rule is obvious.

33

Where the chairman is out of tune with the majority of his committee, or even the parent body, and is obdurate or autocratic in the use of his powers, he can constitute a very serious road block, for, as has been already mentioned, his powers are very great. Yet a number of remedies are open. By law a majority of a committee can do almost anything within the function of the chairman, provided it can find a chance to vote on the issues. A revolt in the House Government Operations Committee in the Eighty-third Congress transferred most of the powers from its chairman to subcommittees. During Senator McKellar's old age, Senator Hayden unselfishly took over the burden of the work of the Senate Appropriations Committee, while allowing his colleague to retain the chairmanship with its prerogatives. If the chairman—or the committee as a whole, for that matter—is out of harmony with the will of its parent body, other adaptations are available. A bill can be referred to a more friendly committee. A special committee can be set up, and the standing committee bypassed. The discharge rule can be invoked. To cite an extreme case, the Civil Rights Act of 1957 bypassed altogether the Senate Judiciary Committee and its chairman, Senator Eastland, and was considered directly on the floor of the Senate.

Adaptations of the types suggested have gone far toward mitigating the evils and disadvantages of the seniority rule. It is at this point that another approach is relevant. Evils there are and evils there always will be, but what are the alternatives? The more usual proposals call for selection of chairmen either by the party machinery or by vote of the committee. In either instance the ever-present struggle for power is intensified. Basically, the members of Congress are overwhelmingly in favor of removing to the sphere of automatic operation a matter as controversial, as likely to produce personal animosities, as unpredictable in its results, as susceptible of clandestine or even sinister forces as the election of committee chairmen.

This is but one example, of which there are many, of the ways whereby these men are better able to live and work with each other. When there is added to these negative arguments against alternatives the affirmative consideration of guaranteed long experience under seniority, Congress would far rather approach the problem by adaptations than by drastic change.

The only type of alternative which would bypass these dangers and at the same time might mitigate some of the evils of the seniority rule would appear to be to limit the term of the chairman to eight or ten years. At the expiration of this period he would be succeeded by the second in length of service. Such a proposal has never really been taken seriously outside of academic circles. Within Congress, the members believe that this type of proposal would greatly and perhaps fatally injure the prestige of a member in his own district.

Centers of power are necessary in any body that would accomplish things, and the desideratum is that this power be responsibly exercised. When it becomes too concentrated or too arbitrary, as in the case of Speaker Joseph G. Cannon in 1910, there is revolt; but new centers necessarily arise. As of today, power is fairly well diffused, though in the House the Speaker and the Majority Leader, partly in their own right and partly because of their close relations and influence with the President if of his party, are the two most powerful single members. They as well as the Minority Leader are buttressed by an effective party whip organization.[10] Party policy committees have developed in the Senate and on the Republican side in the House and wield some measure of power. The House Democrats have been reluctant too much to crystalize formal party activity, caucus or otherwise, so as not to exacerbate their North-South cleavage. Within his own bailiwick, a House committee chairman ordinarily can have

---

[10] See Randall B. Ripley, "The Party Whip Organizations in the United States House of Representatives," *American Political Science Review*, September 1964, pp. 561–76.

his way in blocking legislation, and often in promoting it as well.

The House Rules Committee is obviously a powerful force. It may refuse to report out a bill unless discharged by a petition signed by a majority of the House or unless the bill is called under a special procedure on "Calendar Wednesday," if luck of location favors the bill, or unless, after twenty-one days, the Speaker obtains a majority vote for calling it out. It may grant any one of several types of rule, certain of which are favorable and others unfavorable to the prospects of a given measure. It can make a favorable rule conditional upon an amendment which it favors, either after it has been referred to it or in negotiations with the parent committee prior to the latter's reporting out. A rule, by the way, for those who are not familiar with the term in this connection, is the regulation stipulating the kind, the control, and the extent of floor debate on a given measure.[11] It may also cover matters such as the date or conditions of effectiveness, limitations or amendment, conditions governing points of order. The rule under which a bill is reported may be influential in or even determinative of the subsequent action. Thus a rule forbidding floor amendment, especially in tax bills, is a means of preventing raids by special interests.[12]

These rules are near the heart of the way the House organizes the final legislative stages of a given measure. The Senate, incidentally, is much less formal or rigid. Its principal traffic manager is not its Rules and Administration Committee but its Majority Leadership or Policy Committee.

---

[11] See J. A. Robinson, "The Role of the Rules Committee in Arranging the Program of the United States House of Representatives," *Western Political Quarterly,* September 1959, pp. 653–69. Robinson's *The House Rules Committee* (Indianapolis: Bobbs-Merrill, 1963) is the standard work on the subject.

[12] For an excellent study of the Rules Committee's views of its role and other aspects, see Robert L. Peabody, "The Enlarged Rules Committee" in Robert L. Peabody and Nelson W. Polsby, eds., *New Perspectives on the House of Representatives* (Chicago: Rand-McNally, 1963), chap. 6.

One of the traditional functions attributed to Congress is the illumination of issues with the consequent education of the public. It is doubtful whether this objective has figured very much in any conscious fashion in the evolution of organization and procedure. Nevertheless, the accord given to the right of the minority to be heard, expressed in such a fashion as the usual equal division of time in floor debate in the House and the frequent unlimited facilities in the Senate; the value put upon dramatization in hearings, through the custom of securing "headliners" as witnesses; the emphasis on open hearings written into the Reorganization Act—all these are evidence that a consciousness of the values inherent in education of the electorate has not been without its influence.

Finally, no one can be intimately related to Congress for long without a genuine appreciation of the role played by a desire to promote and safeguard the general welfare as expressed in its organization and procedure.

A good organization and procedure should include the following: [13]

(1) Time for reflection. Except in crises, delay in passage should be such as to give the members opportunity to study measures, not so much for their major substantive content as for their probable public reception in detail. Committee scrutiny, bicameralism, the split session are devices thus used. In other words, the operability of a measure in terms of the cultural setting is the type of question on which a legislature is competent to pass; and delay should be sufficient to permit study with this objective in mind.

(2) Time and opportunity for public reaction. This is closely related to (1). It argues for a procedure which assures public debate at two stages—the introduction of the measure and the time immediately prior to its final passage. Our bicameralism is an inferior substitute for a system of two debates with intervals in a single house. Various rules of procedure can assure two such public discussions. In England, the objective is attained by allowing debate on the general principles of a bill at the so-called "second reading," and then again

---

[13] Ernest S. Griffith, *The Impasse of Democracy* (New York: Harrison-Hilton Books, 1939), pp. 144 ff.

when it has come out of committee just prior to final passage or rejection. If a nation's written or unwritten constitution provides for an economic advisory committee or other devices to obtain the reactions of interest groups, procedure might perhaps provide for remission to them.[14] In any event, the procedure should be such that the main issues are so clarified at the initial public debate as to permit public reaction. Hearings and petitions are the usual ways to render such reaction articulate.

(3) Full public debate to be confined to essentials. This is necessary if a legislative body is to perform its important function of educating the electorate. Debates on the budget, votes of no confidence, and other devices provide the opportunity for reviewing the success or failure of the general policy of the leadership in power at a given moment. Power given to the presiding officer to rule certain types of debate out of order in full session, as belonging rather in committees; time limits; and, most of all, a party procedural leadership and a sense of individual responsibility that will apportion most time to the essential issues—all these will go far toward promoting the type of discussion which will facilitate the education of the electorate. It is nothing short of criminal that a filibuster should sometimes be necessary to direct attention to a vital issue.

(4) Proportionate consideration. This should apply as between measures and as between clauses within a specific measure. With rare exceptions the procedural leadership should ultimately determine what measures should be introduced, the amount of time which should be allocated to each bill and each clause, and the order of their consideration. These latter two provisos should be subject to overruling provisos indicated under (2) and (5). In most nations, the procedural leader will be the majority party leader or steering committee.

(5) Respect for opposition and minorities. Procedure should grant equal time in all discussions to the opposition. It should also allow the opposition equal time at the presentation of the budget; and by one device or another allow a certain number of days each session for criticism and discussion of general policy. These should be under the absolute control of the opposition as regards subject matter, but an equal amount of time should be allowed the incumbent leadership to defend itself.

(6) Opportunities for detailed amendment. For the most part, legislation will tend more and more to follow the French example and be couched in general terms. Yet this is always a relative matter, and procedure should always provide an opportunity for informed

---

[14] On the other hand, it might be better to incorporate these advisory devices at the stage of administrative maturing rather than during legislative deliberation and amendment.

criticism on the basis of additional information, chiefly such information as would be comprised under the term "public reaction." Committee is obviously the place for this, for the entire house would not have the time for such detail. Whether the British system with its non-specialized committees or the more usual American system of specialized ones is adopted, the function is the same. The latter is more intelligent, the former less dispersive.

(7) Facility. Delays other than those contemplated under (1) and (2) must not be allowed in this day and age. Restrictions on debate must bear some relationship to the amount of business to be transacted. In Chapters 16, 25, and 26 below, the possibilities of devolving a large number of decisions upon subordinate bodies will be considered; but in any event facility and absence of undue obstruction can only be obtained, I think, through vesting semi-autocratic powers either in leadership or in an impartial presiding officer, or in both, to control time and order of debate and voting. The safeguards proposed under (1), (2), (5), and (6) will mitigate the obvious dangers of this procedure.

(8) Clarity of ultimate phraseology. The drafting of the original bill should be by experts. After the amending stage is over, the bill should again be submitted to these draftsmen, for recommendations as to ultimate phraseology.

(9) No "riders" or irrelevancies. Procedural rules should be adopted making it illegal to include "riders" or clauses dealing with matters outside of the main subject of a bill. Such irrelevancies are unthinkable in most legislatures, and the time is long overdue for reform of the practice in the United States.

(10) All private or special legislation should be relegated to subordinate legislation in one of the departments.

We may add three other rules of procedure designed especially to facilitate the type of criticism of the administration which will render the latter more alert and responsive.

(11) Regular opportunity for questioning administrators. This can be done in committee or in regular session. It is not essential that it follow the ritual of the British Parliamentary system whereby the cabinet member is the one questioned. Under either the parliamentary or presidential system it should be part of the normal procedure to bring the key administrators onto the floor of the house or into committee, there to be questioned.

(12) Supervision of subordinate legislation. Where appropriate, procedure should provide for delegated legislation to "lie on the table" for a stated period. During this period either a member or a party or a certain number of members may, by simple request, force either its withdrawal or consideration by an appropriately constituted committee of the house itself. Inasmuch as this legislation is not of a uniform

type, it would probably be unwise to stereotype its supervision in any one fashion. However, three or four more or less standardized rules for requiring and obtaining further consideration (should such be desired) would be sufficient.

(13) Use of *ad hoc* commissions. In the nature of the case, probably formal procedural rules cannot provide for such commissions. The rules can, however, somewhat regularize their use. For the most part, the traditions or mores of a legislative body should be such that fairly frequently major recommendations for change of policy or the unsatisfactory functioning of existing policy should be made the subject of inquiry by a commission constituted for the purpose. Customarily this device should also be used by the legislature to deal with questions affecting the vested interests of the civil service itself—salaries, personnel policies, overlapping, coordination, dispersive tendencies. A "Joint Standing Committee on the Public Service" might well be set up, whose business it would be to propose the formation of such *ad hoc* commissions. Important committee chairmen from the two houses might constitute its personnel.

Among these criteria, Congress is probably at its best as regards 1, 2, 5, 6, 8, 11; it is weakest as regards 3, 9, 10, 12.

Political parties are the basis for the organization of Congress. They play a less important role in Congress' policies.[15] From an organizational standpoint, they determine the membership of the committees in each house, especially the number of positions allocated to the majority and minority respectively. In determining individual committee personnel, their influence is severely limited by the seniority convention and the tradition that a member once on a committee remains there, if he so wills. Modifications of this convention and tradition necessarily take place when a majority party becomes the minority and occasionally under other circumstances when deemed appropriate. Rarely is removal from a committee an instrument of party discipline, though transfer to a more desirable committee may be a party reward.

Initial committee assignments are made by committees chosen by the party, and somewhat influenced by the party leaders, especially in the Senate. Assistance to a member in

---

[15] Cf. chap. 17.

40

his re-election, geography, suitability, endorsements, his own desires are all factors.[16]   In the Senate the custom has developed of appointing each new member to at least one major committee prior to the older members having two such assignments.   On the other hand, the influence within the Senate of what Senator Clark of Pennsylvania calls the conservative "establishment" has given a measure of priority to the senators sharing its views.[17]   "The power of the President has been institutionalized; the powers of the congressional committees and their chairman have been institutionalized; but the power of the central leaders of Congress remains personal, *ad hoc,* and transitory." [18]

Organization and procedure are woven into a seamless fabric through all the aspects of congressional activity.   Some aspects are sharply criticized; others are highly praised.   Neither praise nor blame is attempted here.   Where organization is defective, adaptation and custom frequently come to the rescue.   The use of the special committee and subcommittee to mitigate the handicaps of the seniority rule has already been mentioned.   So with many another device.   Things are not always what they seem.   Nor are smoothness and speed of operation by any means the highest rung on the hierarchical ladder of values.   Given things as they are—the nature of the electorate, the size of Congress, the complexity, number, and magnitude of the issues—congressional organization and procedure do not come off badly, especially when it is borne in mind that failure to act may in some instances be a deliberately chosen wiser course, with procedural devices the instrument making such failure to act practicable.

---

[16] Samuel P. Huntington, "Congressional Response to the Twentieth Century," in David B. Truman, *The Congress and America's Future* (Englewood Cliffs: Prentice-Hall, 1965), p. 22.

[17] Joseph S. Clark, *Congress: The Sapless Branch* (New York: Harper, 1964), p. 26.

[18] For the best concrete study of the process in the House, see Nicholas A. Masters, "Committee Assignments," *American Political Science Review,* June 1961, pp. 345–57.

CHAPTER FIVE

Executive-Legislative Relations: the Weapons in the Struggle

FAR more attention has been paid to the clashes, rivalries, and differences between the executive in general, and the President in particular, on the one hand and Congress on the other than to their co-operation. We must grant that it is sociologically inherent that two co-ordinate centers of power operating in a common area will be jealous of each other and will each strive to gain the ascendancy. But it is also psychologically true that there will be accommodation when the shared end is great enough to command a common loyalty or urgent enough to force a solution. If the persons involved are public-spirited, naturally friendly, and broadgauged—and more often than not the President, the department heads, and the congressmen are all three—the government becomes workable. Their mutually independent positions also have this advantage, that each usually is required to convince the other—always a humbling and wholesome experience—before effective action can be taken.

A closer awareness of the inner workings of our government would differentiate between the presidency and the bureaucracy. The former faces some of the same problems faced by Congress in controlling the latter. This is especially true insofar as the Bureau of the Budget and an appropriations subcommittee both look toward economies. It is also true, though in a lesser degree, in matters of policy. So vast is our government and so readily may a bureau whirl in its own orbit that the White House finds much the same need for watchfulness and co-ordination over against a bureau's activity that is felt by the committee of Congress concerned. When a bureau also has its protectors and advocates within Congress, the latter rather than the President may find itself calling the tune. Under such circumstances the difficulties may multiply for both.

In matters of policy as distinct from administration the struggle is chiefly between Congress and the presidency. In this struggle each branch has a number of weapons.

Of the President's formal constitutional powers, Corwin and others have written ably and at length. The veto power and the power of appointment (with the derivative lever of patronage) are the most obvious. Only under exceptional circumstances is the veto overridden. One reason is that certain members vote for a particular measure for political reasons, knowing that it will be vetoed. Without the veto, and with a Congress wholly responsible, the result occasionally would have been different.

A considerable amount of independence is allowed a member before he is black-listed as regards patronage, whether in the matter of jobs for constituents, or public works or other advantages for his district or state. The use of patronage as a lever to obtain compliance has been somewhat exaggerated. In extremely close situations on measures important to the administration, patronage may turn the trick. On the other hand, the streamlining of patronage in appointments by Franklin Roosevelt may in the long run have operated in reverse. It is admitted that a large number of appointees even within the classified service go through the form of presenting a letter of congressional endorsement. Such letters do not ordinarily constitute patronage, for rare is the person whose hostility to the party in power has been so cogently expressed that he will be denied such a letter if he requests it. Genuine pressure upon an agency by a member in behalf of someone especially favored is another thing and results in the type of appointment for which some *quid pro quo* is often expected—even if it is no more than a measure of good will on the part of the member. This may be expressed when legislation or an appropriation of interest to the department making the appointment is up for consideration.

It should be borne in mind that patronage is as often geographic as it is personal in the sense that there is considerable discretion in the military, the water resource agencies, the post office, and elsewhere in the location of new construction. This is occasionally effective in securing support for or opposition to certain measures regarded as important by the executive. It takes the form of threats of withdrawal as well as promises of benefits to a given state or district. Logrolling and the pork barrel exist also in the executive, but their actual extent in both branches is likely to be over-estimated.

Under Presidents Kennedy and Johnson, and under the immediate direction of Lawrence O'Brien of the White House staff, perhaps the most systematic and intensive study ever of individual congressmen's attitudes toward particular measures was coupled with the most detailed campaigns to win particular votes. No legitimate stones were left unturned in the shape of arguments, favors, and—at times—threats real or implied.[1] However, even here the general attitude of a member on specific issues was probably more involved than the usually resented "blackmail."

Occasionally the President diverts, or leaves unused, funds appropriated for some specific purpose of which he does not approve. This invariably leaves Congress with a certain feeling of impotence or frustration; although, if economy has been promoted thereby, the objection may be somewhat muted. This particular weapon is used sparingly. Somewhat akin to this is the selective enforcement of laws or selective carrying

---

[1] Cf. Daniel Berman, *In Congress Assembled* (New York: Macmillan, 1964), pp. 84–91.

out of programs when Congress fails to appropriate the amount that the executive has proposed as adequate for the total activity of an agency. If the cut has been drastic, it is often suspected in Congress that the agency then selects for curtailment those items likely to result in the greatest public outcry.

There is another type of weapon against which Congress can do but little. This is the *fait accompli,* most evident in the President's power as commander in chief of the armed services, but not unknown in his other functions. It is a dangerous weapon, to be used sparingly and only when it is reasonably clear that there will be ultimate vindication in the results of the action.

The President has never been conspicuously successful in singling out individual congressmen for attack. Within his own party, even Franklin Roosevelt could not claim real victory in his attempted "purges." Truman seldom attempted such a purge in Congress, not even with its "Dixiecrat" members.[2] Eisenhower indicated disapproval, not by overt attack but by lukewarmness of support. When the President attacks a member of the opposite party by name, the public enjoys it, as it enjoys any good scrap, but probably this does not greatly affect the future of the particular member. It may even build him up to a prominence he would not otherwise have enjoyed.

The prestige of the President and his office is enormous. Even members of the opposition party cannot help being influenced somewhat by these factors, if and when they are called into council at the White House. President Johnson has brought such powers of persuasion to an all time high.

The President can command the headlines at any time. Franklin Roosevelt devoted more time and attention to the press than to Congress. If a President has a message for the people a radio audience is assured. The televised press con-

---

[2] An exception was his successful effort to oust Representative Slaughter of Missouri, but this was in Truman's own home district.

ferences of Eisenhower, Kennedy, and Johnson were most effective. Under a skilled President, the marshaling of public opinion in his support is almost irresistible against a recalcitrant Congress. But there are limits. These limits are of two sorts: if the appeal is used on issues in which the public is not very much interested, as in the creation of a Department of Transportation, or if the public fundamentally differs, as on Truman's call for repeal of the Taft-Hartley Act. In this latter instance the President may actually have been trying much more to consolidate his support from a particular group than to influence Congress.

Finally, during the decades since the turn of the century, the executive branch until relatively recently had a preponderance of access to facts, both because of experience in dealing with problems and because of its extensive research bureaus. Thus Congress had great difficulty in formulating an intelligent alternative policy on many issues, except in a few fields, such as taxation, in which it had a staff of its own. It was this superior command of information more than any other one factor that for many years gave the executive-legislative struggle the appearance of a losing battle for the latter. "It (Congress) can violently disturb, but it cannot often fathom, the waters of the sea in which the bigger fish of the civil service swim and feed." So wrote Woodrow Wilson in his *Congressional Government*.[3]

But Congress likewise is not without formidable weapons in the struggle. Chief among these are the appropriating and investigating powers. The use of these powers by Congress is more relevant to its relations with the bureaucracy than with the presidency. In a sense it is trying by these means to make the bureaus directly responsible to itself rather than indirectly through the President.

Appropriations (or lack of them) are not merely matters of economy in management. They are used in important

---

[3] First edition, p. 27.

fashions to indicate likes and dislikes of persons and policies in particular agencies and activities. If Congress increases an appropriation beyond the figure requested, the executive apparently still may have the last word, by declining to spend the larger sum, but this seldom happens. It is in the reductions, however, that the more significant policy guidance is given. Even the removal of an obnoxious employee may be indicated indirectly, if not directly, by an appropriation action.

A congressional investigation may be either by a standing committee (or subcommittee) or by a special committee created for the purpose. In any event it is greatly feared when its focus of attention is directed toward the executive branch. The fear of an investigation influences, if it does not dominate, bureau practice. Even a question asked by a single member in a speech on the floor is often enough to change or head off certain administrative decisions. Many investigations are actually the expanded questionings of one man. The practice of naming as chairman of a special investigating committee the member who first urged it (provided he is a member of the majority party) is a standing invitation to the more alert members to make such proposals.

Naturally, investigations of the executive branch are only a minority of the total number of inquiries. The largest single group consists of inquiries into problems, the outcome of which may be to recommend legislation. However, even this group almost necessarily passes in review existing policies and practices of the government.

A heroic effort was made under the Reorganization Act[4] to regularize or systematize these congressional investigations. It was formally provided in the Act that a watchful oversight of the appropriate agency or agencies was to be one of the major functions of the various standing committees. By this means it was hoped that a principal reason for the rash of

---

[4] Public Law 601, Seventy-ninth Congress.

special committees would be removed. To a considerable extent this hope has been realized. In the second session of the Eighty-first Congress, for example, out of the sixteen special investigations authorized, only five were entrusted to special committees.[5] In the second session of the Eighty-third Congress, the number had risen to thirty-nine, but only six were by special or select committees. The remainder of the investigations were handled by the standing committees. In the second session of the Eighty-sixth Congress, there were nine such special investigating committees, but two of these were quite minor. In the first session of the Eighty-ninth Congress the number of special committees sank to two—on the Aging and on the Reorganization of Congress. The Senate and House continued their Select Committees on Small Business, and the former added a permanent Select Committee on Standards and Conduct.

These investigations, whether by special or standing committees, range all the way from the frankly punitive to those specifically designed to advance the interests of a particular department. Where the agency investigated is sure of its ground, it naturally does what it can to convert the investigation into a forum for its vindication or to gain support and understanding. Where the chairman and committee are hostile or irresponsible, the hearings may become a battle of wits, with the executive at times even refusing relevant papers or records.

This latter circumstance has become somewhat more frequent of late, chiefly under the impetus of the loyalty investigations and the subsequent investigations of the security program itself—but also with substantial assistance from the fact that during the 1950's opposite parties controlled Congress and the presidency for most of the period. The execu-

---

[5] Campaign Expenditures, Chemicals and Food Production, Lobbying Activities, Small Business (House), and Organized Crime (Senate).

tive alleges the confidential character of many of its papers, especially of its personnel records.

In the loyalty investigations where the Federal Bureau of Investigation was involved, an additional alleged reason for secrecy entered, insofar as a disclosure of the papers would have imperiled the methods by which the F.B.I. obtained much of its information. Yet, rightly or wrongly, Congress believed that it had had a clearer picture, and for longer, of the menace of communism. It further believed that it had been more zealous than the executive in rooting out subversive elements from the latter. Consequently it did not trust the motives of the executive in withholding the papers and was concerned with ways and means of securing them. This raised an interesting and important point in regard to the congressional power in the matter. It was a point of wider application than merely in the field mentioned.

Section 134(a) of the Legislative Reorganization Act reads: [6]

Each standing committee of the Senate, including any subcommittee of any such committee, is authorized to hold such hearings, . . . to require by subpoena or otherwise the attendance of such witnesses and the production of such correspondence, books, papers, and documents, to take such testimony . . . as it deems advisable. Each such committee may make investigations into any matter within its jurisdiction. . . .

In general, contests of power between the two branches, arising out of investigations, have not been fought in the courts. In *McGrain* v. *Daugherty* (1927) 273 U.S. 135, involving the Teapot Dome Scandal and the congressional investigation of Attorney General Daugherty and his office, the Supreme Court made the nearest approach to a flat recognition of the fitness and propriety of the investigative process in relation to the supervisory power of Congress over

---

[6] The House of Representatives has preferred to treat each committee separately in this regard.

executive administration. The Court, however, went only so far as to declare the investigation of the Attorney General necessary and proper on the ground that the information requested was needed for the efficient exercise of the legislative function. The Court said:

> We are of opinion that the power of inquiry—with process to enforce it—is an essential and appropriate auxiliary to the legislative function. It was so regarded and employed in American legislatures before the Constitution was framed and ratified. Both houses of Congress took this view of it early in their history—the House of Representatives with the approving votes of Mr. Madison and other members whose service in the convention which framed the Constitution gives special significance to their action—and both houses have employed the power accordingly up to the present time. The acts of 1798 and 1857, judged by the comprehensive terms, were intended to recognize the existence of this power in both houses and to enable them to employ it "more effectually" than before. So, when their practice in the matter is appraised according to the circumstances in which it was begun and to those in which it has been continued, it falls nothing short of a practical construction, long continued, of the constitutional provisions respecting their powers, and therefore should be taken as fixing the meaning of those provisions, if otherwise doubtful.
>
> We are further of opinion that the provisions are not of doubtful meaning, but, as was held by this Court in the cases we have reviewed, are intended to be effectively exercised, and therefore to carry with them such auxiliary powers as are necessary and appropriate to that end. While the power to exact information in aid of the legislative function was not involved in those cases, the rule of interpretation applied there is applicable here. A legislative body cannot legislate wisely or effectively in the absence of information respecting the conditions which the legislation is intended to affect or change; and where the legislative body does not itself possess the requisite information— which not infrequently is true—recourse must be had to others who do possess it. Experience has taught that mere requests for such information often are unavailing, and also that information which is volunteered is not always accurate or complete; so some means of compulsion are essential to obtain what is needed. All this was true before and when the Constitution was framed and adopted. In that period the power of inquiry—with enforcing process—was regarded and employed as a necessary and appropriate attribute of the power to legislate—indeed, was treated as inhering in it. Thus there is am-

ple warrant for thinking, as we do, that the constitutional provisions which commit the legislative function to the two houses are intended to include this attribute to the end that the function may be effectively exercised.'

With regard to the Senate resolution involved, the Court further said:

It is quite true that the resolution directing the investigation does not in terms avow that it is intended to be in aid of legislation; but it does show that the subject to be investigated was the administration of the Department of Justice—whether its functions were being properly discharged or were being neglected or misdirected, and particularly whether the Attorney General and his assistants were performing or neglecting their duties in respect of the institution and prosecution of proceedings to punish crimes and enforce appropriate remedies against the wrongdoers—specific instances of alleged neglect being recited. Plainly the subject was one on which legislation could be had and would be materially aided by the information which the investigation was calculated to elicit. This becomes manifest when it is reflected that the functions of the Department of Justice, the powers and duties of the Attorney General and the duties of his assistants, are all subject to regulation by congressional legislation, and that the department is maintained and its activities are carried on under such appropriations as in the judgment of Congress are needed from year to year.

The only legitimate object the Senate could have in ordering the investigation was to aid it in legislating; and we think the subject-matter was such that the presumption should be indulged that this was the real object. An express avowal of the object would have been better; but in view of the particular subject-matter was not indispensable.[7]

Mr. Horne, in the same brief, indicates a possible procedure to test congressional powers:

. . . precedents are not definitive in instances where an executive officer has refused to appear before a Congressional committee or has refused to produce books and papers. If, in the absence of definitive judicial decisions on the precise point of Congressional inquiry into the Executive Branch, the Senate wishes to force the issue on the basis of the general propositions previously set forth, it should do so by enforcing its own process. See Reed v. County Commissioners (1928)

---

[7] Quoted from a manuscript entitled "Subpoenaing Files from an Executive Department," prepared by Frank B. Horne, Legislative Reference Service, May 26, 1949.

277 U.S. 376, 388. To do this the subcommittee should report the incident to the full Committee on the Judiciary and ask that the Chairman be authorized to report it to the Senate and to ask the Senate to order the President pro tempore to issue a warrant directing the Sergeant at Arms to take the person into custody and to bring him before the bar of the Senate to answer for his refusal. Upon further refusal before the bar of the Senate, the Senate could order (1) that the person be continued in the close custody of the Sergeant at Arms, or (2) that he be committed to the common jail of the District of Columbia, or (3) that he be kept by the Sergeant at Arms in close confinement in the guardroom of the Capitol Police. Volume III of Hinds' Precedents of the House of Representatives (Secs. 1669, 1684, 1672, 1686, and 1690) will furnish precedents for this procedure inasmuch as the Senate has in the past looked to the House for guidance in dealing with such persons. These precedents are conveniently outlined in the Senate Committee Print entitled "Memorandum on Proceedings Involving Contempt of Congress and Its Committees" printed for the use of the Committee on the Judiciary. See particularly pages 6 and 10. The matter probably would be placed immediately before the courts by means of a petition for a writ of habeas corpus and a definitive pronouncement would thus be obtained.

It is obvious that such a pronouncement could not be obtained from the courts under R.S. 102 (U.S.C. 2:192), first because the Executive Department would be required to prosecute an officer in the Executive Branch whose refusal is based on a Presidential directive, and second because this section carries a statutory penalty which the President probably could pardon in advance. See Taft, *Our Chief Magistrate and His Powers*, 1925 edition, pages 121–124. It is doubtful if the President could, however, take a definitive action in this manner with regard to a person being held under an order of the Senate. See *Ex Parte Grossman* (1925) 267 U.S. 87, 118.

In *Touhy* v. *Ragen*,[8] the Court apparently settled the question as regards subordinate officials by upholding the refusal of the agent to honor a *subpoena duces tecum* under instructions from the Attorney General. It did this on narrow grounds, without passing judgment on the authority of the Attorney General himself, to refuse or comply.

Former President Truman refused to honor a congressional subpoena. On April 22, 1948, the House of Representatives passed a resolution directing the Secretary of Commerce to

---

[8] 340 U.S. 462 (1950).

transmit a letter with respect to Dr. Edward Condon. The letter was not produced, and the House took no further action.

Mr. Horne in 1954 [9] summarized the current situation as follows:

(a) That the scope of a congressional investigation is as broad as the legislative purpose requires (*Townsend* v. *U.S.* [1938] 95 F. [2d] 352, 361).

(b) That the subpoena of a duly authorized investigatory committee of Congress is no more restricted than that of a grand jury.

(c) That the right of a legislative body to demand and receive, from the executive branch, information and papers which it deems pertinent to the legislative process is established.

(d) That this established right has been vigorously asserted at times by the Congress of the United States against the President and executive officers.

(e) That the President and the executive officers have vigorously opposed such asserted right on the basis of the fundamental doctrine of separation of powers of the executive, legislative, and judicial branches of the Federal Government.

(f) That the Congress has merely asserted its right to obtain information without attempting to enforce it.

(g) That the Congress has never attempted to invoke against executive officers the law which provides that every person who, having been summoned by either House to give testimony or to produce papers upon a matter under inquiry, willfully makes default, is criminally liable.

Having dealt at length with the constitutional problems presented by executive refusals, it should be added that such refusals are the exception. In general the executive complies with such requests for data or responses to questions. Congress has numerous indirect sanctions with which to punish a non-co-operative administration.

Apparently the Supreme Court today is prepared to stretch the investigative power almost to the limit, for Justice Frankfurter speaking for the Court in *Tenney* v. *Brandhove* [10] declares as follows: "Investigations, whether by standing or

---

[9] Senate Document 99, Eighty-third Congress, second session. Congressional Power of Investigation, p. 21. The document develops the points in some detail.

[10] 341 U.S. 367 (1951).

special committees, are an established part of representative government. . . . To find that a committee's investigation has exceeded the bounds of legislative power it must be obvious that there was a usurpation of functions exclusively vested in the Judiciary or the Executive. . . ."

That congressional investigations of the bureaucracy, if constructively handled, can be enormously useful has no stronger witness than the story of the Truman War Investigating Committee in World War II. Here was an example of how the very independence of Congress prevented any white-washing and permitted a genuine watchdog function. In general, the congressional investigation, in addition to other roles, performs the function of the question hour in the British House of Commons, and performs it considerably better.

The occasion of confirmation of presidential appointments is often used by Congress to indicate attitudes. Congressional fears of radicalism, and dislikes of particular aspects of foreign or other policies, are frequently voiced at the time a name is up for consideration; these attitudes are not without their effect, even if the nominee is in fact confirmed. "Senatorial courtesy" in the matter of appointments is a special case—resulting for practical purposes in appointments by the senators [11] (if of the majority party), rather than by the President, of officials whose duties are within the bounds of a single state. It may be regarded as something of an offset against the President's use of patronage to obtain his will. Such "courtesy" is influential but not usually decisive in appointments to positions of national scope.

There is a type of congressional influence which is not well understood by the public and which is difficult to ferret out in all its ramifications. This is found in the informal but direct relationships set up between certain members or committees and particular bureaus or persons in the executive. The ties

---

[11] Or occasionally by members of the House. Cf. p. 217 for other aspects.

are various. Sometimes the bureau chief involved is one originally recommended by a member of Congress. Sometimes assiduous cultivation of a particular committee or friendship arising out of common interests is responsible. Perhaps the bureau itself was originally the creation of a particular committee and was designed to carry out the economic or other interests represented by the members. "Government by whirlpools" characterizes much of the Washington scene.

One cannot live in Washington for long without being conscious that it has these whirlpools or centers of activity focusing on particular problems. The persons who are thus active—in agriculture, in power, in labor, in foreign trade, and the parts thereof—are variously composed. Some are civil servants, some are active members of the appropriate committees in the House and Senate, some are lobbyists, some are unofficial research authorities, connected perhaps with the Brookings Institution or with one of the universities, or even entirely private individuals. Perhaps special correspondents of newspapers are included. These people in their various permutations and combinations are continually meeting in each other's offices, at various clubs, lunching together, and participating in legislative hearings or serving on important but obscure committees set up within the departments. Among such human beings interested in a common problem, ideas are bound to emerge—ideas for programs, ideas for strategy. . . .

Clearance for the idea would be obtained from one's chief, if he were not one of those originally participating. There is nothing really mysterious about this sort of government. It is essentially "of men" and these men behave very naturally. "Who says what to whom, and what is the reaction?" This question, if we could obtain enough answers, would capture the spirit, the genius of our own or any government. It is my opinion that ordinarily the relationship among these men—legislators, administrators, lobbyists, scholars—who are interested in a common problem is a much more real relationship than the relationship between congressmen generally or between administrators generally. In other words, he who would understand the prevailing pattern of our present governmental behavior, instead of studying the formal institutions or even generalizations in the relationships between these institutions or organs, important though all these are, may possibly obtain a better picture of the way things really happen if he would study these "whirlpools" of special social interest and problems.[12]

---

[12] Griffith, *The Impasse of Democracy*, p. 182.

It is this type of congressional-bureaucratic relationship that underlies the reluctance of Congress to give department heads effective control over their bureau chiefs. The first Hoover Commission correctly pointed to this situation as handicapping effective control by the President over much of the administration. Moreover, the independent commissions with terms of office overlapping presidential elections were created in this fashion originally so as to be relatively free from presidential control.

Illustrative of the fashion in which bureaus with congressional connections can circumvent or even defy presidential intent is the position of the Engineer Corps of the Department of the Army. Even orders from President Roosevelt were impotent to prevent its angling for and securing the Kings River project.[13] The Engineer Corps and its twin or rival, the Bureau of Reclamation, are the great construction agencies of the Federal Government. Even Bureau of the Budget disapproval is not enough to block their projects, especially in the case of projects sponsored by the Corps. While it is true that the Bureau of Reclamation sometimes by-passes the Bureau of the Budget by dealing directly with the President, the Corps deals directly with Congress, and support for a project is consolidated prior to any Budget Bureau submission. The secret of the power of these agencies lies in the value to a district or state of the construction and subsequent operation of such water resources projects. This is especially true when, as with the construction under direction of the Corps, the cost is usually centrally borne. Of late, it is quite possible that the power of both of these agencies is exceeded by that of the Bureau of Public Roads. This latter has largesse at its disposal approaching $100,000,000,000; together with the state highway agencies it subsidizes, the

---

13 See Commission on Organization of Executive Branch, *Task Force Report on Natural Resources* (Washington, D.C.: United States Government Printing Office, 1949), pp. 149 ff.

contractors who perform the construction, and the automobile industry that uses the end product, it constitutes a whirlpool of tremendous power. Its story has not yet been documented.

In other words, insofar as there is a struggle between Congress and the President, it is an oversimplification to say that the latter can count on all the agencies and bureaus siding with him, even though he may have appointed the chief or the majority of the commissioners. Many an agency has its way of by-passing the chief executive and working with those in Congress whose interests parallel its own. In fact, a strong case can be made out that we actually have "four-way" government instead of the classic tripartite. Congress, the presidency, the bureaucracy, and the judiciary are the four. A full understanding would require close examination of the relationship of each of these with the others.[14]

The power of impeachment is normally among the weapons of Congress, but it has been invoked only twice against officers of the executive branch—once against the President, and once against the Secretary of War. Both instances resulted in acquittals. It is thus virtually a dead letter as regards the executive.

It was contemplated under the Legislative Reorganization Act that the General Accounting Office would play a much more affirmative role than it now does as an agent of Congress. Section 206 reads as follows:

The Comptroller General is authorized and directed to make an expenditure analysis of each agency in the executive branch of the Government (including Government corporations), which, in the opinion of the Comptroller General, will enable Congress to determine whether public funds have been economically and efficiently administered and expended. Reports on such analyses shall be submitted by the Comptroller General, from time to time, to the Committees on Expenditures [i.e., Government Operations], to the Appropriations Committee, and

---

14 In this connection, see Richard E. Neustadt, "Politicians and Bureaucrats," in David B. Truman, ed., *The Congress and America's Future* (Englewood Cliffs: Prentice-Hall, 1965), pp. 102–20; Peter Woll, *American Bureaucracy* (New York: Norton, 1963).

to the legislative committees having jurisdiction over legislation relating to the operations of the respective agencies, of the two Houses.

This provision has never been implemented with the necessary appropriation. However, the General Accounting Office is one of the sources for "leads," especially for the Committees on Government Operations, when these committees undertake to fulfill one of their statutory functions in

(A) receiving and examining reports of the Comptroller General of the United States and of submitting such recommendation to the Senate (to the House) as it deems necessary or desirable in connection with the subject matter of such reports;
(B) studying the operation of government activities of all levels with a view to determining its economy and efficiency; . . .[15]

Especially in war years, but increasingly of late in peacetime as well, Congress has used statutory time limits in the original act as a device to circumvent a possible presidential veto of some future measure designed to change a particular policy to which it has given reluctant or experimental agreement. Its best-known uses have been in the fields of foreign trade and executive reorganization. International co-operation is apparently also a favorite field for imposition of such time limits. A few programs and agencies, including incidentally the Office of Economic Opportunity, require annual authorizations as well as appropriations. The Agricultural Trade Development and Assistance Act of 1954 carries a three-year limit to the power of entering into agreements concerning use of foreign currencies, emergency relief, and other matters. Export control powers were originally to terminate in 1951, but they have been twice extended. The power to guarantee overseas investment for certain projects under the current Mutual Security Act terminates June 30, 1967. The original Act limited the transfer of military supplies to Japan to June 30, 1955. The date of the authority to draft doctors and dentists has again been extended, but there is a terminal

---

[15] Legislative Reorganization Act of 1946, Sec. 102 (g) (2), Sec. 121 (b) (1), (h) (2).

date. One hesitates to read into these laws too much significance, but it may well be that at least an incipient amendment of the Constitution is emerging by which any *withdrawal* of powers granted the President shall not be subject to veto, if Congress so decides.

Akin to this is the extension of the use of Concurrent Resolutions, which type of legislative action is not subject to presidential veto. Provisions are made in the original statute for amendment of detail to be subject to such an instrument. This is still rare, but it is worthy of note that in some instances it is provided that powers granted may be terminated in this fashion. Also a few statutes provide that certain administrative actions are subject to review by a congressional committee. Certain real estate transactions of the armed services have been so restricted.[16] In 1965 President Johnson vetoed a bill which would have required the approval of the Armed Services Committee for the closing of military bases. The Omnibus Rivers and Harbors Act of 1965 in authorizing smaller water resource projects (costing under $10,000,000) required the specific approval of the Public Works Committees of both Houses prior to spending on a specific project. The President, claiming that this was a derogation of his authority, announced his intention of non-use and seeking repeal. The Appropriations Bill for the Department of Defense for fiscal year 1956 contained a proviso requiring approval of the committee chairmen prior to the Department divesting itself of a business activity by turning it over to a private concern. President Eisenhower, through the Attorney General, challenged the constitutionality of this and indicated his intention of ignoring it. In all these and similar instances Congress is in search of a flexible device under which detailed administrative acts may be subject to review without having to be made the subject of special legislation.[17]

---

[16] Cf. Robert W. Ginnane, "Control of Federal Administration by Congressional Resolutions and Committees," *Harvard Law Review,* February 1953.

[17] See p. 135.

Occasionally Congress passes resolutions directed toward the executive branch, especially in international policy, and this is one of its powers which is capable of considerably greater development. Such resolutions are not binding on the executive, but they can be warnings or encouragements, as the case may be. This will be discussed further when we consider the role of Congress in international affairs.[18]

Finally, one should note the acquisition by Congress of a fairly substantial permanent professional staff. For the most part, this staff is attached to the standing committees or has been added to the Legislative Reference Service.[19] No longer is it so difficult for Congress itself to analyze the proposals of the executive—and, if it sees fit, to formulate alternative policies.[20]

Thus have checks and balances evolved in practice, revealing ramifications often unforeseen and yet making certain that irresponsible power is still virtually unknown under our Constitution.

Certainly the exercise of these weapons is often complicating. For example, it is always dangerous, though not necessarily harmful, for a bureau to have two masters. Yet there are compensations, and usages have arisen whereby co-operation may modify conflict. To these we next turn.

---

[18] Cf. chap. 13.

[19] The Appropriations Committees, the Joint Committee on Internal Revenue Taxation, and the Office of the Legislative Counsel were staffed earlier.

[20] Cf. chap. 7 for an extended discussion of congressional staff services.

CHAPTER SIX

Co-operation in Executive-Legislative Relations

To THE political party is customarily assigned the central role in legislative-executive co-operation. Separation of powers largely precludes
the type of semienforced co-operation which parliaments such
as the British enjoy, thanks to the sanction of dissolution in
the hands of the Prime Minister and the power of the party
to deny candidacy to a recalcitrant member. There are sanctions or weapons in the hands of both the President and Congress available for the one over against the other, as we have
already seen. Yet the scales are relatively even, and each
branch preserves substantial zones of independence. Thus
there must be a voluntary element in working together which
arises out of inner convictions—such as a common loyalty
to party or a common desire to support those measures which
will result in re-election or a common belief in the soundness of specific means and ends. The President and his party
mates in Congress do share a common electoral interest, but
this is less than would be supposed—in part because they
have different constituencies and in part because of the value
the voters place on independence and the way they respond
favorably to a "fighter," whether President or congressman.
During the twentieth century we as a people have come to
have a comparatively weak sense of party loyalty or solidarity.
In practice our national parties are loose federations of local
organizations, and neither cohesive nor integrated. Least of
all, would they think of or be able to wield all-powerful

61

sanctions. Moreover, supraparty considerations, especially a common loyalty to the national interest, are frequently more powerful factors than party loyalty could ever be. Especially is this so, because the points of view of the two parties on major issues are so often indistinguishable. Hence even for party co-operation we are again thrown back largely upon voluntary elements, of which the skill of the President in exercising qualities of leadership is one of the greatest.

The Constitution itself prescribes certain procedures making for executive-legislative co-operation, though many of these have usually been regarded as falling into the more hostile category of checks and balances. For example, the power of the Senate to confirm appointments does result in a constant flow into key political posts in the administration of men who have in some measure the confidence of the legislative branch. When we consider that a large number of such appointees have also had to be cleared with the senators of their home states, and were frequently recommended by them, the scales are weighted still more strongly in the direction of co-operation. Moreover, one might almost say that at long last the requirement of a two-thirds vote in treaty ratification has come to be regarded, not as obstructive, but as an invitation for the President to seek the Senate's co-operation even in the stages of treaty negotiation—its "advice" as well as its "consent." Similarly the possibility of a presidential veto in connection with many important measures has brought consultation and compromise prior to passage that have forestalled the veto.

The presidential message has grown enormously in the frequency of its use and probably also in the attention paid to it by Congress. It has come to be an expected element in leadership at the time of any national crisis.

Laws have also made some contribution to the devices potentially favoring free co-operation. Under the Legislative Reorganization Act of 1946, the most systematic attempt in history was made to see that the committees of Congress corresponded to the agencies and structure of the executive branch.

Furthermore, under the terms of the Act, each of these committees was charged with "watchfulness" over the corresponding agency or agencies. In a few instances this has resulted in invitations to the agency or agencies to come in and tell their story to the committee—with no set agenda and no formal bills. Relations between committee members and staffs on the one side and high officials on the other have extended considerably beyond their institutionalization in committee procedures.

Ingenuity with an assist from a benevolent Supreme Court [1] has brought into being a device of considerable promise. This is a kind of legislative veto over details of executive administrative action in areas in which it is desirable to introduce much greater flexibility than is feasible in ordinary legislation and at the same time permit Congress to exercise a measure of control. The principal case in recent operation is in the field of executive reorganization. The various plans for reorganizing the executive branch were subject to disapproval by either house of Congress during a period of sixty days by a majority vote of its total membership. Similar powers of disapproval appeared in subsequent extensions of these reorganization acts. It may be noted that certain deportation actions and court rule changes are subject to a similar legislative veto. A similar device has been proposed for agreements in international trade and for local District of Columbia legislation in the event of home rule. Such a "veto" by Congress as a whole would seem to be in a different category from attempts on the part of individual committees to require their approval for particular administrative acts. This latter innovation seemingly does violence to the intent of the Constitution, although here again the simpler procedure may be the better one.[2]

Certain departments, notably State, have elevated congres-

---

[1] In *Sibbach* v. *Wilson & Co.*, 312 U.S. 1 (1941).

[2] See Joseph P. Harris, *Congressional Control of Administration* (Washington: Brookings Institution, 1964), chap. 8.

sional liaison to the level of an assistant secretaryship whereas in other instances the head of the agency himself prefers to handle this aspect of his job. A number of departments maintain liaison offices on Capitol Hill. Under the Johnson and Kennedy administrations, legislative liaison officers increased greatly in number. In 1963 a total of 737 persons were involved, partly in services to members, partly in lobbying activities. To a considerable extent they became the eyes and ears of the White House on Capitol Hill. Under Lawrence O'Brien, considerable coordination took place, and there was evidence that these departmental officers were somewhat offsetting the sub-system relationships between bureau chiefs and members. This development is well worth watching.[3]

Usage has gone further than law, but is correspondingly less stable. At the top level are the regular conferences between the President and the leadership of his party in Congress. Moreover, no one can read the White House appointment list without realizing that there is a constant and highly flexible use of conferences with members of Congress on matters of mutual interest—with the initiative divided between the two branches. Chairmen of important committees have frequent conferences with the President with respect to legislative program. It is not at all certain that a formalizing of these various arrangements would necessarily increase the measure of co-operation which in practice they now achieve. Flexibility is a strongly favorable factor in assuring the reality of these relationships, and by these means those in the opposition party can also be called in council. This is especially important in Congresses in which the two branches are controlled by opposite parties. Moreover, flexibility permits the neutralizing of some of the less fortunate results of the seniority rule, which would have to be lived with under

---

[3] See the very interesting article in the *Public Administration Review* of March 1966, pp. 14–24, by G. Russel Pipe.

formalized arrangements. In any event, consultations between the White House and Congress are common practice to an extent and with an influence that only those close to the situation can really appreciate.

In this connection it is worthy of comment that Presidential Assistant Lawrence O'Brien saw to it that under the Kennedy and Johnson administrations all new members of Congress had the opportunity for direct dialogue with the President.

If conferences between the President and members of Congress are increasingly frequent, so also are conferences between cabinet and other members of the administration and appropriate congressmen. These occur scores (and perhaps hundreds) of times a week. The network of informal liaison relationships is one of the keys to the successful operation of our Constitution.

In many, perhaps most, committees the practice has grown up of referring most or all relevant bills to the appropriate departments for comment prior to action. In minor legislation, an unfavorable report from a department is likely to be decisive. A favorable report, however, carries no corresponding assurance, unless it falls within the "whirlpool" pattern discussed later.[4] In such instances, when the interests of a bureau and a pressure group correspond to the predilections of a number of the committee members, the probability of passage is greatly increased. It is this type of situation which is often one of the best illustrations of the previously mentioned situation in which the relationship between a bureau and a committee is more powerful than between the bureau and the presidency.

Of growing importance also are conferences at the "staff level," between members of Congress or the employees of congressional committees and key men in the administration. The two-way flow of advice and opinion, of information as to administrative problems and information as to congres-

---

[4] P. 144 f. Cf. also p. 55 f.

sional attitude, is prolific in its contribution to understanding. Staffs of the Appropriations Committees come to learn which agency budget officers they can trust as sources of information. Analysts on the staff of the Legislative Reference Service make it a point to check with representatives of the departments in connection with most important relevant reports prepared for Congress—a check designed to make certain that the account herein given of the official administration point of view is in fact accurate, though the treatment of that point of view in the report often includes not only a critique of it as well as the arguments in its favor but also a presentation and analysis of alternatives.

Of recent years Congress has frowned upon the earlier practice of borrowing experts from the executive to serve its committees. In any clash of loyalties it was their permanent connection that allegedly prevailed. On the other hand, the proviso of the Legislative Reorganization Act has been abolished that required that a year's interval must elapse prior to a former member of the professional staff of a committee taking a job with the executive. A modest flow of personnel to the executive from Congress and its committee staffs has set in, in part to make it possible for agencies to understand Congress better, in part doubtless to capitalize on congressional connections. A similar hiring in the other direction is not unusual. Thirty-five former employees of the executive branch were employed on the professional staffs of committees during the Eightieth Congress.[5] In the long run, the practice of interchange is largely to the good. Congress operates to a great extent on informal understandings and usages, and the introduction of the factor of exchange of personnel is likely to influence co-operation more than the small numbers involved would indicate.

The use of members of Congress as representatives at in-

---

[5] G. Kammerer, *The Staffing of the Committees of Congress* (Lexington: University of Kentucky Bureau of Government Research, 1949), pp. 44 ff.

ternational and other conferences is a highly important device making for co-operation. This is better considered at length in connection with the congressional role in international affairs.[6] At this point it is enough to call attention to its potentialities in other fields as well. The technique of the joint legislative-executive commission utilized in the Temporary National Economic Committee, the two Commissions on the Organization of the Executive Branch (the Hoover Commissions), and the Commission on Intergovernmental Relations is as yet exceptional. However, the greater measure of success accorded the recommendations of the first Hoover Commission as compared with earlier, purely executive efforts would seem to call for similar creative use of such a device in other fields. The timidity of the executive and its reluctance to share real deliberations because of the "complicating" nature of congressional participation are likely to prove obstacles to such extension.

Patronage has been deplored, and rightly so, as undermining the integrity and quality of the civil service. It is doubtful whether such contribution as it may make to better understanding between the two branches really compensates. It does presumably purchase a measure of co-operation in some congressional circles through fear of its loss, but whether co-operation won in this fashion is in the public interest is doubtful. Other rewards for party regularity fall into the same category. It ought to be appreciated more than it is by the advocates of "responsible" party government that it is on sanctions of this character that a strengthening of party must in a measure rest.

The influence of the President is very great indeed. Upon his nation-wide election, upon his incomparable command of the mediums of communication, upon the glamour surrounding him as the head of the world's greatest nation, upon his superior command of information, upon all these and many

---

[6] Cf. p. 183.

other factors, the President may rely when he wishes to exert his personal influence with Congress in behalf of a particular course of action. Surely these factors are enough; more would introduce elements making for the operation of less worthy motives on the part of congressmen. These motives in the end might be self-defeating in that their cumulative effect might so lower the quality of representative government as to render it less capable of performing its roles of critic and generator of alternative policies.

Of late years the sense of urgency has been ever with the nation. Anyone reading the record must have been deeply impressed with the readiness of Congress to rise to the occasion—first, with the antidepression measures of the mid-thirties, then with the needful measures during our period of belligerent neutrality, then with the war, the reconstruction, the growing Russian menace, the crisis of Korea, the continuation of the cold war, the aggressiveness of communist China. Measures by executive fiat would doubtless have been quicker, but that they would have been sounder and would have obtained that measure of popular acceptance accompanying congressional discussion and decision seems highly unlikely. When there is no urgency in a given field, the pace is slower, the co-operation less readily forthcoming, and we resume our normal pattern of waiting for concurrent majorities to reveal themselves. Nor are our country and our people in fact less well off economically and otherwise than those nations whose problem of executive-legislative co-operation has been solved by the domination of the executive.[7] Nor are our executive's actions arbitrary and doctrinaire as they frequently are in these other nations. Thus we are somewhat hesitant to attach decisive importance to the arguments of those who are impatient with Congress and who read into its isolationism

---

[7] Too much should not be read into this statement. All that is really meant is that certainly the burden of proof lies with the other side to isolate and evaluate this factor in a situation of multiple causation.

following the First World War a pattern for all time and into its frequent economic conservatism obstruction to an alleged progress.

Nevertheless, proposals working toward greater free co-operation between the two branches as between equals are in order. Chiefly these call for the formalizing of devices which have operated in informal fashion, and for increasing the use of ones which thus far have been employed only occasionally.

Corwin and Hyneman would establish joint councils. The Corwin proposal [8] calls for reconstruction of the Cabinet so as to contain the leading members of a joint legislative council. Heads of departments and agencies would be members only as the occasion demands. The Hyneman proposal [9] calls for a central council selected by the President. It would have the function of formulating the program of the government and directing its execution. Membership would include a small group from Congress, some of the key administrators, and probably a few men of great standing who held no other formal governmental office.

The LaFollette-Monroney Committee [10] had several devices of this type presented to it, and in its *Report* recommended the formation of a joint legislative and executive council tied in with a strengthening of party responsibility. The congressional members would consist of the majority policy committees of the two houses with the occasional inclusion of the minority policy committees. In addition, as has been noted elsewhere,[11] the *Report* laid great stress upon a committee structure of Congress which paralleled the administrative structure of the executive.

---

[8] Corwin, *The President: Office and Powers,* pp. 297 ff.

[9] Charles S. Hyneman, *Bureaucracy in a Democracy* (New York: Harper, 1950), pp. 571 ff.

[10] Joint Committee on the Organization of Congress. Established under House Concurrent Resolution 18, Seventy-ninth Congress, first session.

[11] Cf. pp. 43, 57 f.

Senator Kefauver, one of the most recent in a long but intermittent tradition, was a strong exponent of bringing members of the Cabinet onto the floor of the houses for questioning, thus extending to the whole Congress (with the by-product of a wider publicity) a device now commonly used by the committees. Opposition to and support of such a measure exists in both Congress and the executive.

Boards of visitors to the departments, presumably from the appropriate congressional committees, are offered as a device aiming partly at watchfulness, partly at mutual understanding. Informally, such visiting already often takes place and is even formalized in the shape of certain of the committee investigations involving travel to various parts of the United States or abroad. Proposals for congressional advisers for specific agencies are somewhat similar in nature but involve a more affirmative approach in that they contemplate not merely watchfulness but also a measure of participation in policy formation. Under the Thomas-Ives Bill,[12] joint investigating commissions would have been authorized, made up of appointees by the President from a panel of citizens and appointees by Congress from its own membership.

Lasswell proposes the formation of national security committees within Congress (made up of representatives of appropriate other committees), the chairmen of which might sit with the National Security Council.[13]

Paralleling the relationships between the President's Council of Economic Advisers and the Joint Committee on the Economic Report, Wallace Parks suggests a joint committee on foreign economic policy, also to receive a report from the executive.[14]

Kurt Borchardt calls attention to the need for more insti-

---

[12] S. 3775, Eighty-first Congress.
[13] Harold D. Lasswell, *National Security and Individual Freedom* (New York: McGraw-Hill, 1950), pp. 106 ff.
[14] Wallace Parks, *United States Administration of Its International Economic Affairs* (Baltimore: The Johns Hopkins Press, 1951), pp. 287 f.

tutionalized opportunities for both the executive and Congress to deal with over-all programs, instancing the budget and the economic report. He would institute similar opportunities in foreign policy and national security.[15]

Of late there have been relatively few new concrete proposals. Such fresh thinking as has taken place appears to be in the direction of strengthening the national party in its liaison function. Stephen K. Bailey recommends national party headquarters, official and social, located in the Mall, designed to promote fraternization and consultation. He also would have House and Senate elections coincide with that of the President. In the case of the Senate, these elections would be for eight-year terms, half of the senators being elected each four years.[16] James M. Burns in similar vein calls upon the next President to co-operate in establishing the images of a liberal Democratic party and a conservative Republican party by insisting upon unified party policy between the presidential and congressional wings.[17]

One of the most interesting developments has been the annual "President's program." This really started with President Truman. It was consolidated under Eisenhower, except for his first year when time did not allow. Kennedy and Johnson have followed the same general precedent. The program has centered in the three messages, on the "State of the Union," the budget, and the Economic Report. Each item proposed is then normally followed by an administration drafted bill. An interesting by-product has been the leverage these procedures give the President over his departments and agencies.

---

[15] Joint Committee on the Organization of Congress, *Suggestions for Strengthening Congress* ([Joint Committee Print, Seventy-ninth Congress, second session, June 1946], Washington, D.C.: United States Government Printing Office, 1946), pp. 43–45.

[16] Stephen K. Bailey, *The Condition of Our National Political Parties* (New York: Fund for the Republic, 1959), pp. 12 f.

[17] James M. Burns, "Memo to the Next President," *Atlantic Monthly,* April 1960, pp. 64–68.

Why has Congress not only not resented these programs but increasingly welcomed them? Several factors are operative at this point. In the first place, the great majority of items had been before Congress for a number of years. Presidential endorsement became a matter to some extent of timing, the identification of the right moment for throwing his weight back of a proposal. In the second place, Congress with its increasingly developed and available expertise has felt much more secure in dealing with such recommendations. It is able to screen, amend, reject, substitute, or accept, after full hearings and exhaustive analysis. Under these circumstances, especially as there is nothing to prevent Congress adding items, if it wishes, the "President's program" none the less plays a most convenient role in furnishing an outline agenda for the session. Back of the messages may well lie very considerable informal consultations with key congressmen, a give and take which furnishes the initial step in consensus building.

With the tacit acceptance of this "President's program" in the aforementioned roles, new importance attaches itself to the congressional role in "incubating" ideas. The earlier introduction of bills on a subject by individual members, the eventual inquiries and scheduling of hearings on the part of committees, the reporting out or even the passage of a measure in one house all are part of this clearly identifiable congressional role. Issues are illuminated, support is developed, alternatives are explored—all very important steps preparatory to that day on which a president makes a given measure his own. The leadership function is thus seen as a much more diffused one than is popularly supposed.

In conclusion, be it noted that much more has been accomplished already in the direction of co-operation than is generally supposed. This co-operation is not of the rubber-stamp character apparently desired by some and allegedly realized at certain times in our national history. Nor is it the reluctant co-operation induced by bribing or bludgeoning. Rather it is becoming a two-way street, each party making its own peculiar contribution to the end result. The last thirty-five years may have been unusual in that in such large measure there was usually present in a domestic or world crisis an overriding sense of the necessity of placing the national welfare first. Usages of co-operation somewhat haphazardly acquired might crumble in a less favorable climate. It is this hazard, among other considerations, that has led so many political thinkers to call for a strengthening of party discipline as an instrument of party responsibility and to call for party responsibility as a means of enacting an integrated national program. At present, the more informal, freer system allows for flexibility to match the great variables in the case—variables in persons in key positions, variables in subject matter, variables in the degree of crisis, variables as to whether the party of the President is or is not in control of one or both houses of Congress. The burden of proof lies with those who would formalize or strait-jacket the institutional arrangements, especially party control, as a way of furthering the already growing measure of co-operation. In the end, such proposals may prove self-defeating.

CHAPTER SEVEN

The Congressional Response to a Technical Age

THE principal difficulty faced by Congress in carrying out its contemplated functions may be put in question form. How can a group of non-specialists, elected as representatives of the electorate, really function in a specialized and technological age? For surely no one will deny that the overwhelming majority of the great problems facing the government are complex to such a degree that the most skilled specialization and the most profound wisdom are none too great to deal with them.

It is this factor that in most industrialized nations has given the major impetus to a growing bureaucratic domination.

The effects of the multiplication of problems and of their growing complexity have revealed themselves largely in three ways. They have increased the demand upon the members' time by the individual constituent; they have forced an adaptation in the direction of specialization and reliance upon *expertise;* and they have created a dispersiveness in the electorate that has reflected itself in the rise of the pressure group and in an erosion of congressional party responsibility. In all probability each of these trends is irreversible, given separation of powers and our present election system. Fortunately, there are advantages as well as disadvantages to the general welfare in these developments.

Until the end of the Civil War there were seldom more than two or three major issues facing a given Congress. The rest of the world kept its distance for much of the time, though

74

even a slight interference tended to be felt deeply by the self-conscious rising nationalism of the young republic. Slavery was an issue, complex it is true, but maturing over many decades. The detailed development of governmental functions was largely a state and local matter. Continuous intervention in economic and other matters—apart from the tariff—was almost unknown. The opening up of the public domain was perhaps the only exception.

Let us examine somewhat more closely the implications of this relatively simple state of affairs in the spheres already noted.

In the first place, the necessary attention to individual constituents consisted largely (after Andrew Jackson's time) of attention to job seekers and, occasionally, land-grabbers. Districts possessed less than half the population of the present districts, even toward the end of the period. The number of voting constituents was further cut in half by the absence of woman suffrage. In many states the Negro was disfranchised even after the War between the States. Difficulties in transportation precluded visits to Washington on the part of all save the relatively well-to-do few. Congress was in session only a few months of the year. Members were not granted secretarial help, nor did they need it till well on in the century. In other words, the members of Congress had the time to spend in thought and deliberation on issues. At the same time the really major issues were few, usually slow in maturing, and predominantly nontechnical in nature.

It was this nontechnical character of public questions that lent itself to their resolution in an atmosphere of "principle" and party loyalty rather than through study and discussion. The average member knew, or thought he knew, the answers. Where principles were not immediately forthcoming, party supplied them. Party cohesiveness was practicable in an age of few, but persistent, major issues. Debate was leisurely, but in spite of this frequently resulted in more heat than light.

To this day, many are still somewhat under the illusion that a single principle exhausts the meaning of a given issue; there were few then who doubted it. Debates marked the clash of principles, which gave them a certain aura of moral quality, but they contained much less of a truly objective, factual nature than is evident today.[1]

Pressure groups naturally existed, but the average constituency, even the average state, was relatively homogeneous. North *versus* South, commerce *versus* manufacturing, debtor *versus* creditor—these were the relatively simple cleavages that translated themselves into national policy, and seldom did a given member need to suffer from political schizophrenia. The intricate crisscrossing of conflicting groups of today's era of statism was not present to complicate at one and the same time a legislator's conscience and his chances for re-election. The party machinery was more influential than the committee in major decisions, even though the committee system was a relatively early adaptation to the need for detailed preliminary consideration of measures.

The contrast with the present day is tremendous. Congress functions in a different world. By the second or third decade of the twentieth century, labor and agriculture and the veterans had learned the lesson that business had learned earlier: that political action can be a powerful weapon in the arsenal of economic struggle. *Laissez faire,* even in the lip service paid to it, crumbled before the hard realities of the 1930's. The United States became a great power in the world arena; by 1945 it found itself at least potentially "the" great power; in 1960 it shared its world influence with a basically hostile rival of similar magnitude.

The result of these and other forces in the legislative field was revolutionary. Governmental regulation in some fashion or other extended to every business; government controls

---

[1] Here again the expansion westward, with the problems and policies associated with the public domain, may be regarded as an exception.

reached most of the farmers; government contracts could make or break thousands of firms; veterans' benefits probably reached the majority of families; government projects and construction were forthcoming with increasing largesse.

The first and most obvious effect of this was in the changed relationship between a member of Congress and his constituents. No longer were the importunities of job seekers the major relationship of this sort. Perhaps the majority of the voters had an individual economic stake, not merely in the legislation before Congress, but in the fashion in which laws already passed were being administered. In fact, law in the sense of a generalized rule of conduct was no longer the characteristic governmental expression. Laws of the present day—at least the more important ones—characteristically set an objective, create (or designate) an agency to attain that objective, and define the metes and bounds of the agency's conduct. They then leave it to the agency to administer or adjust in the light of the objective the specified sector (usually economic) of national life by some process of continuous intervention. Great discretion is often allowed the agency in particular cases. In such a process countless individuals are affected. To these individuals their member of Congress often appears as a delegate or representative, providentially placed both geographically and in the hierarchy of authority to intervene in their behalf. It is this type of activity which today the member finds particularly time-consuming. True, his power in these matters is greatly exaggerated; his intent to upset normal administrative processes often is even more exaggerated, when it exists at all. But the constituent seldom knows this, and by letter, telephone, or in person he asks or demands help. Constituencies in the House now average about 450,000; in the Senate, almost 4,000,000. Women as well as men vote; the vestiges of racial barriers are crumbling. Modern travel and a greatly improved standard of living bring people to Washington in astronomical numbers. High-school and college students are encouraged to write to their congressman for information and to visit him when in the city. Individual claims for attention vary. A member may be asked to appear before a regulatory commission, to obtain funds to dredge a harbor, to change the route of a highway, to inquire about the cause for delay of a pension, to obtain an exception to the rules governing federal aid to a local housing project, to intervene to secure a contract, to protest at a questionnaire sent a business firm, to appear as a witness in a labor dispute before a federal mediator, to obtain a higher acreage quota for a particular crop.

Certain deeper meanings of this type of activity in the direction of preservation of localism will be left for later analysis.[2] The emphasis at this point is on the demands made upon a member's time and attention as the result of the tremendous increase in the span of governmental activity, and to call attention to the fact that the portion of the demand here discussed bears little relationship to the member's responsibilities for national policy. He does, it is true, learn something of the workings of particular measures from these constituent requests, just as the executive branch learns in its day-to-day administration, but the chief effect is the sheer time consumed, time necessarily subtracted from the larger consideration of general policy. Quantitatively, it is not too easy to set a figure, but some earlier studies have indicated that it was not unusual for a member to devote up to eighty per cent of his time to his dealings with his constituents. On the other hand, more recent studies would put the average between twenty-five and thirty per cent—too much, but probably indicating an increasing reliance upon office staff.[3] Most of what has been said has been on the assumption that mem-

---

[2] Cf. chap. 16.
[3] Warren H. Butler, "Administering Congress: The Role of the Staff," *Public Administration Review,* March 1966, p. 6.

bers of Congress should concern themselves primarily with legislative tasks. This is true, but the other side should not be downgraded. In a government as complex as ours, surely there is much to be said for the individual citizen having an advocate in his behalf, if he feels in some fashion helpless before a gigantic bureaucracy. To serve in this manner is by no means the least important function of a congressman.

His adaptations to this situation are numerous and relatively obvious. Office staffs at public and even at his private expense have grown considerably. Departments have established liaison offices and information bureaus to simplify his problems of contact. Questions of concern to constituents dealt with by the Legislative Reference Service have grown from about three hundred to about six thousand a month in the last twenty-five years. He works longer hours, and Congress remains in session for more of the year—though other factors must bear primary responsibilitiy for the latter. Ghost writers may help him with his speeches and his letters. He develops techniques of courteous refusal. The ways of patronage are streamlined while its channels are limited. Yet, when all is said and done, the problem of the demands on his time remains—unsurmounted and probably insurmountable. Alleviations are possible—such as Home Rule for the District of Columbia, for example.[4] Considerably more hope may lie in the appointment of an "ombudsman," following Scandinavian precedent, to whom congressmen may refer many of the complaints which he and his staff now investigate. Such an agent of Congress could take these matters up with the executive agency and report back to the member.[5] Still another hopeful possibility is the establishment in and by Congress of a consultative service on congressional office

---

[4] This particular reform is desirable for its own sake, but detailed consideration is beyond the scope of this work.

[5] See Henry S. Reuss, "An 'Ombudsman' for America," *New York Times Magazine*, September 13, 1964, p. 30, Walter S. Gellhorn, *Ombudsmen and Others* (Cambridge: Harvard University Press, 1966).

management. This service could survey existing office establishments as well as assist new members.

More serious, because more fundamental, are the problems inherent in the complexity and magnitude of the legislative output itself. The great difficulty is not even the fact that in a given session of Congress there are forty or fifty major issues. It is rather what is inherent in the nature of the issues themselves. The measures proposed are generally urgent (especially in foreign affairs); they are almost invariably far-reaching, but obscure in their derivative or secondary effects; they are often drastic in their primary impact, but in a complex and disturbing way; they are highly specialized; they may involve a multitude of principles, often conflicting; they always involve a quantity of facts for background. All this is only to say that they are a reflection of a specialized, but interlocked, technical age whose social and economic and political structure is intricate, sensitive, dynamic, and at the same time scarcely understood even by the wisest and the best informed of men.

Here, for example, is a partial list of really major issues and measures that faced the first session of the Eighty-fourth Congress. In international relations these included adjustment to the changing and perplexing tactics of the Soviet; the salvaging of Vietnam; protection of Formosa and its attendant islands; the arming of West Germany and its entry into NATO; economic crises in Japan and Brazil; dealings with communist China; amending the United Nations Charter; the Bricker Amendment; Arab-Israel relations; policies toward Spain, India, Yugoslavia; foreign aid, economic, military, technical; the Austrian Treaty; Guatemala; the renewal or modification of the Reciprocal Trade program; the refugee program; our overseas information program; atoms for peace; political crises in Pakistan, Indonesia, France, and elsewhere; control of atomic weapons.

On the home front, the list was even longer: modifications

of our social security program; federal aid to school construction; peaceful uses of atomic energy; the Dixon-Yates contract; a national highway program; re-examination of the security program; the Upper Colorado, Hells Canyon, and other water resource projects; agricultural surpluses; extension of the draft; adequate reserves for the armed services; nuclear warfare; integration of the armed services; conflicts over aircraft carriers and the size of the Air Force; dangers of inflation; automation; minimum wage; national health programs; polio vaccine; juvenile delinquency; antitrust legislation; integration of the races; the role and ethics of congressional investigations; reduction of governmental activities, especially if competitive with private enterprise; governmental reorganization; federal-state relations; balancing the budget; major changes in tax policy; reform of the electoral college; veterans' benefits; federal pay scales; the stock exchange; postal rates; statehood for Alaska and Hawaii; internal subversion.

By the Eighty-ninth Congress, in the international field, the Austrian Treaty and the Bricker Amendment were off the agenda. All the other items were still present in the same or somewhat altered fashion: Crises in Africa, a number of Latin-American republics, Syria, and Yemen were added; deGaulle was threatening to turn NATO into a shambles; communist China had become a nuclear power; Cuba constituted a challenge; the Peace Corps had emerged.

On the home front, the list included almost every topic in the Eighty-fourth Congress plus a number of others. Some problems, such as federal aid to education, health, and civil rights programs, were expanding rapidly, once the principle of federal intervention had been established. Statehood for Alaska and Hawaii was settled. However, the "Great Society" had begun to involve the federal government much more than earlier in matters such as urban renewal, stream pollution, auto safety, medicare, birth control, stubborn problems of poverty, highway beautification, outer space, desalinization, the fostering of the arts, interurban transportation, recreation resources, and many other facets of life. In addition, Congress was confronted with the "one man, one vote" issue in reapportioning state legislatures, weather modification, immigration policy, the "right to work" issue, outflow of gold, cigarette advertising,—to mention only a few of the other more important issues.

In such a setting the changes in Congress have been profound and far-reaching during recent years. Actually the last three decades have been but the climax to a trend that was already noticeable during the latter part of the last century, and certain congressional adaptations trace to this period or even earlier. For convenience, we may group the adaptations under three interrelated headings: procedural changes, a growth in specialization, and an increasing reliance upon technical experts.

The whole question of congressional procedure has received excellent descriptive and analytic treatment in the writings of Cannon, Luce, Galloway, Riddick, and others, and need not detain us here save for a few observations. In both House and Senate, it is steeped in precedent, and a member who masters it has elements of effectiveness denied to the uninitiated. The House by its tendency to divide time equally between supporters and opponents of a measure, the Senate by its virtually unlimited debate—these bear eloquent witness to our overriding belief in the rights of minorities to be heard and in the efficacy of discussion. In the House, the minority is occasionally of the opinion that the more rigid limitations set by the House on total debate place it at a disadvantage as compared with the Senate. In the latter the rules more than compensate for any disadvantages facing the minority in the House. Whether the delays and filibusters of the Senate are too high a price to pay in comparison with the greater order and expeditiousness of the House is a matter of opinion. The

House does manage to transact an enormous amount of business, considering its size. Neither house has mastered the problem of the congestion of business toward the end of the session.

The Legislative Reorganization Act of 1946 made certain minor procedural contributions in the direction of limiting the number of private bills and in setting up a more orderly committee structure. It also curtailed somewhat the power of a committee chairman to obstruct the course of legislation with which he did not agree. Ancient procedures are jealously guarded by those who have learned how to use them, and adaptation rather than change has been perhaps the principal response to needs in this procedural field. The one recommendation I would make at this point would be that in some fashion the Senate should modify its cloture rule, so that a filibuster ultimately can be more easily broken.

Deserving of somewhat more attention is the increasing tendency of Congress toward division of labor and specialization within its own membership. The most obvious expression is in the committee system. Among the changes brought in by the aforesaid Reorganization Act was the replacing of the old committee structure by fewer and, in the Senate, smaller committees. In this fashion the average House member finds himself on one or two committees only,[6] and the average senator on two or three. This in itself has brought a higher degree of specialization within the membership, especially on the part of the House. By one means or another there was naturally some gravitation on the part of an individual member toward the committee whose subject matter he already knew best, or was most interested in, or which dealt with the problems which meant most to his district. These three provisos frequently coincided and rein-

---

[6] The trend is in the direction of two committees, usually pairing one of the third rank with one of the second rank. See Louis C. Gawthrop, "Changing Membership Patterns in House Committees," *American Political Science Review,* June 1966, pp. 366–73.

forced each other in a given instance, and after a modest amount of service a member might find himself looked upon as an "authority" on a given subject among his colleagues. Deference would be paid then not only to his membership on the committee responsible for a given measure but also to his substantive knowledge. It is thus that the individual member often attains influence as well as power. Between one–fifth and one–quarter of the members of most committees have served ten years or more.

And so the habit more and more prevails, on the one hand of reluctance to go counter to a committee recommendation, on the other, of looking to different people for guidance on different subjects. This cuts squarely across party membership and is certainly one of the factors which weakens it. It is the instinctive as well as rational triumph of superior knowledge in a technical age. It operates within a committee as well as between the committee members and the Congress as a whole. It may operate, and frequently does, in the respect paid to a well-informed member who is not a member of the relevant committee at all.

All of the foregoing is written in full knowledge of the extent to which clientele interests are concentrated in certain committees. It is highly probable that such committees find their bills more frequently subject to floor amendment. Yet a bi-partisan committee recommendation of the great majority of a committee is rarely altered or revised on the floor. Where eighty per cent or more of a committee are in agreement, a bill which reaches the floor is virtually certain to pass.

Both before and after the Reorganization Act through the same tendency toward specialization subcommittees proliferated, and also special or select committees, though to a less extent than before. The former as well as the latter are frequently galvanized into life to secure intensive examination of a given problem. Each makes it possible to utilize as chairman a member of special talent. Such a member might under the seniority rule have had to wait years before having the opportunity to contribute through his peculiar qualifications in a given area by serving as chairman of the appropriate standing committee.

The third major adaptation of Congress to the problems of a technological age lies in its use of experts outside its own membership. The story is an interesting and important one, extending in its implications far into executive-legislative relations, the role of lobbies, and the prospects for representative government itself. Because the story is less familiar than that of the other adaptations, it will be told at greater length.

Toward the end of the nineteenth century, questions and problems concerning business and industry came to the fore. The establishment of the Interstate Commerce Commission and the passage of the Sherman Antitrust Act illustrated the trend. With the presidency of Theodore Roosevelt, the extent of such concern with economic life grew more marked, and Woodrow Wilson's "New Freedom" put the seal on the development.

The congressional response to the pressure of these problems was not to rely on its own native equipment, as it tended to rely in the earlier period of its existence, but to call on experts from the interests involved for advice. Characteristically, though not exclusively, this took the form of a major development of the committee hearing as an institutional device to bring such experience to bear upon pending problems and legislation. Thus reliance on the experts connected with the special interests was not nearly the sinister affair that might be inferred, for legislation was often the product of conflicting interests, each of which had the opportunity of appearing before the committee. Where there was no apparent conflict, it was nevertheless part of the American mores to believe that what benefited business or agriculture benefited the nation as a whole. Thus there was no inner conflict in a member's mind between the special interest and the general good. This method seemed right and proper for another reason also. The majority of congressmen were (and still are) lawyers, and, to a lawyer, truth emerges from a battle of protagonists. Undoubtedly this strengthened greatly the use and prestige of the hearing, which was for the lawyer member the courtroom in which he and his colleagues served, as it were, as judge and jury. If in connection with the appearance of a particular witness a member occasionally forgot his normal role and became prosecuting attorney or the counsel for the defense, who shall say that this, too, was not part of a way of dealing with problems which was an expression of his customary occupational thinking.

Even when the time came at which the representatives of organized labor marshaled experts as able as those of industry or agriculture, the result still fell considerably short of presenting a complete and unbiased picture. This held true, even though the belief that the general welfare equaled the sum of the welfares of the special groups showed something of the same tenacity as a kind of "group utilitarianism" which the individualistic utilitarianism of Adam Smith and Bentham possessed. In this earlier form the general welfare was equated to the sum total of individual desires. The flaw in both individual and group utilitarianism was the same. Just as there were conflicts between individuals in which general welfare not only did not coincide with the triumph of the stronger over the weaker but might be something quite different from the desires of either or even a compromise between the two, so in the larger group conflicts and relationships there was often a public interest identifiable that was something other than the victory of one side or the other, or other than even a compromise between these two. Third, fourth, and fifth parties entered in. The over-all interest of the consumer was surely part of the total picture that was of concern to Congress; so also were national strength and the interest of future generations.

Under these circumstances it is not surprising that eventually experts other than those from the special interests came to be called upon and in the end to be accorded an influence as great as or greater than the latter. In the first instance these were most often spokesmen from the executive branch.

The turning point came with the election of Franklin Roosevelt to the presidency in 1933. Industry and finance were flat on their respective backs and to a considerable extent discredited as well as uncertain in their own minds. The outlooks of organized labor and organized agriculture were still extremely limited and were confined almost entirely to preoccupation with solutions for their own particular problems without much reference to the economy as a whole. With one accord these groups turned to government for the answers. The problems were real. The new brain trust and the old bureaus ground out a program to meet them. Measure after measure of major importance went from the White House to Capitol Hill. Many of them were quite gratuitously labeled "must" legislation, for Congress had more or less lost any momentum of policy formulation it once possessed and was ready for strong and informed leadership. Gigantic research and action bureaus grew almost overnight and generated still further legislation. The evidence concerning these first two or three years would indicate that fully eighty per cent of the important legislation was for practical purposes White House and bureau generated (and, much of it, drafted as well), rather than originating in Congress itself. This still held true even if there were included as a congressional product that which resulted from the prodding and counsel of experts of the special interests and other sources.

This was a development more important and far-reaching than might at first be supposed. Under the parliamentary system of government there had come to be a world-wide trend in the industrialized nations in this direction. In Great Britain, for example, behind the façade of the Cabinet were the permanent civil servants, tirelessly and ceaselessly advising the individual ministers as regards indicated legislation on the basis of their (the civil servants') study and experience. Except for certain trends in the electorate, tidal in their nature, which reflected themselves in shifts in party allegiance and a consequent shift in general direction in a limited number of spheres of legislation, the permanent officials matured virtually all the legislative proposals. This left to Parliament only a bit of polishing and now and again a delay or a rejection.

These were the days in which many writers, including the author, predicted that a similar set of usages would emerge behind the façade of our own Constitution. We saw Congress reduced largely to a ratifying role, with the executive in an ascendancy, based ultimately upon the superior technical competence of its personnel. As in Great Britain, so in our own country these expert-devised programs would be pushed by a partisan executive with the various devices of party discipline at his command.

Actually the net result was not too greatly different from reliance upon the representation of the special interests, for the latter on a broad scale transferred much of their attention to the executive branch, often by establishing bureaus in the executive branch which became their respective spokesmen. These bureaus in turn generated legislative proposals more or less agreeable to their respective clienteles. Hence new, but still unappreciated, conflicts took place in the resultant legislation. This particular defect must be reserved for special analysis later.[7] Other defects or shortcomings were more immediately noticeable.

By the end of the decade Congress had become increas-

---

[7] Cf. chaps. 10 and 11.

ingly restless. Many factors were involved, among them a sociologically understandable institutional jealousy and, more important, a feeling that all was not well in a setting in which the number of unemployed was still over 10,000,000 in spite of all the effort. There was also present a strong feeling of frustration and resentment, in that the executive seemed to have most of the chips in the form of vastly greater research facilities, at times approaching a kind of monopoly. Almost the only alternative experts available to Congress were the still considerably discredited specialists and representatives from the commercial and industrial corporations. More fundamentally there had come to be a sincere and genuine appreciation that reliance upon the executive for fact finding and analysis had also some serious limitations.

In the first place, the President was elected in a political campaign. The heads of the agencies were mostly his partisan appointees. By the very nature of the democratic process, declarations of policy were made in the course of such a campaign that constituted the surface reason for subsequent legislative proposals. Similar public policy declarations would be made during the years following an election, not only by the President, but also by his appointees. It soon came to be noted in Congress that the findings and testimony of the experts from the several agencies were almost invariably such as to constitute an endorsement of these publicly assumed positions of the political chief. This might be cause as well as effect, of course, for the chief might well have taken the position in question because he had become familiar with the facts and analyses of his experts; but this was not always so. Often the roles were reversed.

I well remember a characterization of government research I once heard in an address by Luther Gulick. He took us in imagination to a huge room whose walls were covered with files and pigeonholes labeled "Facts." In and out of the room came and went a continuous procession of men carrying sheets of paper. When the men came in, their sheets were blank, save for the conclusions. Diligent search would then be made among the files and pigeonholes for facts which would add up to the preconceived conclusions. Such facts, when found, were duly entered, and, with the documents thus prepared to the satisfaction of the researcher, he would leave the room. This, said Gulick, was "government research"—of sorts, no doubt, but a characterization with a sufficient element of truth in it to evoke an appreciative response from his listeners.

Conversely, those in Congress who held positions on issues other than those held by the executive found themselves severely limited both in inquiry and in debate. Leaks from dissenters within the executive, private research organizations, special interests—these were hardly a match for the mass of facts and figures presented by an executive cloaked with the aura of the "public interest" and monolithic in its rejoinders to any criticism.

A second weakness lay more within the bureaus themselves than in the political pronouncements of their chiefs and the President. This was the very human tendency to stay in a rut, or to find it difficult to change one's mind once a position had been assumed. While prevalent in all walks of life and in all varieties of bureaucrat, it was and is especially dangerous if and when it is found in the armed services. A legislative body is peculiarly powerless in this area of policy because to the mysteries of the technical are added the further mysteries of the secrecy that must necessarily surround so much that may be basic to a wise decision. Yet the legislative body cannot and dare not delegate all responsibility in this area. Witness, for example, the reliance the French Chamber of Deputies placed upon the Maginot line on advice of its General Staff and the near-fatal consequences thereof. Illustrations might be given drawn from other departments. The insistence on the part of certain of our officials that Chiang Kai-shek must be superseded will also serve by way of illustration. The real question at this point is not so much whether a given expert in the executive branch was right or wrong in a particular instance but whether there were alternative policies that merited consideration along with the executive viewpoint.

In the third place, a bureaucrat normally recommends policies that involve expansion of his own staff and powers. This is not unnatural, nor need the sinister or selfish motives of "empire building," at times present, necessarily be brought into the picture for its understanding. Each chief who is worth his salt believes in the objectives of his agency. It therefore normally follows that, given a larger staff or given extended powers to enable him to control more of the factors influencing the attainment of these objectives, he feels that he can do a better job. This is not itself an evil, provided he must justify his recommendations before a body commanding the same authoritative technical competence and one which, at the same time, has no vested interest in or drive toward such expansion. If the congressional committee which, under the usages of our Constitution, has the primary responsibility to pass judgment on the request does not itself have in its own membership or in the alternative sources of information and analysis open to it a roughly comparable competence in the specific field in question, it is naturally at a very considerable disadvantage in passing judgment on the request for greater staff or greater powers. The result may be as great an evil, if in blind resentment or perplexity a Congress rejects any and all such requests, as it is if a Congress is the unwitting dupe of the executive in granting them. The fact that Congress in practice has never become a prey to either of these extremes does not remove the danger of falling measurably short of the best decision in a given instance through lack of mastery of its subject matter.

Here then were at least three defects in predominant reliance upon executive research, analysis, recommendations, and expertness—defects which Congress felt were occurring, if not universally, at least with sufficient frequency to cast considerable doubt on even apparently well-documented proposals. Congress was frankly uneasy, and this uneasiness grew steadily until it crystallized in the mid-forties into a major expansion of Congress' own staff agencies.

These staff agencies marked a third stage in the development of the use of *expertise* in the meeting of this major challenge to the effectiveness of representative government in a technological and specialized age. Not that such use of staffs of its own was unknown to Congress before the forties. It had long been customary, especially in a major congressional investigation, for a committee of Congress to assemble for the purpose an *ad hoc* staff often of very great technical competence. However, the quality of such staffs was not always uniformly high. Their temporary nature contained its own limitations. Furthermore, a laudable desire for economy often led to a congressional committee's borrowing such experts from the executive branch. The latter was usually quite ready to loan, inasmuch as something regarding the future course of the lending agency was often the subject under discussion. On the other hand, over the years certain committees developed in their clerks persons of great professional competence and on a nonpartisan basis. The career of Marcellus Sheild, for twenty-nine years Clerk of the House Appropriations Committee, is perhaps the best known but is by no means unique. For many years both houses had had in their offices of legislative counsel a skilled legislative drafting service. Finally in 1926 the Joint Committee on Internal Revenue Taxation was set up and granted a professional staff of modest size. Over the ensuing years this staff functioned continuously as a high level congressional audit on Treasury proposals, not hesitating to bring forward documentary support for forms of taxation alternative to those advanced by the executive; or to challenge Treasury estimates of prospective revenues.

The first further tangible expression of this awakening desire of Congress for its own permanent professional staff was found in some modest increases in the appropriations for the Legislative Reference Service in the early forties. Notable among these was the one which made possible the appointment in 1945 of the first really top-flight experts (later to be known as "senior specialists") in the four fields of foreign relations, taxation, American law, and labor relations. It was in part the satisfactory initial experience with these men that led in 1946 to the authorized extension of senior specialist appointments to all fields under the Legislative Reorganization Act.

This Act marked the real birth of a full-fledged congressional staff. It was a major response to needs already indicated. The major provisions affected the offices of the legislative counsels, the standing committees, and the Legislative Reference Service. A separate act gave each senator an administrative assistant and authorized small staffs for the policy committees of the two parties. An as yet unimplemented provision was included, expanding the investigatory role of the General Accounting Office at the behest of Congress. The authorized appropriations for the legislative counsels were increased to $250,000. The standing committees were each allowed to engage up to four professional staff members at substantial salaries and "without regard to political affiliations and solely on the basis of fitness to perform the duties of the office. . . ."[8]

While differing authorizing provisions were made for additional staffs for the Appropriations Committees of the two houses, each marked a substantial increase. The Legislative Reference Service was also greatly expanded over the next

---

[8] Sec. 202(a).

two decades. It was assigned two roles in the general scheme of things: supplementary aid to committees and primary aid to individual members. Expressed in appropriation terms, the increase in total congressional staff aid of a research and reference character was striking. Committee staff appropriations increased from $944,280 for the fiscal year 1944 to $4,117,800 for the fiscal year 1951, to $5,432,690 for 1956, to $6,054,335 for 1961, and to $8,972,410 for 1965.[9] Appropriations for the offices of the legislative counsels increased from $83,000 to $199,500 for 1951, to $290,000 for 1956, to $416,950 for 1961, and to $603,000 for 1965, and for the Legislative Reference Service from $166,300 [10] to $790,000 for 1951, to $1,061,000 for 1956, to $1,660,-200 for 1961 and to $2,524,000 for 1965. The House Coordinator of Information received $136,000 for 1965; it was nonexistent as an office in 1944. The grand total of these items shows an increase from $1,193,580 to $12,235,410 over the total period. In addition, over $9,000,000 was set aside for special investigations.

The resulting pattern of staff work and utilization is still exceedingly uneven—uneven as between members, between committees, between subject fields. The offices of the legislative counsels are perhaps the best established. Their tenure and the essentially nonpartisan character of their staff are not in question. With the exception of one year, the trend in the Legislative Reference Service has been steadily upward for the last twenty-five years, if quantitative and qualitative use and the sums appropriated and transferred from committee funds are fair measurements. Its nonpartisanship and scholarly character have been acknowledged in Congress. The staffs

---

[9] Appropriation Acts, var. Includes clerical but does not include amounts set aside for subsequent special investigations. Senate Majority and Minority Policy Committee staffs included but not Joint Committee on Printing.

[10] Includes a portion of appropriation for Index to State Legislation attributable to research.

of the standing committees present a less clear picture. Some have survived changes in party control without impairment, largely in instances in which party considerations did not influence the original appointments. In other instances a reasonable stability has been secured by the division of appointments between the parties. Others have been partisan. By 1965 the long-continued Democratic majority and the tendency in many committees for the chairmen and majority party to monopolize the staff led to an intensified demand among many House Republicans for assured minority staffing. As of 1965 this demand had not been granted. Practice in the Senate has, however, tended in this direction.

Lawyers and journalists have been employed in considerable numbers, economists and subject specialists perhaps somewhat less so than would have been anticipated. However, the tradition of permanence soon makes specialists of all of them. A few staff members have been obtained on loan from the Legislative Reference Service, and this has resulted in almost perfect integration of the two groups in the work of those committees in which this took place. The trend seems still in the direction of nonpartisanship and permanence.[11]

It is possible that in certain respects Congress may even be overstaffed. In addition to the permanent professional staffs of the committees, each session sees a burgeoning of special investigations, usually with a considerable number of temporary personnel. The quality and purpose of these differ greatly. Some are patronage and political; others are led by persons of great ability who serve at a sacrifice. Some are allegedly created in response to pressures and suggestions from the temporary staffs of expiring investigations so as to retain their congressional connections. The costs of such special investigations in the Senate increased from $170,268 in 1940 to $692,603 in 1947, $1,936,217 in 1954, and $4,361,956 in

---

[11] The principal treatise in this field is Kenneth Kofmehl, *Professional Staffs of Congress* (West Lafayette: Purdue University Press, 1962).

1965. Some of this increase is accounted for by the fact that pay scales are higher and that staff is no longer freely borrowed from the administration, but the growth of investigations is much the largest factor.[12]

More important has been the effect of staffing upon the role of Congress in the total picture, and for the purpose of the present discussion the staffs may be considered as constituting a single corps. The trends are unmistakable. For example, on every major and most minor issues one group or the other is called upon to make an independent, objective study—called upon either by the appropriate committee as a whole or by the minority or by an individual member or members. Thus there is introduced a "third force" of experts, usually designed as a corrective to the bias of the special interests and to any shortcomings in the substantive recommendations of the executive. For the most part this third force does not itself make recommendations. As regards the Legislative Reference Service always and as regards the committee staffs in many and perhaps most instances, the staff objective is to present an unbiased total picture—neither hostile to nor in support of the picture presented by the executive branch or the special interests, but filling in the gaps, assessing the factual base, outlining possible alternative courses of action. Sometimes this operates in the direction of reinforcing, though usually in considerably amended form, the recommendations of the executive, as in the Marshall Plan, revisions of the Social Security Act, and various programs of federal aid to the states. Sometimes it contributes to a decision to postpone action to force a more thorough and impartial assessment of a situation by the executive, as in the cases of the Fair Labor Standards Act and proposals for universal military service or the St. Lawrence Seaway. At other times, it aids Congress in developing an independent policy in the teeth of presidential opposition, as in the Taft-Hartley and Landrum-Griffin Acts,

---

[12] Senator Ellender in *Congressional Record*, March 18, 1955, p. 2692.

and in the Smith-Ferguson-McCarran Act against subversives. And at still other times, though this might not be admitted by the executive, it has been a strong factor in bringing the latter to a definite change in the direction of its policy—as, for example, in proposals for strengthening the United Nations and altering its structure so as to avoid the veto and to promote immediate action against an aggressor.

The respective contributions of the staff services and of the members themselves can never be accurately assessed in instances like the foregoing; and there are certain hazards in even mentioning such specific instances. Nevertheless it is my sincere conviction based upon many, many more instances than I would ever be at liberty to disclose, that the enlargement and strengthening of the staffs of Congress have in fact been a major factor in arresting and probably reversing a trend that had set in in the United States as well as in every other industrialized nation. This is the trend in the direction of the ascendancy or even the virtually complete dominance of the bureaucracy over the legislative branch through the former's near-monopoly of the facts and the technical and specialized competence on the basis of which decisions are ultimately made. Other legislative bodies—the British Parliament through its Royal Commissions, the Swedish Riksdag through its "remiss" and commission devices—do from time to time tap alternative expert sources. The new Japanese Diet and the German Bundestag have instituted legislative staff services on the American model that have great potentialities. Yet by and large the Congress of the United States still remains as yet the only major legislative assembly of which it can unmistakably be said that its independent, creative functioning has grown steadily more effective in the last twenty-five years or so. The time elapsed is naturally still too short to be certain that this will be a permanent achievement.

It is not that Congress does not continue to use the services of the experts of the executive or that it will not continue to use them. It is rather that the trend is in the direction of these experts becoming witnesses—respected witnesses, it is true—but witnesses only, whereas for many years previously they had been the advisers and consultants whose word had carried the day. The change is seen in the end results. Where a witness from the executive has come unprepared, he may well find himself literally demolished in a committee hearing. Where his case is "solid," a consensus usually results. It is specialization on the part of members and staff alike that has made Congress effective.[13]

In a subtle fashion, the nature of many of the hearings has changed. No longer are witnesses confined as they once were largely to representatives of special interests and of the executive branch. Specialists from the public at large are increasingly called in by invitation of the committees themselves. In some instances these hearings have developed into full-scale panels, when the experts in question fall into differing schools of thought, and appear in discussions under committee auspices. Here also the advice of staff in the selection of such witnesses has been invaluable.

Congress has thus mastered, or has provided itself with the tools to master, the problem of assuring itself of an unbiased, competent source of expert information and analysis which is its very own. By the same token it has mastered the problem of recapturing its constitutional role as the independent policy determiner—a self-respecting coequal of the bureaucracy, its legal master in policy matters, in practice its competent partner or its intelligent critic. Congress has done

---

[13] Former Congressman and Undersecretary of Treasury Joseph Barr, in a public address, September 20, 1965, before the Washington Chapter of the American Society for Public Administration, commented that he had learned far more in his chosen field of international finance in his two years in the House than in his two graduate years at Harvard. Not only did he have the high order expertise of the members and staff of the Ways and Means Committee to call on, but he used freely the assistance available from the various agencies in Washington.

this without sacrificing its own amateur standing as the elected representatives of the people. This has been no small contribution to the content of governance in a complex and technical age.

It is worth summarizing the analysis thus far of legislative-executive relations. Reference was made at the outset to these relations as an "institutionalized mutual responsibility of coequals." [14] In the light of the development of *expertise,* this characterization may now be given a richer meaning. The mutual responsibility is seen to be much more than that of coequal power in the formal sense. Power to be effective must be buttressed by knowledge and Congress now has this knowledge. For either branch to have its way it must now convince the other as to the wisdom, operative as well as political, of a proposed course of action.

[14] Cf. p. 7.

CHAPTER EIGHT

Appropriations

THE appropriating process is almost the only point in the congressional agenda at which the program of the government passes in review in its totality. Here legislative intent can be enhanced and promoted; here also it can be hampered or strangled altogether. Economy and largesse struggle. Here is an arena in which the philosophies of statism and individualism may lock in combat. The pressure groups beat upon the committee doors. The executive masses its persuasion and its coerciveness, its facts and its subterfuges. The Appropriations Committees have the largest memberships and the largest staffs of any of the standing committees. Their tasks are incomparably the most difficult.

Some of these difficulties are patent. The sheer size of the total budget is one. Is it to be forty billion or one hundred billion dollars? Use of trust funds with earmarked revenues now exceeds twenty billion annually. These are in addition to the normal budget. Figures cease to have meaning and leave the average individual dazed. Close examination, apart from sampling here and there, is simply impossible in a situation of such unbelievable complexity. If appropriations are to be considered in detail, there are not days, weeks, and months enough to cover the ground. If it is in lump sums, who is to judge whether the amount is too much or too little to attain the end? Occasionally work-load measurements lend a color of objectivity to changes in size of staff; but these conditions are exceptional, and there is seldom assurance that the original base was itself a sound one. Whole sections of expenditure, especially in the military, are shrouded in secrecy and must be accepted largely on faith. Occasionally, functions declining in their magnitude or largely obsolete are retained year after year at their old figure, principally for want of a substantive analysis of the work itself. Then, too, the approach employed by the executive retains the fiction of the equal importance of all items in the estimates, and what would be enormously valuable assistance from the Bureau of the Budget or the agency itself, in assessing priorities, is not forthcoming. Duplications, especially in research and intelligence, are covered up through emphasis on minor differences. Their detection is the more difficult because they usually fall within the province of different subcommittees, and it is in the subcommittees that the detailed examination of estimates takes place. Pressures from the interests involved and from their congressional spokesmen are overtly and subtly exerted. At any time a Spartan decision in the direction of economy on the part of the committee may be overthrown in a quick vote on the floor or by the committee of the other house, which may hold a different view. Moreover, a very large part of the estimated expenditure is contractual in nature and not subject to cutting: interest on the debt, subsidies to the states that rest upon a legislative formula, veterans' benefits, pensions, subsidies for agriculture—all are substantial money users and on all of these the Appropriations Committees are virtually powerless, unless the legislative requirements are themselves changed.[1] Of a similar nature are the self-financing activities, chiefly loans, which contain appropriations as well as authorizations in the original act.

The Appropriations Committees are unlike any others in many respects. In the House the Committee is an "exclusive" one, membership on any other standing committee being exceptional in the extreme.[2] For several years, five to seven

[1] See Arthur Smithies, *The Budgetary Process in the United States* (New York: McGraw-Hill, 1955) var.; R. A. Wallace, "Congressional Control of the Budget," *Midwest Journal of Political Science,* May 1959, pp. 151–67.

[2] In the second session of the Eighty-ninth Congress, two members were also members of the Joint Committee on Atomic Energy and one of the House Administration Committee.

101

men gave their whole committee time to the appropriations of a single agency or group of agencies. This allowed a high degree of specialization, particularly when a member served year after year on the same subcommittee. Customarily, the same staff member served the same subcommittee each year. Some duplication of membership did take place in connection with certain special subcommittees, such as the one on foreign aid and the one on the legislative branch. At the beginning of the Eighty-fourth Congress, the individual subcommittees were enlarged considerably and their jurisdictions regrouped. This increased to two or more the subcommittee responsibilities of the individual members.

Continuity is highly important, as regards both members and staff. Most members in the House are from "safe" districts, and rarely change to other committees. Unlike the ordinary legislative standing committee, most of its business each year is "old" business. The agency presenting its estimates and the estimates themselves have a tradition and a content for the most part familiar over the years to those who have served on or served the subcommittee for long periods. The measure of an agency's officials and especially of its budget officer is taken, and action on their requests colored thereby. Studies made in earlier years can be brought up to date for comparative purposes.

Members of the Appropriations Committee develop certain occupational characteristics. Conscientiousness and a thick skin exist in about equal proportions in a good Appropriations Committee member. Notably in the House, the self-image of hard work and budget-cutting prevails. Norms of expected behavior include deference to seniority within a subcommittee, reciprocity based on specialization, nonpartisanship with exceptions.[3]

---

[3] See Richard F. Fenno, Jr., "The House Appropriations Committee as a Political System," *American Political Science Review*, June 1962, p. 310–24, for the best study of this aspect of the House Committee.

The Senate Appropriations Committee exhibits certain differences. The smaller membership of the Senate does not permit exclusive committee assignments, and hence the average senator can spend less time on details. On certain of the subcommittees there are three ex-officio members from the appropriate standing committee serving as liaison. This holds true of Agriculture and Forestry, Civil Service, Armed Services, Atomic Energy, District of Columbia, Public Works, and Foreign Relations.

Normally, the Senate takes up consideration of an appropriation after the House has acted, but occasionally Committee consideration may be simultaneous. However, in such instances the Senate subcommittees do not report until after they have heard from the House. To a very considerable extent the Senate thus acts as a board of review, giving special attention to the cuts made by the House, the restoration of which is most vigorously pushed. However, it is somewhat sensitive to the allegation frequently voiced on the House side that it (the Senate) often undoes the work of the House and does not really believe in economy. For this and other reasons, it will normally make certain cuts of its own in a given estimate.

Each year the Appropriations Committees and Congress set forth seemingly formidable total reductions as their basis for claims of substantial economies. Each year these are criticized as largely "bookkeeping" devices. Some of them result from decisions to postpone or slow down recommended construction. If these are ultimately undertaken and completed, the economy involved is somewhat dubious—unless indeed they subsequently serve as deterrents of requests for still further construction. Some of the most substantial cuts represent lowered estimates on the part of the Committees as to what will be needed for certain statutory expenditures, such as veterans' benefits or agricultural subsidies. These are accompanied by directives to the agency to bring in a supple-

103

mental or deficiency estimate, if experience shows the need. Supplemental and deficiency appropriations for these and other similar items are of the magnitude of two to four billion dollars in the usual year. Some economies are directives to shrink unspent balances. When all these items are taken into account, congressional economies in reality are much more modest than usually claimed.

In the performance of their duties the Appropriations Committees occasionally receive assistance apart from their own staff. On request, the Bureau of the Budget will make special studies. According to the letter of the Reorganization Act, the General Accounting Office was assigned the function of making studies of the efficiency of agency operations, but this provision has never been implemented by the appropriating of the necessary funds. Nevertheless, the G.A.O. does from time to time render certain assistance. Its audit reports are particularly valuable. Tips about examples of waste and extravagance as well as maladministration are constantly received by the Committees. Many of these are investigated prior to the hearings or form the subject of questions at the time of an agency's appearance.

Floor amendments are fairly numerous, but the majority are defeated. The minority party may at times use this occasion to dramatize some issue. Floor time is equally divided between the parties. The ranking majority and minority members of the subcommittees usually act as leaders of the debates on their bills and are usually in agreement.

Floor amendments customarily fall into three groups. The first group arises quite naturally from the fact that even with the best will in the world to the contrary—and the will is often conspicuously lacking—cuts or increases or even granting the sum requested in appropriations are inevitably to some degree policy verdicts on the activities of the agency in question. Consequently, proposals to increase or decrease the funds for a particular activity are ways in which the House

104

or Senate as a whole may express a verdict on the activity. This is especially true in highly controversial issues, such as foreign aid, veterans' hospitals, the composition of the Air Force, and public power. Amendments at this point, though expressed in money terms, really concern policy matters. Note especially the activity on the part of certain members for their favorite agencies.

Of another type are the "economy" amendments, offered either in succession on a number of estimates or as an overall cut on a percentage or lump-sum basis or otherwise. This type gained some favor during the forties and fifties, in part as the response of a frustrated Congress to the extreme difficulties involved in obtaining substantial economies by the alternative channel of the detailed consideration of a budget so increased in size and complexity as to be virtually past comprehension. On the other hand, this method has been severely attacked as constituting the virtual abdication by Congress of its appropriating responsibilities because in effect it restores discretionary spending to the executive, especially if the agency or agencies to which the cut is to be applied are not specified. It is at this point that the item veto calls for mention. Actually the President does from time to time decline to spend certain appropriated funds, and Congress has not required of him that he spend them. The item veto, especially if applied to public works, would regularize and encourage this practice.

An amendment of a third type is the effort of a member in behalf of a particular project for his own district. This is not dissimilar from the first type but is more essentially local in character. Such amendments seldom succeed, but they do "make a record" for the member.

Nor does the action of either house singly represent the final verdict. Time and again, conference committee action is decisive in controversial policy matters.

When finally passed, what do the appropriation measures

singly and collectively express? Many things, for they often represent the real thinking of Congress on national policy as distinct from its frequent response to the special interests in substantive legislation.

For this very reason there have been valiant efforts in the last few years to achieve an over-all view at the fiscal policy level. The first of these was the legislative budget provided for under the Reorganization Act, whereby all receipts and expenditures were to be brought together for simultaneous fixing of targets. There were two major attempts to make the provision operative. For practical purposes, these must be written down as almost complete failures. The reasons lie deep in the fiscal timetable and to some extent in the nature of the appropriation process as now established.

At the very least, the President would have to send the estimates to Congress much earlier, and this would present grave problems in forecasting needs so far in advance. Moreover, this would assume at least preliminary consideration of its various parts by the relevant subcommittees, and the process would be not too greatly different from the omnibus measure of the Eighty-first Congress. Conceivably Congress itself might speed up its processes. The House during the session of 1950 gave rather an impressive demonstration of dispatch. In the end, however, it was late August before the appropriations bills finally became law. Alternatively, the beginning of the fiscal year might be fixed at September first. This has much to commend it in any event, inasmuch as final congressional consideration rarely is complete much before this date. One other possibility would be joint hearings of the subcommittees of the two houses, but this suggestion has had but little support in Congress and has evoked considerable opposition. A still more drastic possibility would be to place the review function in Congress itself, which would be equivalent to an elimination of the executive budget.

During 1950 a new method was used to give an opportunity to register over-all fiscal policy. This was in the form of the single measure, the omnibus appropriation bill.[4] Changes in the revenue system were incorporated in a separate tax bill, but its estimated total figured largely in the floor discussions of appropriations as well. Conversely, these over-all aspects seem to have played relatively little part in the subcommittee consideration of separate items. The subcommittees of both houses functioned much as before. Such reports as leaked out of the executive sessions of the full Committees would seem to indicate that these Committees made little, if any, change in their subcommittees' reports. The really significant change brought about by the omnibus method took the form of far-reaching action on the floors of both houses and in conference. The most significant action did not relate to the details of individual items but took the form of over-all reductions aiming at the total. These were first urged in the form of percentage cuts, applicable to all save certain items or agencies. There also passed the House a provision forbidding the filling of all except a small fraction of vacancies as they arose. The ultimate form assumed by this over-all consideration was a vote of a cut of $550,000,000, to be applied at the discretion of the executive, but again with certain exemptions. Opinion is divided regarding whether the economy thereby effected compensated for the alleged abdication of congressional discretion and the presumed necessity of cuts in activities deemed important. The method itself had from time to time been applied to individual appropriations, in which an agency had been asked to absorb a cut or the cost of a new activity or its pay increases. The fact of the matter is that it is good for an agency to go through this type of wringer occasionally, provided it is not repeated too often and

---

[4] Foreign aid and certain other items were contined in separate bills, but Congress was well aware of their general contour.

does not go too far, for it forces re-examination of the staffing of particular units regardless of vested interests and sacred cows. What eventuates is likely to be more streamlined as well as more economical.

The omnibus bill was dropped after the one session, and separate subcommittees again mature separate bills for the grand divisions of the government.

Occasional other over-all cuts should be noted. Sometimes these apply to specific types of expenditure, such as construction in the light of a corresponding fall in price level. Sometimes these express a policy, such as forbidding the purchase of new typewriters or restricting the staff of personnel officers to a certain percentage of the total agency staff.

Moreover, the appropriating process is often Congress' corrective for that which, in default of such a corrective, would otherwise be deemed its legislative intent. To pass a law or grant an authorization does not complete the legislative action on a given subject. So intricate is the pattern of group pressures and trades that very frequently the laws and authorizations require "correction" through curtailed appropriations—or omitting an appropriation altogether—in order to register the real judgment of Congress. At other times a curtailed appropriation represents something more personal with the Committee, for departments and agencies and activities and the heads of each vary in popularity. If the Committee strains too far the general opinion of the House, floor amendments are moved. Sometimes the "corrective" is more substantive, and directives or riders are introduced which seem to some to transgress the prohibition against legislation in an appropriation act. Unless there is a closed rule, this may be raised as a "point of order" on the floor, which, if sustained, will eliminate the offending clause. But by and large, in spite of jealousies between the Appropriations Committees and the other standing committees, there is a widespread, grudging admiration for the former and a wish for them to be "hard-boiled." They are one of the great restraining factors on Congress as a whole.

Once in a while Congress, speaking through its Appropriations Committees or on the floor, will reverse the process and write into the appropriations bill some increases over the President's budget for favored agencies or projects. The Air Force has been a recipient of such endorsement on two occasions, only to have the extra funds impounded in the executive the first time; and, while the funds were spent the second time, a corresponding reduction in next year's requests ensued. Projects of the Corps of Engineers are favorite subjects for inclusion, over and above those provided for in Bureau of the Budget estimates. This applies even to the addition of projects on which the Bureau has reported adversely. In the rate of expenditure on projects already commenced, Congress often tends to economize for the time being by slowing down construction.

All in all, the appropriating function of our government has come to be more and more its program function—first as the Bureau of the Budget believes the President sees it, and then as Congress would have it. Yet, unlike the British Parliament, Congress still looks upon the estimates more as a means of expenditure control than as an instrument of national planning. Nevertheless, the amounts and activities involved are too tremendous and far-flung to suppose that Congress as a whole, or even very many of its members, can grasp them in their totality. No one can master them in detail. They are a program, vast and far-reaching—of defense, of welfare, of world outlook, of development of resources, of the political economy of the wealthiest and most powerful nation in the world. It is as trustees of this program that the Appropriations Committees and Congress in its appropriating function serve.

The program is not only the sums appropriated; it is what is not appropriated also. It is found in an economy and a lowered tax rate that leave consumer purchasing power the greater and consumer choices by so much the freer. It is found in a restraint that refuses to extend the boundaries of collectivism. It is found in the valiant fight through this weapon also to make and keep our bureaucracy responsible.

CHAPTER NINE

Congressional Investigations

CONGRESSIONAL investigations play a multitude of roles. Yet in each of these roles there are alternative instruments available.

The congressional investigation furnishes a basis for legislation. This role it shares with research, with executive recommendations, with the presentments of lobbyists and others. It is an instrument of oversight of the executive branch. There are also other instruments: the appropriations process, floor debate, and contacts both formal and informal. Many times the investigation finds itself operating in the pre-legislative twilight zone in which the very fact of illumination influences conduct, sometimes rendering legislation unnecessary. Congressional speeches, on and off the floor, or even the mere introduction of a bill, may likewise bring about such a desired result. The investigation is one of Congress' striking ways of educating the public, along with floor debate, research reports, and constituent contacts. It also is a means of obtaining reelection, one among many ways of sharpening the image of congressmen as conscientious and vigorous servants of the public interest.

In other words, the investigation is not unique in any of its roles; nor can one always say in any particular instance which of the various potential roles it is designed chiefly to serve, nor how many it will end by serving.

George Galloway observes the following in his work on the congressional legislative process: [1]

Aside from its informative and disciplinary functions, the congressional investigating committee is often used by group interests to exploit

---

[1] George B. Galloway, *Legislative Process in Congress* (New York: Thomas Crowell, 1953), pp. 487, 627.

crisis situations, to expose and attack rival groups and practices, and to mobilize public opinion against opposing groups and the governmental agencies associated with them. . . .

The scope and conduct of congressional investigations have been subjects of controversy throughout the history of the Republic. Their powers and procedures have been bitterly attacked and vigorously defended. . . . It is now well settled that the congressional committee of inquiry is a device appropriate for use in the performance by Congress of its legislative, supervisory, and informing functions.

Again in a later work, Dr. Galloway calls attention to the "variety of practical uses. Their most important function has been to collect facts so as to enable committee members to make informed judgments regarding legislative proposals. . . . A second use of the hearing process is the safety valve function, . . . A third use . . . is as a political sounding board for the legislature, furnishing a barometer to gauge public opinion." [2]

The Reorganization Act [3] was an attempt to systematize the many congressional investigations by assigning the overseeing of certain agencies to appropriate standing committees. The Act has had the effect of at least reducing the number of committees created especially to conduct investigations.[4]

Attempts have been made to draw the line between an investigation and the ordinary hearing, but without too much success. Occasionally an investigation will be ordered and separately financed without any hearings at all ensuing. A line can perhaps be drawn as to whether the investigation is conducted by a standing committee or by a special or select committee. Lines can also be drawn between inquiries requiring supplemental funds and those conducted by the permanent staff. Some investigations use the subpoena power; others do not even ask for it.

The truth of the matter is that the investigation in essence

---

[2] George B. Galloway, *History of the House of Representatives* (New York: Thomas Crowell, 1961), p. 89.
[3] Public Law 601, Seventy-ninth Congress.
[4] See p. 119.

is a *process* and not a single, definable instrument. It lends itself to the performance of many functions. It is highly adaptable in the detail of its rituals. It is a most useful tool. According to whether they are narrowly or broadly defined, one may count fifteen to several hundred investigations in a given session.

Some investigations are of persons. Most of these are by appropriate committees of the Senate, prior to action upon presidential nominations. Occasionally they take on the guise of witch hunts, and still more rarely are preludes to impeachment.

Responsibility for oversight of the administration results in a number of investigations.[5] Some, such as the recent succession of investigations of the regulatory commissions by the House Interstate and Foreign Commerce Committee's Subcommittee on Legislative Oversight, and the Special Committee on Federally Supported Research and Development Programs, concern themselves rather widely with the conduct and functioning of entire units. Others, such as those concerned with the removal of General MacArthur, the U-2 flight, the Otepka Security Case, and the TFX contract, deal with single episodes or acts. Of this sort was the investigation of the Pearl Harbor disaster. These investigations often end by ranging widely if they uncover some general weakness in the executive branch. Some arise in the course of the appropriations process, seeking economy or assurance of the execution of legislative intent. The Government Operations Committees, working closely with the General Accounting Office, have a continuous mandate, a roving commission to investigate almost anything in the administration that seems to need it. Still others are concerned with executive reorganization, focusing upon a resolution either to approve or to disapprove a specific plan submitted by the President.

---

[5] See chaps. 5 and 10 for a fuller analysis of this aspect.

Most frequent are the inquiries conducted in connection with bills and ratification of treaties. These "hearings" are in some circles not considered investigations at all; but, if we are thinking in terms of a "process," they most certainly qualify.

Finally there are the investigations of "problems." Crime, the communist conspiracy, disarmament, racketeering in labor unions, tax-exempt foundations, the war in Vietnam, are among the most famous of recent years. Under this heading undoubtedly fall the annual inquiries as to the state of the nation's economic health by the Joint Economic Committee, and its widely ranging analyses of the major aspects of our political economy. The investigations of problems and the hearings on bills are largely interchangeable, for often it is the multiplicity of bills on a subject that leads to an investigation of a problem, and the existence of a problem is not infrequently recognized by focusing consideration upon a specific bill.

The investigation as "process" follows many patterns. Before considering variants, desirable or undesirable, it is a useful analytic tool to sketch the stages likely to be followed in the ideal full-fledged inquiry. First is a clear definition or demarcation of the problem or question. If a specific bill is under consideration, its content will serve initially as such demarcation. If not, then the problem will be defined. This is followed by the allocation of staff, or the request for and the obtaining of additional funds for the expense of the inquiry. At about this stage, a request is often made of the Legislative Reference Service to conduct a preliminary "skirmish," by preparing a bibliography and summarizing the existing writings on the subject. If staff is to be added, a staff director is selected on merit and he proceeds to select additional staff. Liaison with the Legislative Reference Service is established, either by borrowing a specialist from the Service or by designation of a contact man from the committee staff. The next stage is to plan the hearings. A balanced panel consisting of a cross section of expert witnesses is named. Questions to be explored are determined. These are questions interesting to the committee members or suggested by staff analysis. These pre-hearing conferences serve to focus the hearings. In the hearings themselves individual committee members are given the chance to develop particular points. Organizations concerned with the problem are invited to make their views known, although they seldom need an invitation. So also are appropriate agencies in the executive branch. Moot questions quickly develop and staff studies are commissioned thereon. Supplementary witnesses may be invited to appear to assist the committee. Following this stage, the committee holds a number of executive sessions in which the general outlines of the findings are first determined, and then the report and/or bill is drafted in detail. These are then presented to the parent body along with recommendations. If a bill results and is passed and sent to the other House, then the appropriate committee of the latter should (and often does) ask its staff to brief it on the nature, substance, and results of the investigation prior to its own considerations.

A surprising number of investigations conform in all essentials to the process as thus outlined. A large number of others fall short in one or more particulars, and it is these shortcomings that raise serious questions as to the process itself, and even as to the responsibility of Congress.

Some investigations range widely and irresponsibly. Some become mere "fishing expeditions." It was this type of excess that led to the case of *Watkins* v. *U. S.*,[6] in which the Court declared in succession that there must be a legislative purpose, that the purpose must be defined, that there is no general authority to investigate individuals or to expose for the sake of exposure, that inquiries "designed to 'punish' those investigated are indefensible," that witnesses have their consti-

---

[6] 354 U.S. 178 (1957).

tutional rights which Congress must respect.[7]   Yet in general the power of inquiry is coterminous with its legislative competence.[8]

Other investigations make extravagant demands for funds, usually associated with excessive travel "junkets" or patronage appointments of the staff.   Akin to these are the investigations allegedly "dreamed up" by temporary staffs so as to continue their own tenure.   The phrase "permanent temporaries" is semihumorously used by certain committees to characterize these personnel.

Some committees "stack" the witnesses, giving far more time and preferred positions to one side—usually the position held by the chairman—than to the other.   Questions and treatment of witnesses may be motivated by headline hunting rather than a search for truth.   Committee members may rely upon their immunities in making random or baseless charges.   The rights of witnesses may be grossly infringed—much less now than before Congress gave attention to the problem.   Investigations may be punitive in intent, arising out of resentment at certain administrative decisions.   The "prosecuting attorney approach" may badger witnesses unmercifully.   These and other abuses have led many committees to adopt codes of fair procedure.   These have many elements in common—the right to counsel, the right to defend oneself against charges, the obligation of members to treat witnesses with courtesy.   On March 23, 1955, under the so-called Doyle resolution, the House amended its standing rules to incorporate such a code for its investigations henceforth.[9]

---

[7] See "Congress v. the Courts: Limitations on Congressional Investigations," *Univ. of Chicago Law Review,* Summer 1957, pp. 740–51.

[8] See the recent reaffirmation of this in *Barenblatt* v. *U. S.,* 360 U.S. 109 (1959).

[9] See House Manual, Sect. 735, Rule XI, subsection h-q, pp. 366–68 (1960).   Attention is also called to the study of the McCarthy hearings in Alan Barth, *Government by Investigation* (New York: Viking, 1955). The book is a disturbing, though one-sided, account of the extravagances of the McCarthy era.

Criticism is occasionally voiced in the executive branch that members of certain committee staffs exact as their price for support of a bill the inclusion of a specific point favored by a staff member, though opposed by the executive. The assumption here is that the members themselves are too busy to master the details of the bill, and necessarily rely upon staff advice. On the other hand, the staff member may well be speaking on the basis of what he knows of the members' real intent.

These criticisms are important. Yet on balance no one seriously advocates abolition of the process or even its serious curtailment. What is devoutly to be hoped is that, with the passing of the years, these discrediting and harmful elements will continue to decrease, as they have for the most part decreased in recent years. They never affected more than a minority of the committees, although they obtained a far greater proportion of public attention. Meanwhile, be it instrument or process, the investigation will find the roles assigned to it a challenge to perform more adequately, skillfully, and responsibly.

A few supplementary observations are in order. For the most part the chairman makes or breaks an investigation. As Truman did when he headed the War Investigating Committee, he can pursue the investigation thoroughly and constructively. He can give each of the other committee members his chance to develop lines of questioning without reference to party. He can use staff intelligently and permit his colleagues to do the same. Above all, he can impart a "tone" to the whole proceedings that is worthy of the occasion.

The type of staff utilized makes a genuine difference. Those with permanence of tenure and appointed on a nonpartisan basis will seek to retain the confidence of the committee by the conscientiousness of their work, and by not obtruding their own points of view. In the type of investigation which is an extension of the particular interest and drive

117

of the chairman, the committee counsel should ordinarily be one engaged for the occasion and in full sympathy with the chairman's intent. Partly because of their skill in analysis and cross-questioning, there is a disposition to use lawyers in this capacity rather more than subject specialists. To the latter, either on the committee staff or in the Legislative Reference Service, is more frequently assigned the preparation of the staff research papers.

If the staffs are party hacks or the recipients of patronage, they can be quite wasteful, for such persons are rarely experts, and much time must be spent on their own education. Then, too, there is the ever-present danger of distortion so as to please the one to whom they owe their appointment.

Reference has been made to the "permanent temporaries" and the suggestion that these may on occasion have stimulated unnecessary investigations in order to retain employment. There is, however, another side of the coin. Many standing committees undoubtedly have continuing agenda and responsibilities in excess of the four or (occasionally) more professional staff members normally allowed them. What may be lost in occasional overstaffing may be more than made up by the experience of these men who are retained year after year for a series of special investigations financed by *ad hoc* funds. This is undoubtedly a factor favoring the assignment of investigations to standing committees rather than to special committees, which latter, by the nature of their establishment, must recruit new and often inexperienced staff on a purely temporary basis. It is not surprising, therefore, to find these special committees occasionally borrowing on a reimbursable basis from the experienced and immediately useful staffs of other committees, the executive, or the Legislative Reference Service. This was notably true in the case of special committees set up to formulate the National Aeronautics and Space Act of 1958. Such staff members retain their earlier tenure, and return to their original agency when the committee no longer needs them.

In the House a committee wishing to sponsor a special investigation requiring funds presents the case to the Committee on House Administration, usually after clearing in principle with the Speaker. The latter's opposition is usually tantamount to a veto, and his influence on what is to be investigated is one of his principal sources of power and influence. In the Senate almost any senator of the majority party can successfully propose an investigation if he wishes to do so. This is subject to the consent of the committee which would normally claim subject-matter jurisdiction, if a special committee is contemplated. More usual in the Senate is for a senator to work from within a standing committee and be named as chairman of a subcommittee to deal with the problem in question. In some committees such assignments are perennial, extended from Congress to Congress, with successive grants of funds. The Senate Judiciary Committee has engaged in this practice to an extent unparalleled by any other committee. Its expenditure in the last few sessions has averaged nearly $2,000,000 a session.

In both houses, it is usual for the member sponsoring a successful resolution setting up a special committee to be named chairman thereof. This adds to his prestige as well as his opportunity for service. It also widens considerably the committee-leadership base, supplementing the seniority rule by often drawing upon the rank and file for chairmen. Under rare and extraordinary circumstances, the party majority leaders may serve as chairmen, as they did in the full-dress investigations in space and astronautics following the advent of the first sputnik.

In conclusion, we repeat that the investigation has not one role, but several. It is a process, an instrument, if you will, to carry out a number of functions. It has grown greatly in

119

frequency and prestige, as the agenda of Congress has multiplied many times, and as the problems facing the nation have grown in magnitude and complexity. Trends are observable, chiefly in the direction of perfecting its technique and safeguarding it against abuses. Skill in questioning, focusing upon the relevant, buttressing by research at both the preparatory and the synthesizing stages, streamlining of press relations, increasing nonpartisanship, development of codes of fair and orderly procedure—these and other trends are making the congressional investigation a potent and dramatic instrument in governance. It is the major factor in legislative-executive relations, the major educator of the public in dramatizing issues (rivaled only by the President's press conference), one among several tools to serve as the basis for congressional decisions. We venture to predict that, as it makes further gains in responsibility and precision, it will appear more and more clearly as a vital part of the democratic process.

CHAPTER TEN

Congress and
Administration

Only the naïve believe that Congress legislates and the President administers—that is, that our tripartite government observes protocol by each part staying out of the others' provinces. The founding fathers were well aware that their neat division of separation of powers into the legislative, executive, and judicial had been deliberately overlaid or complicated by the principle of checks and balances in the text of the Constitution. Informal usages have found many a further interstice in the formal document, until there are few major sectors of governance to which at least at some time or other both Congress and the President have not laid claim.

Yet outside of Congress itself there has been surprisingly little criticism of the extent to which the executive has matured legislation, legislation which in its more or less finished form is sent to Congress with high hope of enactment. Nor has there been much but rear-guard criticism of the powers delegated to the bureaucracy of making "regulations" in great profuseness, for these have seemed an inevitable development from the very nature of present-day governance. Where these trends have been criticized, it has most frequently been by those who have objected to the substance and not to the process; Congress has itself had its share of criticism for passing the enabling legislation in the first place.

On the other hand, the ventures of Congress into what administrators customarily regard as their peculiar sphere have been subjected to widespread censure. This censure is not only on the part of a substantial majority of students of gov-

121

ernment, but also takes the form of intense but underbreath resentment on the part of the administrators themselves. The gulf between what Congress has operatively considered to be its role in administration, and what the administrators in their candid moments are prepared to concede such a role to be is one of the most fundamental and pervasive conflicts in the whole national picture. It is not growing any the less with the years.

It has been correctly urged that the line between policy and administration is impossible to draw. Congressmen, no less than other students of the problem, are keenly aware of the extent to which many an administrator forms policy in his day-to-day decisions. This is especially true, for example, in actions of the regulatory commissions and in the State Department, but it is equally true wherever discretion is implicitly or explicitly vested in an agency. The subject has been vigorously explored, not only in the journals and reviews, but also in the committee hearings of Congress itself. It furnishes a measure of justification for much of the congressional interest in the kind of person administering even in the lower echelons. The fact is that Congress and especially its committees seek to bend the departments and agencies to their will.

The Constitution is both ambivalent and ambiguous on the congressional role in administration. It declares that the President shall be the seat of executive power; it gives confirmation of appointments and the appropriating function to Congress. In the several legislative powers entrusted to Congress it makes no stipulation of or sets no limit to the detail that may mark a law; and statutory detail is or may be carried so far that in effect it is administration. The watchful oversight of the executive, especially in recent years, has been conceded to be an appropriate legislative function, but the differences are sharp and widespread on what is appropriate overseeing, and even more, what is correctly bracketed under the elusive concept of "control." The term, "monitoring," has become increasingly popular, though this is somewhat more limited. "To monitor means to test, to educate, to criticize, to publicize, to question, to compel explanations, to oversee performance, and thus to establish limits of tolerance and expectation." [1]

For our purposes, it may be useful to consider our subject under the three headings of control or supervision, standards, and specific decisions, and then consider each in turn.

The word "control" is popularly so loosely used that it is important at the outset to understand what is really meant.[2] We face in the bureaucracy the emergence of a force of tremendous potential power—a force which, if it operates within legally prescribed limits and according to popular intent as reflected in the policies of elected officials and other media, may be an instrument of far-reaching effectiveness for the public interest. Conversely, it can become a Frankenstein monster, a law unto itself, interested largely in its own perpetuation and expansion. Many view the transformation of the original revolutionary zeal of Soviet communism into the present police state as of this character. Then, too, there is the vitally important question of its honesty and integrity. Controls internal and external can do much to assure that this tremendous machine does not fall into the hands of the unscrupulous, though the final verdict in these matters rests rather with the spiritual forces that so largely determine the mores of a people. In the popular mind, the problem of control involves efficient operation—that is, economy, effectiveness in performance of the several functions, co-ordination in the bureaucracy as a whole. With the growth in

---

[1] Holbert N. Carroll, *The House of Representatives and Foreign Affairs,* rev. ed. (Boston: Little, Brown, 1966), p. 367. See also J. M. Smith and C. P. Cotter, "Administrative Accountability," *Western Political Quarterly,* December 1956, pp. 955–66; June 1957, pp. 405–15.

[2] Pp. 123–31 draw heavily upon the author's *American System of Government,* 4th ed. (New York: Frederick A. Praeger, Inc., 1965), chap. 10.

numbers, with the advent of so much that is discretionary in officialdom and so much that can vitally affect the individuals and groups with which officialdom deals, the bureaucracy has come to have very great political power of its own. All too frequently this is capable of influencing the very electoral process on which its control so largely depends. Moreover, in American eyes, there is a new and important element requiring control, an element of loyalty which in times past has been taken for granted, but no longer can be so. Finally, much of policy determination itself is inherent in administration. For example, there is the power in foreign relations and in direction of the armed services to create major *faits accomplis*. Another example is the weight of authority which experience with problems gives to a government agency administering a field such as agriculture when it proposes new legislation. Thus it becomes all too obvious that general policy as well as detail is a sphere in which the issue of control of the bureaucracy is vital. All these elements—legality, intent, honesty, integrity, efficiency, political power, loyalty, policy—are parts or aspects of the problem of control.

Limited roles in control are played also by the courts and the General Accounting Office, but our concern here is not with them. Also the built-in controls of the "presidency," especially of the Bureau of the Budget, and of the Civil Service Commission, are of major importance in any over-all consideration, but are relevant here only in that they constitute the alternative instruments offered by those who criticize or resent the role of Congress.

Legality on the part of the administration is scarcely the responsibility of the legislative branch, nor does it claim it as such. The courts and the General Accounting Office are the normal enforcing agents, but occasionally a speech will charge illegality, or a congressional investigation will uncover information that the committee members believe they are justified in sending on to the Attorney General, or the Committees on Government Operations will raise questions on disturbing information received from the General Accounting Office.

Distortion of legislative intent is another matter. This is a province that Congress regards as peculiarly its own. Apart from amending the law, which is not likely to be too practicable a remedy because of the probability of a presidential veto, the chief weapons of Congress in this field are publicity and appropriations. Theoretically, there should be no problem, if laws are carefully drawn, but they are not always so drawn. Then, too, many laws are purposely drawn in general terms to allow a very considerable measure of administrative discretion. Laws whose chief content is the declaration of objectives and the creation of instruments to carry them out lend themselves readily to subsequent administrative modification of these objectives. The administration of certain laws may legally be entirely correct; while at the same time, administration may be in such a fashion as to incorporate the philosophy of the administrator rather than of Congress. Moreover, Congress may never have made its intention clear in the first place. Price controls can be administered to limit profits more than—or less than—wages. Public power development can be administered to favor public over private distribution thereof, in the absence of any law on the subject. With so many laws actually matured in the bureaucracy, the Congress can never be quite certain what "sleepers" or hidden powers and meanings may be concealed within the text. In Britain what seems to be a relative absence of such problems is probably accounted for by two circumstances—the general loyalty of the civil servant to the intent of the Minister and the desire to save him embarrassment; plus the assumption on the part of the Government of public responsibility for all the consequences of a given law, even though it may not have realized them at the time of passage. Separation of the executive from the legislative under the American system lessens the former's loyalty to the legislative branch, while at the same

125

time it gives greater subsequent assurance that such deviation from understood intent will be ruthlessly exposed in floor debate and committee investigations. Retribution for noncompliance will be exacted most probably through cuts or directives in appropriations.

A word of caution should be added at this point against crediting as true all accusations in Congress as to distorted intent. It is common practice for individual members or groups, unable to secure the general support of their colleagues, to charge such distortion, on points that were perhaps not even foreseen, let alone specifically passed upon at time of enactment. It is also standard tactics of the minority to try to pin the badges of illegality, unconstitutionality, and irresponsibility upon the party in power. These charges may or may not be true, especially to the extent alleged. None the less, the nature of government today is such that a large measure of discretion must inevitably fall to the bureaucracy; and it is surely of importance that the way be open and used to prevent this discretion being employed contrary to the intent of the body passing the original law.

Crude peculation in the administration is not a serious problem, and in any event is likely to be uncovered by the ordinary internal accounting controls. Scandals such as the recent ones in the Bureau of Internal Revenue, whereby tax favors were extended for personal considerations, represent a more difficult type to detect. An alert Congress has been invaluable in this regard; and Senators Kefauver and Williams became national heroes for their role in investigations. Another approach is that urged by men like Senator Douglas and Representative Bennett, who would have Congress formulate a code of ethics for public officials. This code would go beyond the law, and serve as a crystallized norm for all public officials in place of the confusion we have already mentioned. In 1966 the Senate set up a Select Committee on Standards and Conduct.

The weapon of congressional investigation is essential. Leaving investigations wholly to the executive invites the temptation to cover up, lest exposure should weaken its prestige. The American electorate rightly honors its crusaders and this puts a premium on success in this regard by a member. Congressional investigations not only have their own special staffs, they also have a considerable measure of concrete assistance in obtaining information from inside the executive and from members of the public. Such investigations are peculiarly adapted to those situations in which no law has been violated, but in which there has been an apparent betrayal of public trust. By focusing on ethics rather than legality, they can perform the highly important function of crystallizing opinion on what things are or are not "done." This is not to say that all investigations are noble in motive or nobly conducted. Many fall far short of such standards. Yet Madison's point made more than a century and a half ago retains much of its pristine validity: the American system harnesses the self-interest of different institutions to check each other in such a way that perhaps the people so governed are better served than they would be by concentration of power and responsibility.

Efficiency as an objective of control requires more precise definition. Actually three principal values seem to be involved in this concept. The first is economy in financial terms, or, more fundamentally, in the use of men and materials. The second is effectiveness, that is, the performance of functions as entrusted accurately, expeditiously, and in full measure. The third has to do with co-ordination, the integrating of the several parts and objectives in such a fashion that there is no incompatibility or lost motion. A word is in order concerning each of these three.

Concerning economy we have already indicated the role played by the Appropriations Committees. The cuts imposed by Congress at the behest of the Appropriations Committees in the estimates that have already been approved by the Budget Bureau are often fairly substantial; though some cynics doubt how far they go beyond what the agency succeeded in including originally in excess of what was vitally needed—expecting some cuts in any event. As regards specific items of extravagance, the congressional Committees are aided from time to time by tips or information from many sources both within and outside of the government. Efforts to establish cost figures based on work load have made some progress in the so-called "performance budget." The staff work of the Committees constitutes another invaluable aid. Yet when all is said and done, Congress is still largely at the mercy of a department, especially the Department of Defense, because of the sheer magnitude and technical nature of its operations. The necessary secrecy surrounding many military matters constitutes another hazard in this particular instance. *Ex post facto* investigation of expenditures is one of the statutory functions of the Congressional Committees on Government Operations; and these Committees occasionally turn out reports of considerable influence in future estimates.

The effectiveness of administration is a subject of constant congressional concern. Much criticism is informal, by telephone or otherwise, and the matter is settled "out of court." It should be borne in mind at this point that far more than is the individual member of Parliament, the member of Congress is looked to by his constituents for redress of grievances or as the recipient of suggestions for improved public service. The President is also written to on matters of this sort. By and large, the agencies are extremely sensitive to criticism, even by a single member of Congress. Thus there goes on through various channels a continuous barrage of reactions from those affected by, or those noticing, ineffective or faulty operations. Conversely there are instances of praise and gratitude as well.

Sometimes criticism reaches the stature of a full-fledged investigation. The investigation may be by the standing committees charged with responsibility for the field, or by one of the Committees on Government Operations, or it may be by a special committee created for the purpose. The investigation is an exceedingly flexible weapon of control. It can range widely; it can focus narrowly. It can be very simple —the result of a mere request on a committee's part for explanation of certain matters, usually, but not always, resulting in the attendance of someone from the agency at a public hearing. On the other hand, as was the case with the recall of General MacArthur, the hearing may go on for months and pass in review matters of the highest importance. Or the investigation may be continuous, as, for example, that by the committee presided over by the then Senator Truman during the war, which ranged widely over much of the war effort. It should be borne in mind that the standing committees of Congress are specifically charged under the Legislative Reorganization Act of 1946 with "watchfulness" over the corresponding agencies in the bureaucracy. Where the committee is itself composed of members largely chosen from regions whose economic interest is coincidental with the purpose that created the agency for which the committee is responsible, the committee is likely to be especially zealous to see that the work is well performed; but it is also likely to be less ready to criticize policy recommendations. Pressure groups in this and other fashions have their spokesmen in Congress. They serve as ready and alert vehicles to see to it, as far as agitation, criticism, and questions will do the job, that the group's interests are furthered up to the intent of the relevant law; and that these interests are not harmed by a hostile administration without a clear showing of authority therefor on the part of the latter. Finally, it should be repeated that the influence and activity of the Appropriations Committees extend considerably beyond considerations of economy. In the language of the Appropriations Bill, in criticism, in informal guidance, or explicit directives, controls are exercised over administration, organization, and policy which make these Committees the most powerful of the weapons in the congressional arsenal of control.

On balance, Congress is highly successful in its efforts to keep the administration even more sensitive to public opinion than it otherwise would have been. In its questions and investigations it goes far beyond what many regard as appropriate. This has undoubtedly discouraged some from entering and remaining in the public service. It has in many instances itself been costly of time and effort. The weapon of investigation has at times been irresponsibly exercised. Yet the public interest aroused; the quality of constant alertness created; the sense of accountability generated, are surely assets of very great value. Over and above this there exists an impressive record of concrete reforms and results; and, conversely, of vindications of agencies through criticism being pursued to a conclusion, a record that makes the general verdict on the particular matter unmistakably favorable.

We leave for later discussion [3] the type of control that looks toward co-ordination.

The problem of the political power of the executive branch especially at election time is one on which congressmen are divided in mind. The temptation to profit thereby themselves is considerable. On the other hand, there are many campaign and election practices that are illegal, and others that are distinctly frowned upon by more than merely the members of Congress whose hold on the electorate is impaired thereby. The manipulation of administrative decisions and activities to create favorable impressions and results at election time evokes an uneasiness even among some of the President's party. It brings criticism rising to rage on the part of the opposition.

[3] Cf. chap. 12.

A word is certainly in order concerning one of the most spectacular and controversial aspects of congressional control of the executive—that involving the loyalty of government employees. As a matter of fact the issues are not too difficult to understand, if one starts with an examination of the premise held by the majority of Congress, to the effect that the free world is now at war. From time to time the war assumes limited military aspects; but for the most part it is held that the war is being fought with other and more sophisticated weapons. Whatever the weapons, and whatever the enemy may say, an extremely strong case can be made out that the enemy has in fact resolved upon our ultimate destruction. Under these circumstances, it is surely not unreasonable for those who believe this to take whatever steps may be necessary to assure themselves that there are none in critical and sensitive positions who may owe allegiance to the enemy. Beyond this, opinion divides; and the fears of people are too often exploited for political purposes with innocent men suffering. It is perhaps not inaccurate to say that there is majority sentiment in Congress for giving the benefit of the doubt to the individual in a noncritical position, but to resolve the doubt against the individual in a sensitive and critical position. The whole subject is highly controversial, but those who would understand the relatively recent congressional attitude must first meet squarely the aforementioned underlying assumption and discuss it in these terms. Congress has undoubtedly forced the pace, but the executive is likewise committed to the view that no Communist may hold an appointive office.

We may summarize the problem by saying that there is agreement that Congress has and should have a highly important role in the control and oversight of the administration, however much people may differ on the proper extent of such control and the skill and objectivity with which Congress in fact exercises it. The investigation is an inevitable response of Congress to the dangers of a technical monopoly on the part of the bureaucracy.[4]

The prescription of administrative standards is another matter. What is in question is not declarations of policy such as "appointment solely on merit" or "full reporting." It is when standards become detailed, with salary scales, retirement, accounting procedures, purchase and disposal of supplies, and similar administrative areas meticulously set out in statutes, and frequently with the laws thereon differing quite irrationally in different departments. These differences may have arisen through differences in the committees that brought in the original bills or through different times and personnel of the same committee, or differences in the political power of the employees concerned. For example, it is difficult to defend on purely rational grounds the singling out of the postal employees for special treatment, as over against the classified service.

However, the fact that laws of this kind may be intricate in their detail may leave a false impression concerning the origin of such detail. For the most part these laws are matured, not in the congressional committee, but in the department or agency of the administration appropriate thereto. Most bills relating to personnel originate in the Civil Service Commission, often it is true aided by at least some prior consultation with the chairmen of the Post Office and Civil Service Committees. These Committees reserve full right to amend the Commission's version and usually exercise it. The two chairmen often differ, and differing versions thus find their way into the two houses, ultimately to be resolved in conference committee, with the executive tactfully but often effectively pressing its point of view. So also bills relating to procurement or disposal of supplies and property or accounting are apt to be formulated in great detail in the legal or

---

[4] An excellent analysis of this oversight function is found in George B. Galloway, *History of the House of Representatives, op. cit.,* chap. 10.

accounting or budget offices of the agencies concerned. They are submitted to Congress for review and formal sanction.

The Appropriations Committees, notably in the House, occasionally attach stipulations to bills, which have the effect of prescription of standards. Many of these are designed to force a shrinkage of staff or expenditure; others in effect reflect policy verdicts. They are usually criticized by the administration as not leaving leeway for adaptation to individual circumstances or as being illogical in their incidence.

Finally, and in the third place, Congress has retained a large degree of power to make specific administrative decisions. The most frequent are those associated with appropriations, public works, and confirmation of appointments.

The appropriating process lends itself to specific decisions, not merely in the detailed sums appropriated or denied, but in the accompanying text of the committee reports. Specific books for overseas informational use may be frowned upon; higher salaries may be allowed specific positions; authorized activities may be sharply curtailed in specific aspects; funds for construction of veterans' hospitals may be tied to specific locations. These and other normally administrative decisions may result from use of the appropriating process to indicate policy judgments or to express the localism inherent in congressional structure.[5] *United States* v. *Lovett*[6] has curbed the use of the appropriation bill for direct removal of individuals, but more subtle tools remain.

Akin to this administrative detail are the numerous immigration and other special or private bills which pass each Congress. The amount of time that Congress spends on such individual decisions may easily be exaggerated. Relatively few members take part in the subcommittee discussion which reviews or screens them, and the members have staff assistance also. In these and other administrative matters in which con-

---

[5] See chaps. 8 and 16 for background.
[6] 328 U.S. 303 (1946).

gressmen intervene formally or informally, one sees a working out of a congressional philosophy that most laws designed to promote general objectives need adjustments to fit particular situations; and that the individual congressman has the responsibility of making such adjustment possible as far as his constituents are concerned. For the most part, such intervention is based on humane considerations; in some instances it reflects the economic interests of his constituent or his district; in still other instances, campaign contributions or a legal retainer to a member's firm may have been not without their influence. In any event the practice of private bills is vigorously and widely defended in Congress itself, and in its end results bears a curious resemblance to the effect on specific administrative decisions which British members of Parliament produce through the instrumentality of the question hour.

Interest in administrative decisions on persons is widespread in Congress. The formal confirmation of appointments has been explored and discussed quite thoroughly many times, and we have little to add. It assures the spotlight on the earlier record of at least the upper ranges among the appointees. Patronage has been excoriated and defended in a multitude of quarters. The firing of employees has been "complicated" both ways by congressional interest—or usually by the interest of individual congressmen. Some employees have incurred enmity; others are admired. Congress protects a Dr. Astin from the enmity of a private interest against which he as Director of the Bureau of Standards has ruled; it makes difficult the retention of a staff member who has lost the confidence of powerful congressmen.

Apart from government employees, there are many other instances of congressional interest in individuals. Certain orders concerning the deportation of aliens are subject to being overruled by the nonvetoable Concurrent Resolution. We have already mentioned the number of individual immigration bills granting exceptions from normal procedure. Much of the grist of congressional investigations has to do with *persons*—loyalty, undue influence, and other matters. The widespread interest on Capitol Hill in formulating rules of committee procedure and codes of ethics has sprung largely from practices in connection with hearings which many members have regarded as unfair in dealings with individuals.

For a long time Congress retained virtually the entire responsibility for final decision on departmental and agency internal organization. Of late the rigidities arising from such procedure have been greatly lessened, yet with ultimate congressional authority safeguarded by procedures under the various reorganization acts. Responsibility for proposing such structural rearrangements has been explicitly vested in the executive, yet the executive has had very great assistance in the studies leading up to such proposals by the two Hoover Commissions. These have been "mixed" commissions, partly appointed by and from Congress, partly by and from the executive, partly chosen by each from outside citizenry. Either house of Congress might reject a reorganization proposal by majority vote of its total membership, within sixty days of submission. Not every plan so formulated has been adopted nor necessarily should it have been, but the method itself has been conspicuously successful compared to any previously used. Most earlier efforts foundered on the shoals of bureau support within Congress buttressed by clientele support among the electorate—examples of the power and autonomy of the "whirlpools" referred to elsewhere.[7]

In performing these [administrative] activities, Congress is acting where it is most competent to act, it is dealing with particulars, not general policies. . . . Committee specialization and committee power enhance rather than detract from the effectiveness of the committees as administrative overseers. In addition, as the great organized interests of society come to be represented more directly in the bureaucracy and administration, the role of Congress as representative of individual citizens becomes all the more important. The congress-

---

[7] See pp. 55, 144 f.

man more often serves their interests by representing them in the administrative process than in the legislative process.[8]

The relationship of Congress to administration is far more pervading and complex than is indicated within the confines of this particular chapter.[9] We have run across it and shall run across it in almost every major consideration in this work —in the executive-legislative struggle and co-operation, in appraising the staff services of Congress, in connection with the pressure groups, the parties, localism, and international policy. All these matters lend color to the theory that separation of powers and checks and balances under our Constitution are the most powerful, the most all-pervading of its principles, save only the principle of the direct election of our officials. From these principles evolves much of the interlocking pluralism in decision-making which has been held both the genius and the despair of the American system.

---

[8] Samuel P. Huntington, "Congressional Responses to the Twentieth Century," in David B. Truman, ed., *The Congress and America's Future* (Englewood Cliffs: Prentice-Hall, 1965), p. 25.

[9] The standard work on the subject is Joseph P. Harris, *Congressional Control of Administration* (Washington: Brookings Institution, 1964). The analysis therein is considerably less favorable to Congress than is the present author's.

The Pressure Groups and Congress

T HE most difficult problem of statecraft today is not the relationship of the govern-
ment and the individual but the relationship of the government
and the groups, economic and otherwise. We recognize our
society as having centers of free and organized activity all
over the place, and for the most part are happy that it is so.
Neither the anarchy of the theoretically possible complete individualism nor the monolithic society of the dictatorship exercises very much hold upon our people. Rather do we see
our society as one of tremendous vitality and ferment—individuals leading and bending others to their more clearly
thought and strongly felt objectives; groups autonomous
within healthy limits, their drive and energy operating (to a
very considerable extent of their own volition) to the common
good; and government the necessary integrator or adjuster
where conflicts arise—either between individual and individual, group and group, individual and group, or individual or
group and the general welfare.

The deeper origins of such a society have often been explored and need detain us only long enough to summarize
the argument and to underscore a certain inevitable quality
therein.

Basically, the origin lies in technology, in the premium put
upon differentiation in the economic processes of production,
distribution, and to some extent consumption. The economic
advantages of specialization over the self-contained and self-
supporting household economy have long since established
themselves. The derivative effects of such specialization are

137

first of all sociological, and then as a corollary, political. Within a specialized group—dairy farmers, bricklayers, bankers, doctors, steel manufacturers, steelworkers—the initial earlier impact or emphasis was to a very considerable extent competitive, but this consciousness of the competitive element with its individualistic connotations has long since been accompanied or even overshadowed by an awareness of the common interests of the group as a whole over against other groups or society at large. More sophisticated reasoning has enabled the members of many of these groups to differentiate between the two—to compete vigorously among themselves but also to join forces in areas of common interest to attain common ends.

Moreover, this group consciousness and group action have arisen in a period and in a society whose economic philosophy was at first the rather crude utilitarianism of Adam Smith and Spencer, the universal identification of self-interest with the common good. Later, the more penetrating concept of *function* in the great society emerged, in which each group or industry became more and more conscious of its contribution to national productivity, wealth, and well-being. The Rotary Club and other service clubs mark the full flowering of the mores created by this line of functional thinking.

Members of each of these groups commonly found themselves associated with each other, usually socially as well as in economic activities. They thus inevitably developed like patterns of thought. These patterns included a rationalization of their occupation in terms of its necessary contribution to the welfare of society, a derivative alarm at and resistance to anything that thwarted such a contribution (measured, of course, by the prosperity of their group), the cloaking of the public pronouncements of such alarm and resistance in usually perfectly sincere terms of the general good, and (and this is of cardinal political importance) an eventual full-fledged campaign of political action designed to use the instrumentalities of government to further their ends.

In many areas, these objectives did in fact coincide with the public interest, as, for example, the eight-hour day, the furtherance of agricultural experiment and research, the protection of products against adulteration or misbranding, but in other areas their social value was more problematical. These less fortunate developments were chiefly in state action designed to foster scarcity and consequent higher prices than would otherwise have ruled. Long-range and secondary effects cannot be overlooked in a full appraisal of the relationships of such measures to the public interest. Programs such as crop limitations with parity prices, the closed shop with union control over admission to the union, insistence upon basing point pricing so as to permit identical bidding and division of markets, retail price maintenance—these and many others are certainly of mixed social consequence. But those who strive for them do not think so, for they have long been accustomed to identify their own prosperity with the common good under each and every circumstance.

The sociological consequence of differentiation is dispersiveness; the political consequence is the dispersive state. That is to say, the dominant characteristic of society and state alike is this pattern of organized group activity, often in fact in the interest of the whole (though accidentally so), but often also to a very considerable extent in conflict with such interest. This spontaneous pluralism is technological and sociological in its origin. It is irreversible, but it is capable of being understood. The problem of statecraft is clear. It is how to adjust the intergroup conflicts and how to integrate group action into an over-all program in the common interest but, and this is the catch, without destroying or curbing unduly both the individual and group drive and spontaneity which are the very lifeblood of our dynamic economy. The ultimate judgment on how so to adjust and so to integrate lies with Congress, an inescapable responsibility of the first magnitude.

But these political insistences of the groups do not stop with legislation. The legislation customarily creates a continuing instrument in the shape of an executive agency to further the objectives sought. Sometimes these agencies are arbitral in character, to adjust conflicts between groups; more often they represent the incorporation into the governmental structure of the principle of continuous intervention. Such is the Department of Agriculture. Such is the Civil Aeronautics Authority. Such is the Bureau of Public Roads. Such is the National Labor Relations Board, whose members by an informal understanding for a number of years were "cleared" with the great union organizations. This is not the whole picture, of course, for the very cloaking of these officials with the mantle of the public interest itself affects their behavior and modifies their previous predilections. Yet the pattern of the executive branch, in so far as this group influence is one of its major aspects, nevertheless represents for the most part a pattern of agencies and clientele—the dispersive expression in administration of dispersive legislation; the dispersive legislation, the product of dispersive politics; the dispersive politics, the logical and inexorable outcome of a dispersive society.

Congressmen are themselves the products or creatures of this same dispersive society. Yet when they commence to serve, they come to grasp, more quickly and readily than their constituents with the latter's narrower experience, something of the nature of this problem as it confronts government. Many more of the congressmen than one generally appreciates come to realize that the common good is not, as the "conservatives" would have it, totally bound up with the success of business; nor is it bound up, as the "liberals" would have it, with the effectuating of a union between agriculture and labor by giving to each more or less what it wants without regard to broader social consequences. To many a member of Congress, his problem appears to be that of picking and choosing; of granting to the insistent groups those portions of their demands that in fact minister to the common good; and, as for the remainder of these demands, by one device or another he would foster a disguised and masterly inaction. The groups on the other hand seek to put a member on record, to concentrate on obtaining loyalty to their *total* program, to punish and reward accordingly.

The congressman cannot escape the fact that he is a product of this dispersive society—elected by his state or district as its representative, elected in all probability because he is "one of them," believing as these voters believe, his opinions the product of their social milieu, his mores theirs. If his subsequent education and experience have given him a broader view, a deeper insight, he must not openly stray too far from the pattern of thought of his district or he will not return after the next election. The good he would do, he cannot always do openly, and perhaps not at all. Yet he can and does defend himself in his own conscience by the belief that he is aware of the nature of the problem and will push the public or general interest as far as he can and still remain in office—till the happy day in which he can push it still further. Meanwhile, he will represent his constituents.

Comparatively few members are operatively aware that there is also an over-all, integrating role to be performed. The automatic adjustment of a flexible economy is still a widely held belief, though the collapse of 1929 shook this belief considerably. Whether such an integrating role is to be performed by government directly or by creating the setting in which industry will itself perform it is discussible. That it must in fact be performed is held by virtually all students of political economy. The congressional role in the matter will be treated more at length in a later chapter.[1] At this stage the problem is merely noted.

By and large, what is the pattern of the impact of these

---

[1] Cf. chap. 12.

special interests or pressure groups in and upon Congress? It is so complex that only the broadest of generalizations can be safely made.[2] There are four major groups with very great political power—business, agriculture, labor, veterans. A fifth group, the aged, is emerging on the horizon as one likely to be of similar stature. Government employees, Negroes, consumers, conservationists, international co-operationists, the "patriotic front," represent a second tier. Certain of the professions, notably the lawyers and doctors, are influential within a narrow field.

Of course such a picture is a gross oversimplification. Business is by no means united except on a limited number of issues. Exporters and importers conflict. Rival forms of transportation bring pressures and facts to bear upon the same congressional committees. Big business and little business lobby incessantly. To some extent this is true of agriculture. Irrigation farmers struggle with the ordinary farmers. Intercrop rivalry and intersectional rivalry over the same crop appear here and there in the political picture. The great farm organizations seldom speak with a wholly united voice. Rivalries between the erstwhile great labor federations had their congressional expression. To a greater or less extent the whole intricate pattern of our dispersive society has its counterpart in the pressures that beat upon Congress.

In fairly obvious fashion this relates itself to regional groupings. Urban-rural conflicts are everywhere evident, so much so that those districts and states which are fairly equally divided between the two are more often the most unstable politically, in comparison with those primarily rural or urban. Within a metropolitan area, suburbia compete with the workers' districts. The industrial East and Middle West follow much the same group structure pattern. The South is still mostly conservative, with some influx of laborite liberalism

---

2 See Emanuel Celler, "Pressure Groups in Congress," *Annals of the American Academy,* September 1958, pp. 1–9.

from the industrial Piedmont where voting laws permit. The Prairie States still have a smoldering agrarian radicalism from their debtor days but are essentially "agriculture" rather than Republican or Democrat. The Mountain States have a coloration of their own, centering around the scarcity of water. This finds political expression in the activities of the great water-resources construction agencies of the government. The Pacific Coast States are more complex, and consequently perhaps more involved in controversies involving real issues rather than party lines.

This economic and sectional pattern reflects itself within Congress in a number of ways. Among the most obvious are the coveted memberships on committees which consider the measures most decisive for the region or economic group or groups which the member represents. Members of the Committees on Agriculture are almost wholly from the farm states. The Interior and Insular Affairs Committees draw their membership predominantly from west of the one hundredth meridian. The Labor Committees are chiefly a mixture of members from districts dominated by organized labor and members from areas whose mores are those of conservative capitalism, members whose mission is to prevent the growth of what they deem to be the menace of radicalism. Of the thirty members on the House Merchant Marine and Fisheries Committee, twenty-four are from seacoast and lakefront districts. The pattern is less clear in the great business committees of Interstate and Foreign Commerce, Banking and Currency, Ways and Means, and Finance. Here the individual member may be explainable, but the total membership is complex. The importance attached to memberships, especially on the latter two, results in a heavy representation from among the senior and more experienced members. All pressure groups struggle for sympathetic members on Appropriations or House Rules.

The ways in which individual members can represent or

favor the groups assisting their election are numerous. Committee action is influential, though not necessarily decisive. Committee hearings can favor the presentation of witnesses whose views the committee members share, if the latter thus see fit. Helpful questions may be asked, or embarrassing ones. Attendance and attention may be discriminating. A negative reaction from a committee to a given measure is normally equivalent to a veto, though an affirmative report may not carry equal assurance of its final passage.

Members specialize and members bargain, in each instance largely in fields determined by their constituents' interest and interests. Votes on the floor do not split primarily on party lines. Rather they express or reflect a combination of economic interests involving a member's district and a more detached view on the part of those not intimately concerned with the measure in question. It is the presence of this latter group that, on the one hand, it is true, is an invitation to logrolling and trading of votes but on the other hand contains within itself the best hope of the public interest prevailing through amendment, rejection, or acceptance. This hope is that this group will prove superior to the more special economic or regional interests so frequently expressing themselves in the committee memberships. Those who would strengthen party discipline must be very certain that such party solidarity would in fact bring about the dominance of the general welfare as is commonly argued and not party bargains with the special interests in exchange for support. Thus party discipline would express itself by forcing into line those who have developed so much of detachment and independence.[3]

In concluding this portion of our analysis we again direct attention to the phenomenon of "government by whirlpools." Our dispersive society and our dispersive politics are such that among their greatest realities are these associations to-

---

[3] Cf. chap. 17.

144

gether of like-minded individuals—individuals with a common background of experience, a common set of mores, and common objectives. The spokesmen of the group are not only those paid to speak, or even the members of the group itself in a narrow sense. Spokesmen are also found among the people whose own prosperity, whose standing in their local community, are at least indirectly determined by the flourishing of the groups in question. They are also the government officials whose clientele these groups are. They are the members of Congress from the states and districts whose experience and attitudes are woven from the same fabric and who truly "represent" their district, by experience and conviction as well as by election. In the innumerable conferences and associations, formal and informal, between these various types of persons interested in common objectives, much of what we call government policy is matured. This is the heart of the dispersive state; it is the bedrock or grassroots expression of the inherent pluralism of every industrially mature society. How and how far a more general interest can utilize, discipline, or curb these special interests in the governmental process is a supreme test of a people's economic and political genius. It faces the President in his dealings with the bureaucracy no less than it faces Congress, but it is the latter with which we are most concerned.[4]

Congress over the years has evolved certain devices designed to limit the effectiveness of group pressures to those measures thought to be socially useful.

A congressional hearing is a two-edged instrument. It may serve the purpose of the witness in giving him an opportunity to present his case. On the other hand, under questioning by a skilled exponent of the public interest, such sophistries and rationalizations as may underlie even the most plausible presentation may be exposed. This questioning is

---

[4] Cf. J. Leiper Freeman, *The Political Process: Executive Bureau–Legislative Committee Relations* (Garden City: Doubleday, 1955).

especially effective if the member or members are armed with the necessary factual as well as analytic basis for such cross-examination. Sometimes such information is forthcoming from an executive agency, sometimes from an opposing pressure group, but more and more of late it has come from one or another of the congressional staff agencies in response to a member's request.

Moreover, publicity remains one of democracy's best and most appropriate weapons in other parts of the congressional setting. Lobbies have been and always will be an integral part of the give and take of politics—an influence in making public opinion and legislators' decisions. They are enormously useful; they are also in many of their aspects extremely dangerous; they are also at times just a plain nuisance. In any event, Congress, following the lead of several of our state legislatures, has expressed its formal verdict that, whether useful or harmful, there would be much gain and little if anything lost if the weapon of publicity were brought to bear upon them and lobbies were compelled to declare themselves for what they are. Consequently the Legislative Reorganization Act contained provisions requiring registration, declaration of organization, membership and personnel, and listing of the principal sources of financial support. This portion of the Act seems not to have been too well drawn, and a number of lobbyists have apparently escaped through its interstices. Its workings were made the subject of investigation by a special committee of the House during the Eighty-first Congress. Further investigations were foreshadowed in the Eighty-fourth Congress by the Government Operations Committee of the Senate. The Committee on the Organization of Congress of the Eighty-ninth Congress has also made the problem an item on its agenda. Some strengthening of the Act is certainly in order.

After full public hearings committees customarily resort to executive sessions. At these, members frequently join in searching for ways and means of circumventing the undesirable portions of the legislation pressed for by the special interests. Sometimes vagueness of language is deliberate, to allow the administration of the measure leeway in interpreting the public interest. Informal understandings may be made with responsible members of the other house as regards what will remain and what will be eliminated in conference. Conference committees almost always confine their activities to executive sessions, and modifications in the public interest are apparently much more frequent than the more highly publicized logrolling. Even though theoretically the conferees are supposed to fight for the positions taken by their respective houses, there is no doubt that in the bargaining such zeal is affected by the beliefs of the conferees themselves as regards specific provisions. Executive sessions have normally, as an important part of their agenda, considerations of tactics and strategy, once the ultimately desirable format of a bill has been agreed upon. Informal, unofficial meetings, by no means always confined to members of a single party, are frequently held prior to these formal meetings, if it is felt that others on the committee must be circumvented or placated to obtain the necessary majority for the bloc in question.

Inaction or delaying action are tactics frequently used to trim down the demands of these special interests. A chairman may fail to call a committee meeting. Hearings may be prolonged. In the Senate the filibuster with its various modifications may occasionally perform this type of function, but of late it has been more often used as an instrument of a minority of the membership. Loading a bill with controversial amendments is not unknown as a means to assure defeat. The President's veto, known or understood in advance, is still another device. If an appropriation is called for, it is not always forthcoming. Time and again a "gravy clause" inserted at the behest of a special interest by one house or the other is eliminated in the conference committee of the two houses, and the broader public interest prevails. There are occasional understandings with regard to which house will "play politics" and which house will "play statesman." Sometimes the latter consists merely of an informal assurance that the measure will be bottled up in committee, or will be junked from the calendar to expedite the end of a session. A filibuster may be incubating in the Senate, allowing the House to gain such kudos as may derive from a favorable roll call—without the nation having to be subjected to the passage of the measure in question. Frequently ills are amended in the House in the Committee of the Whole, where formal roll calls are not allowed.

We have also mentioned [5] how the Rules Committee of the House may at times be used in this fashion. A measure may be "bottled up" or granted an unfavorable rule. As often as not, such tactics represent the quiet "better judgment" of a majority of the members, a majority which on roll call might be converted into a minority through political exigency. We have written earlier of the respect paid to committee recommendations.[6] At this point a distinction should be drawn between the "clientele" committees and those with a more broadly based membership. Recommendations from the former are more likely to be subject to floor amendment or (in the House) to be held up, or made subject to agreed upon changes, by the Rules Committee. For example during the decade of the 1940's the House Veterans' Affairs Committee was largely the spokesman of the veterans' lobbies. Only the Rules Committee stood between its recommendations and an embarrassing floor roll call. Similarly the Agriculture Committees have found their recommendations substantially altered by floor amendments.

Party loyalty at the behest of party leadership occasionally allows a member to vote his better judgment as well as his poorer, but this is relatively a minor factor, for it may mark

[5] Cf. p. 29.
[6] Cf. p. 84.

him in his own eyes as well as in the eyes of his constituents as not having independence—and the reputation for a measure of independence is a political asset, especially if the results happen to coincide with the desires and program of politically powerful elements in the electorate.

If the foregoing description of legislative maneuvering appears a bit cynical, it is not so intended. The member who eagerly takes a stand on every issue in accordance with what he believes to be the public interest unfortunately may not survive the next election. Far too many in the electorate feel so intensely on some one issue that a member's total record is ignored. If a member can block action on such an issue by some means other than a direct vote, the nation is more likely to have his services beyond the end of his present term, and he believes that this fact vindicates the necessary tactical obfuscation or "stealthy statesmanship." [7]

The real nub of the matter is this. While for the most part the beliefs of members sincerely reflect the beliefs of the electorate in their district, especially in the battle of economic interests, nevertheless a process of political and economic education inevitably sets in from the first time a member or would-be or future member gives his attention to national issues. He sees that there are two sides to a question, and, as the years pass, he sees also that there is a transcending public interest greater than and perhaps different from either side or even any compromise between the two sides. This realization comes to different persons at different times. It comes with different issues to different persons. To some it never comes. Moreover, the realization rarely, if ever, comes to any one member as regards all issues. Each inevitably has certain blind spots, the product of environment or the penalty paid for not enough time to study. The blind spot is not a defect of motive; it is a flaw in the nature of our society.

---

[7] Cf. p. 246.

But to many members, now on one issue and now on another—and generally to a different set of members on each separate issue—this realization of the contradiction between the special interest and the general interest surely comes. Their horizons are broadening as they witness the conflicts of interests and as they give thought to deeper analyses of problems and the findings of research. On given measures, because of the political and economic composition of their districts, many members enjoy the luxury of voting their convictions without incurring the hostility of any politically significant special groups among their constituents. Still others vote their convictions in any event and take the political consequences. Not infrequently these consequences vindicate their courage, but also they often bring defeat. Still others merely let their convictions dilute the intensity with which they support a measure favored by the insistent group or groups on which they are dependent for re-election. Such low-temperature support may then be the kiss of death for the measure in question. In this setting one must not judge too harshly these other devices whereby with seemingly less courage but frequently with a wisdom which foresees a better, long-range result, members of Congress circumvent the special interests in order to further the general good as they see it. With economic interests frequently so evenly divided politically as they are, the number who so vote or so act need not be very great to be in fact decisive. In the House there are easily twenty or thirty whose votes on most closely argued questions are not predictable in that they habitually approach such questions without earlier commitments or minds set. Whether the strengthening of party discipline would inhibit such statesmanship (as by and large it has in our past history), or enhance it, as much of the recent writing in political science would seem to indicate, will be considered presently.

Broadly speaking, Congress may be thought of as performing, deliberately or otherwise, a kind of "filter" function in its dealings with the pressure groups and the special interests. The vitality and energy of these groups represent the greatest asset of our economic life; their deliberations and decisions make up much of our highly valued pluralism in their multi-plication of decentralized centers of power and decision-making. Yet their dispersiveness, their limited view, and their greed mean that many of their demands are contrary to the general welfare. To filter these out, while not curbing the creative vitality of the private enterprise system—this is the role of Congress; and, as we have seen, many are the devices by which such filtering has become possible.

We conclude this chapter as we began it, by underscoring what is really at stake in the Congress of a dispersive government and society such as ours. Insistent minorities in the form of special interests or pressure groups, by their orga-nized power of political reward or political punishment, can force their will against even a majority if the "temperature" with which that majority feels the opposite is mild and if it is unorganized. Congressmen who fail to comply with the militant minority do so at their peril. But even if two or more groups make common cause—as, for example, labor and agriculture—and constitute a clear majority, there may still be a general interest contradictory to this alliance and perceived by those in Congress who are better informed.

How can or should representative government operate in such a society? That Congress is operating with increasing effectiveness and with an awareness of and conformity to the long-range public interest is the considered judgment of the author. Congress has a right to be judged by its end result, more than by the seemingly less happy aspects of politics which attend the process of attaining that end result. At the very minimum, some such politics of this kind are prob-ably essential to the member's survival in a society kept basically dispersive by its technology and its economic spe-cialization.

CHAPTER TWELVE

Economic Planning
and Congress

FOUR substantive fields in particular raise
serious questions as to the competence of
Congress to deal with them. These are economic planning,
foreign policy, national defense, and science. They are alike
in that they require *expertise* of a high order. They are
all costly. To a major extent they overlap or are interrelated, each one with each of the others. At least the last
three involve very considerable classified material. Together
they involve over three-quarters of the national budget; and
in one fashion or another figure in an even larger percentage
of governmental decisions. The role of Congress in each
merits separate treatment, and this and the three chapters that
follow consider each in turn.

In the discussions thus far, and notably in Chapter VII, the
groundwork has been laid in general terms. Congress has
through specialization on the part of its members, and through
its command of expertise, attempted to meet the onslaught of
a technical age and at the same time preserve the reality of
representative government.

*　　*　　*

The passage of the Employment Act of 1946 was evidence
of the realization in Congress that government has a responsibility to contribute toward the full functioning of the national economy. In the original Senate version there was
present the concept of continuous and, if necessary, vigorous
intervention to promote and sustain full employment, but the
House, and ultimately the conferees, shied away from such
an aggressive approach as marking a path down which we

152

were not yet ready to travel. However, as a very substantial residue, there survived a Council of Economic Advisers in the Office of the President and a Joint Committee on the Economic Report in Congress.[1] The former was to make a continuous audit of the economic state of the nation, and report to the President, and the President, with such additions, deletions, or modifications as he saw fit, was to report at least annually to Congress. The Joint Committee in turn was to report its reactions and reflections on the President's report.

The core idea is not that of broad governmental planning and intervention but of providing stabilizing factors whereby the economy as a whole—relying primarily on private enterprise—may move forward in orderly fashion. Programs as articulated in party platforms, presidential messages, and congressional agenda only incidentally and obliquely deal with these factors—except in the downswing and depth of a depression. Even then, the individual items partake more of the character of relief or support for each group than of recovery as a whole. Far more characteristic of our political thinking is the "program" which ordinarily consists of a series of unintegrated and dispersive items, each in response to the demands of a particular pressure group. If, as is currently being strongly advocated, party government and responsibility are strengthened, the burden of proof certainly is with these advocates that the end results will not be a further intensification of these dispersive factors and an elimination of the correctives of those independent elements in Congress who view the effect of a given proposal on the political economy of the nation as a whole.[2]

---

[1] The name of this latter was subsequently changed to Joint Economic Committee.

[2] Cf. p. 242 f. See also in this connection the study made by J. Roland Pennock of the power of the agricultural interests in Great Britain under the Parliamentary system, "Agriculture Subsidies in England and the United States," *American Political Science Review,* September 1962, pp. 621–33.

There is then, entirely apart from economic programs of the kind mentioned, a type of governmental intervention in the economy which deals with aggregates and over-all relationships—with saving and consumption, with saving and investment, with cash and installment buying, with bank debits and bank reserves, with resources exhaustion and conservation, with taxation and borrowing, with the government zone and the private zone, with the purchasing power of other nations and our own, with exports and imports (including the invisible items), with wages and profits (as affecting some of these relationships), with inventories at the several stages and consumer purchasing, with price level and available purchasing power.

Of something of the same nature is the function of integrating the individual items of a program in an economic sense. This was the crying need of the New Deal, which in its early years was the outstanding example to date of what a party program would be like as regards internal contradictions. Almost simultaneously it invoked measures designed to stimulate exports of our agricultural products and measures raising their prices so much that they began to be priced out of the export market. With the Federal Deposit Insurance Corporation, it brought pressures upon the banks to be cautious in credit extension; under the Federal Reserve policy it urged a loosening or expansion of credit. It raised the threat of public housing which frightened the private builder; it stimulated the same builder to build by extending him credit. It prosecuted for antitrust violations; it promoted such combined action under the N.R.A. There is little wonder that after seven years of this there were still 10,000,000 unemployed. Thus did the dispersiveness, the conflicts, and the contradictions in society and politics translate themselves into governmental action.

To integrate the several parts of a program by harmonizing them, to deal with the over-all forces affecting our economic life—these are the two aspects of what we here emphasize in economic planning.

This is no easy task, even for an omniscient dictator, if there were such. For a democracy it would appear to be considerably more difficult. The insistences of a dispersive society themselves constitute the major political obstacles. So accustomed has each group become to the utilization of government to carve out for itself a greater share of the national income regardless of consequences that over-all co-ordination is most likely to seem a thwarting or blocking of the very heart of what the group deems important to itself and what it has rationalized into identifying with the national welfare.

In the second place, authorities differ materially over what can or should be done in this area of economic stabilization. The economists are far from united in their diagnoses of the malady of depressions and are even more divergent as regards its cure.

The mechanism of the economy is delicate and brittle, especially so at the critical or decisive moments. Too drastic a remedy may bring inflation; too mild a one may allow the forces of deflation to gather irresistible momentum.

Moreover, even the expectation of intervention may precipitate complications. We have witnessed in the early days of the Korean war what happened when wage control and price control were merely authorized without being quickly used. Wage contracts presumably fixed for a much longer period were quickly reopened. Prices advanced without corresponding justification in increased costs. Inasmuch as both of these steps were taken in order to anticipate the controls, inflation gained another notch.

Last, but by no means least, there is a disturbing suspicion that such intervention, far from making government less necessary by obviating the need for action such as took place in the middle thirties, in reality marks still another mile down the long descent into a virtually complete statism. Especially

155

would this be true, it is argued, if such intervention should take the form of further additions to the already dizzy heights of government expenditure. The time may come in the United States which has already appeared in certain other nations, a time at which it becomes political suicide to tax at the rate necessary even to carry current expenses, not to mention debt repayment, and steadily mounting deficit financing would then bring in its train a steady currency depreciation with its attendant evils and ultimate crash.

Without passing judgment on the soundness or unsoundness of the arguments against this line of political and economic thinking, it should be borne in mind that governmental action of some sort becomes in this day and age a political imperative in the event of a recession or depression. Perhaps both the friends and enemies of so-called economic planning therefore might agree that at least that measure of economic integration should be forthcoming which would see to it that contradictions and cross-purposes are removed from any program so adopted and that no item should be included which would be demonstrably harmful to economic stabilization or recovery. Whether even this measure of integration is in fact politically practicable remains to be seen. It was this modest amount of co-ordination of government programs within the pattern of free enterprise that was contemplated in the 1946 Act.

Nor must one suppose that economic foresight of this character is necessarily governmental or that the indicated actions to sustain or restore prosperity are likewise necessarily governmental. Working through organizations like the Committee for Economic Development, industry has shown marked ability to organize its economic thinking and through its various spokesmen has repeatedly admitted the obligation of so conducting itself as to promote higher and higher production and levels of employment.[3]

---

[3] The Committee for Economic Development assigns a role to government also.

Examples of a similar potential economic statesmanship also can be found in labor and agricultural circles, now that their political and economic power has lifted them out of the weak position in which they found themselves until fairly recently. Perhaps a private organization such as the National Planning Association, with representatives therein of industry, labor, and agriculture, may some day command a prestige and acceptance great enough for these major economic groups to accept its leadership and voluntarily govern their policies accordingly without the need for extended government intervention. If they do not, government will most surely further intervene, forced by the politics of the situation, if not by its economics.

But our concern here is with Congress, and its responsibilities in the matter. What machinery does it possess for generating this type of thinking and for allowing it legislative expression?

Curiously enough, perhaps the most effective role hitherto has been performed not by party leadership but by individual members operating in committee or in floor debate and voting. It is at just this point that independent thought is most significant, especially in calling attention to harmful effects of measures designed to carry out the wishes of major pressure groups. For a party as such to do this is to invite the implacable hostility of the group in question, but for individual members to do the same thing, especially if they are from districts in which the group in question is relatively weak, is much more feasible. Such members, possessed of the facts, influence the votes and action of others, and the measure in question may be amended, postponed, or defeated outright. Needless to say, more than the efforts of individual members is needed to undertake the formulation of affirmative measures dealing with over-all aspects, such as the aforementioned economic relationships. Individuals of independence may block or modify harmful elements in legislation; they are ill-suited to mature, or at least to put through, constructive measures. For these there must be some institutional expression in the structure and workings of Congress.

Party policy committees are advocated by many to perform this role, particularly if their membership goes beyond the personnel of one house, or even of Congress. The Senate Minority (Republican) Policy Committee for many years revealed potentialities in this respect, partly because of its personnel and partly because it had equipped itself with an able staff. The House Minority leadership has not chosen to build up any large staff of its own, relying in part upon research at National Party Headquarters. The Majority (Democratic) policy groups almost of political necessity followed presidential leadership under Roosevelt and Truman, though from time to time they influenced materially the channel such leadership took. When the Republican, Eisenhower, was in the White House, it was interesting to observe certain changes in Congress, notably the emergence of the Democratic Majority Leader of the Senate as a rival leader.

The Legislative Reorganization Act provided for a legislative budget or fiscal program with a joint committee to formulate it. This never really functioned and is now seemingly a dead letter. The intent of the Act was, however, sound in its objective that at some stage the provisional totals of appropriations and revenue should be reviewed together and consciously related to each other. Practical difficulties were seemingly too great for it to succeed. However, the Appropriations Committees and the Ways and Means and Finance Committees (either separately or their senior members co-operating as the Joint Committee on Internal Revenue Taxation) do have one of the few opportunities offered, organizationally speaking, to take an over-all view of our national economy. From this standpoint it is perhaps regrettable that Congress did not have the opportunity to perfect the technique of the omnibus appropriations measure. As matters stand, the Appropriations Committee suffers from internal decentralization.

In the deliberations of all these committees, if we are to judge by their reports and floor discussion, the welfare of the total economy is a factor very much present. Various schools of economic thought, though chiefly conservative, seem to be represented among the members. To some extent these committees are also served by professional staffs, a few of whom are trained economists and others of whom have absorbed economics through experience. Certainly in any conscious program of economic stabilization or full employment undertaken by or with the co-operation of Congress, these vital committees, dealing as they do with fiscal policy, are essential to a satisfactory end result.

A complete picture would call attention to other committees that necessarily deal with important sectors of the national economy—Interstate and Foreign Commerce, Foreign Relations, Foreign Affairs, Small Business, Banking and Currency, Labor, Public Works, Interior and Insular Affairs, Agriculture, Merchant Marine and Fisheries—and others which, dealing as they do with governmental structure, personnel, or expenditure, exercise important influence on the political economy of the nation—Post Office and Civil Service, Government Operations, Veterans Affairs. Yet these committees are by nature separate if not dispersive. Many of them are apt to be problem and clientele committees, with over-all matters inherently less easily fitting into their thinking. The Foreign Relations and Foreign Affairs Committees constitute an exception because of the currently decisive importance of foreign affairs in our domestic economy, but this is an exception and may not outlast the present international crises.

Finally, there is the Joint Economic Committee, created as part of the Employment Act of 1946. It is not a legislative committee in the sense that it may sponsor legislation.

159

Narrowly interpreted, it would have only the responsibility of commenting on the President's *Annual Report*. A broad interpretation of its function would take in a responsibility for advice or even leadership in Congress in the whole economic sector of our national life. At present it is still feeling its way. It is as yet relatively unintegrated into the congressional mechanism, and an expanded role might well develop resistances and resentments among the other committees. Nevertheless, here if anywhere is the most likely and logical place for over-all considerations and policies to emerge.

It must always be borne in mind that many members of Congress, like so many in the electorate, are reluctant to accept the fact that our economy is not self-adjusting and that the organized intervention of powerful private groups, such as labor unions or the trade associations, has introduced rigidities with which the ordinary day-to-day operations of the market cannot deal. Such rigidities may be inflationary, or they may prolong a depression. In either event it would appear that community intervention was called for at the policy level. Even more of the members (possibly a majority) are unaware that savings and investment or spending and saving are by no means self-adjusting at the ratios necessary to keep our economy healthy and steadily expanding. What the average member does usually sense is that there are certain harmful effects attendant upon measures laudable in purpose; he senses that governments elsewhere are making administrative decisions affecting our private economy; he sees alternating recession and prosperity and wonders if this is necessary. There is also dramatic evidence that governmental fiscal policy is or can be a major factor. Out of these elements in his frame of reference, it should be possible to derive a measure of attention and support for a congressional instrument focusing on over-all or interrelational economic policy. This is true, in spite of the fact that the special interests of a member's district or home state will inevitably find themselves challenged from time to time in the process.

The practical alternative instruments to the Joint Economic Committee are the party policy committees.[4]

What are the real possibilities offered by the Joint Committee? As presently constituted it is not formally integrated in membership with the operating standing committees. Its chairmen have often been among the most influential men in the Senate and House. Senator Taft was at the same time its chairman and chairman of the Republican Policy Committee and the Committee on Labor and Public Welfare. Senator O'Mahoney, who served as its original chairman, and again in the Eighty-second Congress, was also chairman of the Interior and Insular Affairs Committee, an influential member of the Appropriations Committee, and a member of the Democratic Steering Committee. Representative Wolcott, the third chairman, was also chairman of the Banking and Currency Committee. Representative Patman, the present chairman, is also the present chairman of the Banking and Currency Committee. The former chairman, Senator Douglas, is an important member of both the Banking and Currency and Finance Committees and was and is ubiquitous and persistent in bringing his economic views to bear in floor debate and elsewhere. In the case of all these men, and a number of others of the Committee's membership, there is evidence of definite correlation between their membership on the Economic Committee and these other committees. In its early years its prestige had not been established. Today its membership is drawn very largely from important members of important committees. The stage is set for it to exert very considerable influence.

The Committee conducts important studies; the findings of these studies are sent to all committees, and reprints circulate far and wide throughout the nation. It is usually the

---

[4] Cf. chap. 17 for consideration of the role of the party.

policy of the chairman or staff director to consult with the appropriate standing committees before the Joint Committee undertakes a particular study. Its reports on the President's *Report* are widely circulated and publicized. So also are its minority reports. Undoubtedly the thought and controversy thus evoked are beneficial. The Committee's *Report* and its other publications figure frequently in floor debate on specific measures and in the deliberations of other committees. Its *Economic Indicators* is widely used and has removed its basic data from the area of controversy. Yet only rarely does a standing committee refer a bill to the Joint Economic Committee for comment. Informal contacts are more frequent.

The Committee has over the years divided itself into a number of subcommittees, the scope of which has been quite fluid. Here, as in a number of other committees of Congress, the interest of a particular member in a particular problem may well be determinative in a subcommittee's agenda. Sometimes, as in the cases of the investigation of the reform of the tax system or of glaring inconsistencies in ocean freight rates or of the efficiency of federal procurement, it might have been supposed that one of the other standing committees of Congress would have been a more logical instrument. However, the operation of Congress is supple, and negotiations or overlapping membership seem to have prevented serious jurisdictional clashes.[5]

The long-range picture contains many elements of hope. Because the reports of the Joint Committee have proven in fact to be sound over the years, its prestige is steadily rising, and membership thereon is eagerly sought. The chairmanship can and does carry great weight, especially if the same high caliber can be maintained that has so far prevailed.

---

[5] A very impressive account of the Committee's various achievements may be found in the Committee's publication *Twentieth Anniversary of the Employment Act of 1946* in the statement by John W. Lehan, pp. 87–90.

Moreover, there are a number of suggestions that have been offered for its further effectiveness.

In the first place, it has been suggested that its membership be such that at least one member shall be drawn from each of the standing committees that are of great importance in our political economy. While it would perhaps be too much to expect that the chairman or ranking minority member of a standing committee would have the time for or would give the time to such dual membership, the conscious designation of one from the committee charged with this responsibility could mean much by way of keeping the standing committee aware of the over-all implications of its several actions. Ways and Means, Finance, and Banking and Currency have always been represented.

Whether it would be wise to establish a similar tie with party leadership is less clear. The area of bipartisan agreement among committee members is quite considerable, even though its chief concern is with the heart of the controversial economic order. Recent majority and minority reports have not differed so much in their diagnoses and recommendations as they have in the language in which they were couched. In 1950 the Committee was very near to bringing in a unanimous report, and in April 1951 unanimity was in fact achieved to the extent that one document only emerged, many recommendations were agreed to by all, dissents were noted but not incorporated in a separate report, and differences were not along strictly partisan lines. The 1952 *Report* included supplemental and minority views. No report from the Council was sent in 1953 and hence the Committee issued no report. In 1954 the *Report* was unanimous, although supplemental views were filed on certain points. In 1955 the *Report* was in some particulars unanimous, but more extensive majority and minority "supplementals" were filed. Of late, the need for speed in issuing reports has often precluded identification of the substantial areas of agreement, yet with relatively little difficulty, given the will, such a comparatively bipartisan approach could be resumed. A *Report* could be divided into two parts—an agreed upon portion and a presentation of those items on which there was controversy whether partisan or factional, together with the reasons therefor. Certainly the public interest, as well as the effectiveness of the *Report,* would appear to be enhanced by such widening of the zone of agreement based upon impartial and thorough analyses of facts. To tie the Committee in to party programs is to destroy such hope of its providing truly broad national leadership.

Moreover, it is in accord with congressional practice for committees to route measures under serious consideration to interested parties for comment. Even when the opposition party is in power, most of the seriously considered measures are routed to the appropriate executive agency for its views prior to consideration or decision in committee. The suggestion is therefore all the more reasonable that the important measures before standing committees should similarly be routed to the Joint Committee for its comment if the bill in question is of major economic importance. This could be started in informal fashion by a few committees with an occasional bill and the results observed prior to any generalizing of the practice.

There is a serious inhibiting factor in the Committee's usefulness inherent in the present timetable. The President's *Economic Report* comes in January. By the time the Committee has studied it and issued its own report, it is usually too late in a given session for it to have much influence. A remedy for this which would at least be worth trying would be for the President's *Report* to be sent in July. The Committee's hearings and studies could then take place in time for its own recommendations to greet Congress the following January. These could be pinpointed by standing committees and taken into account along with these committees' legislative programs for the ensuing session. If changes had meanwhile taken place in the economy as a whole, the President could send a supplementary message. Moreover, the Committee or its staff could be given a confidential briefing in November concerning the main points of the President's budget.

Finally, it must be borne in mind that this Committee, like the other committees, possesses a permanent professional staff. There is nothing to prevent a great deal of correlation between committee staffs and also with the senior specialists in the Legislative Reference Service, and such correlation has in fact taken place. There is no danger that these other professional staffs will be dominated by the staff of the Joint Committee or vice versa, for both are or should be outstanding analysts in their own right. However, the very fact that they are presumably scholars leaves the way open for each to learn from the other and thus to bring the influence of such shared thinking to bear upon the staff or the Reference Service reports to the various committees or to Congress as a whole.

The discussion so far has largely overlooked the very important fact that in all probability the major initiatives will necessarily come from the executive in this field. The Council of Economic Advisers is in the Office of the President and thus close to the Bureau of the Budget. Much remains to be done by way of realizing the implications of these relationships and even more in seeing to it that the Council's findings are effectively brought to the notice of the several departments. The time factor usually involved in economic matters of this sort makes it more likely that recommendations will emerge from the executive than from Congress. The role of the latter then comes to be that of critic and facilitator rather than of generator and leader.

Yet here also, as in other areas, we have seen the importance

165

of preserving the opportunity and practice whereby Congress itself may formulate alternatives and assume the lead, if it feels that the executive is dilatory or in error.

Executive and Congress alike are only on the threshold of making the necessary adaptations to the level of mature economic thinking now available—thinking which, if translated into policy and action, can make it possible for our nation to move forward continuously in the direction of ever greater prosperity and an ever higher attendant standard of living. The politics of the special interests, the vested interests of the dispersive state, are ready to block such an outcome. On the other side of the ledger is a world crisis in which we know we must have a strong America.

CHAPTER THIRTEEN

Congress and International Policy

THE myth has grown up that in practice the President is almost completely determinative in our international relations except for the Senate's alleged role as obstructor. There have been times in which the myth has been not far from the truth. Conspicuously has this been so in the events leading up to the American entry into many, if not most, of its wars. Franklin Roosevelt certainly controlled the American end of the events bringing the United States into its status of belligerent neutrality, even though the shooting came unwittingly upon the nation. More dramatically, it was Truman's decision to use defensive force in Korea, a decision, broadened and sanctioned by the United Nations, out of which so many subsequent happenings have logically stemmed. A succession of presidents has accelerated our military commitments in Vietnam. Yet, notwithstanding the power of the President, the initiative and co-operation of Congress have played an integral part in important matters, such as foreign aid, and Congress itself has been in considerable measure influential in setting the pace in the "cold war" and in reorientation of our Far Eastern policy. Moreover, the very power of the President in these matters creates an inherent uneasiness in Congress and leads to the search for ways and means, not so much to circumscribe the President as to insist on a sharing in crucial decisions. In this lay the inherent strength of the support in Congress for the Bricker Amendment. In the material that follows there is no implication that the initiative does not normally lie with the President. He it is who commands the unparalleled intelligence network of the present day. He it is who possesses the instruments of negotiation. These two factors alone make his role the dominant one.

It is apparent that Congress of late is far from being passive or obstructive in international affairs. More and more it is searching for and finding ways of making itself felt in a more constructive and affirmative fashion. The executive must still reckon with the possibility that Congress will refuse to "go along," by nonratification of a treaty, by failure to appropriate funds, by nonimplementation of an executive agreement, by declining to confirm a presidential choice for an important office. This is nothing new. But the affirmative and co-operative support of bold programs in peacetime is probably new in kind as well as degree, and the techniques for winning such support merit careful study. Much more dramatic have been efforts of Congress—the Constitution notwithstanding—to guide international policy, either by further stimulating or accelerating an already noticeable trend or by altering its course altogether. That Congress can nullify, that it can support, is well established; that in the mid-twentieth century it can formulate international policy is not too generally understood.

There are reasons that make an enhanced congressional role inevitable. These reasons lie deep in the area of social change—on the domestic front involving a rising articulateness and discrimination on the part of the electorate, in the international scene marking the advent of total diplomacy with its inextricable interlocking of the political, the economic, the social, the cultural. Popular support and popular participation call for congressional leadership and conviction as well as for presidential negotiation.

Moreover, treaties are relatively less important in international policy than formerly. Of at least equal importance are certain obvious contemporary characteristics and instruments. These may be conveniently described under four headings—not necessarily mutually exclusive in particular instances. First are the bilateral and multilateral trade and economic agreements. Of these, the so-called reciprocal trade agreements have been the most publicized, and probably the most important. Included in this category are also agreements for commodity stabilization and exchange support.

This first type passes rather easily into the joint project, distinguished from the first group more by its magnitude than by any difference in legal status. However, its customary legislative implementation may center more around the amount to be appropriated than around the formalities of approval. The recent great joint projects are the Marshall Plan, exchange stabilization, military aid, and the programs of investment in and technical aid to less developed areas.

This type is not sharply distinguishable from still another type, participation in regional and international organizations. The United Nations [1] and its affiliates constitute one of the great major spheres of our activity. We have proved our interest and loyalty in countless ways, among which the Korean campaign provided the supreme test. The Organization of American States is still important, though relatively speaking it is yielding to the larger world orientation.[2] Neither it nor the United Nations seems capable of prompt and decisive action, if aggression by a communist power is involved. International activity requires appropriations, and it also requires any number of instances of subsequent integration into legislation. The military significance of the co-operation and united action among the nations of the Atlantic Pact bids fair to occupy congressional attention for the foreseeable future, although with the recent lessening of the Berlin crisis, inter-

---

[1] The San Francisco Charter is a treaty; entrance into the United Nations' affiliates has usually required affirmative congressional action.

[2] O.A.S. membership is technically a treaty, ratified by the Senate.

nal differences are weakening the ties. The latest in the family of regional pacts, SEATO, has limited possibilities, even though presently its area is the world's storm center.

In the fourth place, and finally, we find thrust upon us a cultural leadership whereby, as the most powerful nation of the free world, we are of necessity called upon to defend our ideals, not merely in negative fashion, but as something we believe in so much that we would hope others would wish to share them. The democratic way is part of that faith: the way of freedom, of equality of opportunity, of participation. So also is capitalism or private enterprise. So probably also are our educational system, our humanitarianism, and our religious institutions and beliefs. We would use this cultural leadership to strengthen the solidarity of the anti-communist world, to win friends, to raise the standard and quality of living of people everywhere. The *Voice of America,* the democratization of occupied areas, the Fulbright Plan, the social and political aspects of our policy in South Vietnam, are the most obvious concrete examples of our choice of ways and means. The decade of the 1960's opened with a search for or renewal of a "national purpose."

It is with reference to an international policy with characteristics such as these that Congress must perforce function in the present state of world affairs. No President alone can create, install, and execute programs of this nature; no Secretary of State unaided can carry conviction; no constitutional theory of the role of the executive can create *faits accomplis,* which Congress is legally bound to honor. Such an international policy will succeed only if there is a deep, underlying solidarity in popular support—a solidarity which Congress can develop as well as register. That Congress has been able to do this in large measure is remarkable evidence of its current sense of responsibility and maturity—and this without passing judgment on the wisdom of the particular measures. Whether time and posterity will judge them wise or not, there can be

170

only one opinion as regards their motivation. This is that they arose out of a sense of world danger, of world responsibilities, and even of world unity.[3]

It has often been stated that a nation's international policy is an extension of its domestic. Certainly the fear of the growth and the aggression of communism has been a prominent factor, in part selfish, in most of our postwar international activities. More clearly than before, it is likewise apparent that to unchoke the clogged channels of international trade will contribute to our domestic prosperity, and not alone because of our growing export interests. But any economic interpretation of foreign policy with its alleged corollary of power politics is far from representing the entire picture. We really believe in free and representative government as a people, especially after the searchings of heart that have been ours now that we find such government seriously threatened. We believe in it, and rightly or wrongly we have come to believe that we can fully trust only those peoples who also believe in it. For this reason, among others, we would throw our influence into the scales for its extending—and a great "freedom internationale" is being born before our eyes. Deeper yet, we are still a nation of Hebrew-Christian ideals and standards; that is, a nation to which the sacredness of the individual and the brotherhood of man are fighting words. We would project these concepts that lie at the heart of our religious faith into other cultures, and an unofficial "Christian internationale" is at least not beyond the realm of possibility in this day of international movements. We hesitate to utilize official channels in this regard, because of our tradition of the separation of church and state: but foreign policy is not confined to official organs and is made by churches and trade-unions and corporations and business and professional

---

[3] For a thorough analysis of the role of Congress in this "consensus building," see Roger Hilsman, "Congressional-Executive Relations and the Foreign Policy Consensus," *American Political Science Review,* September 1958, pp. 725–44.

associations and other voluntary bodies, and the official can favor the unofficial and operate along parallel lines toward a single goal. All over the world persons are rebelling against inferior status, some violently, some through the ballot box. A revolution of selfhood or personalism is sweeping the developing nations. Foreign aid must take account of this, in stressing those factors making for its realization.

But our domestic policy is also an extension of our international policy—though this is largely unappreciated. More accurately, one might say that domestic and international are inseparable. For this is a total war, a war of cultures and civilizations. Many a time we at home are being influenced by what we would accomplish abroad. What the rest of the world would think is already urged as an argument in many of our domestic issues. Our actions must square with our ideals if we would ask others to share the latter. Our own house must be in order—and international policy projects itself into the domestic.

In such a setting congressional support is absolutely essential to success. Treaties to these ends must be ratified, of course. Even more, appropriations must square with pretensions. The common cause requires equality of sacrifice and not exhortations and alliances alone. Congress must be satisfied before it appropriates billions of dollars a year for foreign aid, with the concomitant increases in the tax burden and indefinite postponement of coveted normalcy at home. Military affairs Congress tends to understand. Its experience during the past decade with the potency of economic factors in national strength has made these factors part of its thinking also. Formal political alliances, international organizations, and international law are not alien to its pattern of thought. It can debate them and understand them, whether it agrees or not. It can raise basic issues with reference to Vietnam.

But what of these great new elements in the international

scene—the cultural, the psychological, the ideological, the things that make men sing, march, and willing to die? These are different in kind from the world we used to know. Can Congress, or any of us for that matter, really understand their significance, in the sense that we make them a basis for our action? Even if we grant that the President and the State Department understand these things—and this is by no means certain—do the Department of Defense, the Department of Commerce, the Department of Justice, understand them? Above all, do the representatives of the people in Congress assembled understand them? Do our editors, our educators, our labor leaders, our clergy, our businessmen, understand them and see their ramifications?

It is not the place of this study to pass judgment on issues but to analyze the setting. There are debates in Congress that give one great hope. Many in Congress understand what is involved. For example, in plans such as those proposed in the Eighty-first Congress by Senator McMahon or Senator Flanders, there was witnessed an insight into the nature of the struggle—and this again without either praising or condemning the proposals themselves.[4] More recently a subcommittee

---

[4] For Senator McMahon's plan for a peace offensive, see *Congressional Record*, February 2, 1950, Vol. XCVI, pp. 1366–72. Senator Flanders' program for carrying psychological warfare behind the Iron Curtain appears in succinct form in a letter presented to President Truman on August 18, 1950, by himself and twenty-seven other senators. The heart of the letter is as follows:

"In view of these critical conditions we urge upon you a psychological and spiritual offensive against the Kremlin, devised to bring the Russian and American people into contact and into relations of mutual brotherhood.

"Let us explain to them the grim necessity of the western world for arming ourselves when we have seen their rulers sweep over nation after nation, destroying their freedom and enslaving their peoples. While the rulers of Russia have been doing this, the capitalist nations have been freeing their colonies for self government.

"Let us tell the Russian people that we want to live in peace with them and hope that their rulers will not compel us to fight them. We would like to help them to get a better life from their rich soil, forests and mines.

"We are now saying this in an indirect and partial way through the Voice of America. We need more funds and a great expansion of facilities. But more than money, we need a new vigor, a new imagination, a new directness and plainness of speech. We need the message to be continuously, indefi-

of the House Foreign Affairs Committee under the chairmanship of Representative Fascell has systematically studied the
non-military and non-economic aspects of the world struggle.
In their understanding they need not fear comparison with
the best that has thus far emerged from the executive
branch.

Of late years the Foreign Relations Committee and other
committees of the Senate have undertaken, either themselves
or by delegation or contract, an impressive series of studies
and inquiries. Some of these have been regional, others have
dealt with long-range goals; still others have considered the
process of foreign policy formation. More recently our Vietnam and China policies have been subjected to review, two
areas especially sensitive politically. Notable studies in the
reduction and control of armaments and the organization for
national security will hold their own with the best that have
been forthcoming from any source. Till relatively recently
they went considerably beyond any visible research efforts in
these areas on the part of the executive branch. Perhaps
theoretically these studies should have emanated either from
the appropriate department or from the office of the President.
The fact is, they did not—and here again, the idea of Congress as an important balance, supplement, or corrective in
the American system of government suggests itself. An interesting by-product was that when the time came for the executive to give attention to these matters, there was an informed
group in Congress ready to share the deliberations and, as
in the Test Ban Treaty, to give effective support.

Similarly, it would appear that Congress, or a substantial

---

nitely reiterated. We need to use means new and old, thought of and un-
thought of, traditional and revolutionary.

"Mr. President, let us declare total mobilization and total engagement of
our psychological and spiritual forces. Thus may we soften and erode the
foundations of the Politburo, escape the appalling expenditure of life and
treasure with which we are faced, and thus escape the totalitarian control
of our lives which neither you, we, nor the American people can contemplate
without dismay."

portion of it, saw the irreconcilable nature of the conflict of civilizations before it was seen—or at least before its logical consequences were acted upon—in the executive branch. It was Congress that forced the purges of the communists and fellow travelers; it was Congress that analyzed correctly the nature of Chinese communism; it was Congress that forced precautions (albeit too late) surrounding the atomic bomb. To say these things is not to say that there are not debit items in the ledger also or that Congress was united in these matters or that the executive was blind. These illustrations are presented rather to document the mood of Congress in its belief that it has an affirmative role to play and to indicate how much there is to be said for such a role. This bi-polar generation of policy may be complicating; it may also be invigorating and make for the ultimate adoption of a sounder policy than would result were the executive alone responsible.

Yet the ways and means of exercising world leadership culturally and ideologically, in so far as these are governmental matters, remain fluid and uncertain. Insofar as they are governmental, they must have the assent and support of Congress if they are to succeed—a support that goes beyond appropriations (though it includes them, discriminatingly, rather than recklessly) and includes much of our internal behavior as well as external action. When to put conditions on our aid to other nations and of what nature they should be, whether this aid should be in loans or grants, what metes and bounds to impose on the *Voice of America,* what foreigners to entertain and how, what technical processes and ideas to export and how, what to learn from our friends and our enemies, how to yield something of what we think is best in the interest of a pooling of the creative ideas of others as well as ourselves, how to stir the somewhat lagging spirit of certain of our Atlantic allies, how to capture the imagination of the uncommitted peoples of the world, how to penetrate the Iron Curtain—these and other issues are crowding upon Congress,

175

making its role in international relations incomparably the most difficult it has ever been asked to perform.

Mention has already been made of the desire in Congress to find ways and means of exercising congressional initiative in international affairs. That this is at times looked at askance by the State Department on the ground of the Department's assumption of superior knowledge or on the basis of its proving an embarrassment or from its sense of invasion of prerogative is well known. Such lack of enthusiasm is at least understandable. Yet when Congress does so exercise initiative, it may well be because its majority is registering some great upsurge of popular opinion—one of those waves of intuition which are not infrequently sounder guides than the supposedly more sophisticated reasonings of the "experts." Such was the nature of the B2H2 and the Fulbright resolutions; [5] such was the search of so many within and without Congress for alternatives to the intolerable exercise of the veto in the United Nations—and even for a world organization minus the Soviet Union. The Congressional Joint Resolution calling for an Atlantic Convention opened up new horizons of political collaboration with our sister democracies.[6] Such may have been the rising tide of criticism of our China policy and of the already mentioned softness with communists. Such is almost certainly the creation of a record and a climate of opinion that will make morally impossible any diplomatic betrayal of the captive Baltic republics and other peoples in the Soviet empire. Some would read the same meaning into congressional activity looking toward the establishment and strengthening of Israel, the aid to Franco's Spain—or even the union of all Ireland. Time will tell which of these represent more than an acceding to the wishes and pressures of highly political minorities. At least the first

---

[5] For the B2H2 resolution, see Senate Resolution 114, Seventy-eighth Congress, first session. For the Fulbright resolution, see House Concurrent Resolution 25, Seventy-eighth Congress, first session.

[6] S.J.R. 170, Eighty-sixth Congress, second session.

named appears to have had very wide general support, and the second has had influential military backing. The "foreign" constituents of congressmen are present, but haphazard in their quantity and distribution as to nations. The present harder and more realistic line in foreign aid owes much to the criticism and prodding of Congress. At this point these and the others mentioned are cited primarily as examples of attempted congressional initiative in a field hitherto regarded for the most part as traditionally and constitutionally the prerogative of executive leadership.[7]

The vehicles or instruments through which Congress exercises its degree of leadership and guidance are chiefly appropriations, laws, resolutions, hearings, and debates. Of these, the appropriating process is more likely to be a tool of censure or disapproval than to be an affirmative instrument. Attempts to add something in this field are few and far between. The most recent examples have to do with the direction rather than the amount of foreign aid. China and Spain were the areas favored, and in these two instances the executive was reluctant to accede. Limitations on aid to Yugoslavia and the United Arab Republic indicated disapproval of the policies of these nations. Riders and provisos are not infrequently used, earmarking funds for particular sectors of a total program or stipulating certain conditions for use of the funds. Displeasure with particular activities, such as broadcasting, can be quickly registered in curtailing of funds. Such a device has also been suggested as a way to express disapproval of sending troops abroad. Congressional investigations may curtail certain undesirable activities, but this may be at the price of a resultant executive timidity and reluctance to operate on the scale or with the imagination necessary to bring maximum results.

---

[7] Cf. in this and other matters covered in this chapter the excellent study by H. Bradford Westerfield, *Foreign Policy and Party Politics* (New Haven: Yale University Press, 1955).

Proposals for actual legislation in the field of international affairs originate sometimes with the executive, sometimes in Congress. They are particularly significant in connection with economic aid and cultural relations. Provisions for foreign scholarships and fellowships, the Pan American Highway, and the International Development Fund have legislative rather than treaty bases. So also, in another field, has foreign military assistance. Both in preliminary negotiations and in amendments the congressional contributions to the content of measures of this sort are likely to be fairly substantial, even if in the first instance they originated with the executive, as many of them do.

Resolutions are usually largely congressional in their origin, and are perhaps the chief affirmative tool available to Congress. Such have been the Connally and Fulbright resolutions.[8] They are obviously capable of greater development than at present. At times they constitute a kind of advance pledge of congressional support for the object of a State Department negotiation previously announced or about to be undertaken. Such pledges in advance were extended by the Senate in connection with the restoration of German sovereignty and by joint resolution sanctioning the use of the armed services in the defense of Formosa. In 1957 the use of force in the Middle East was endorsed, if the President felt it to be necessary. Endorsement of a strong stand in Berlin and Cuba was forthcoming in 1962. More recently the House has gone on record as favoring unilateral intervention on the part of ourselves or other nations in case of the danger of a communist take-over in Latin America. Such resolutions go far to assure or reassure other nations that, even under our Constitution of divided powers, these nations can count on the necessary legislative support if they agree to our official proposals. Similarly, they may serve as warning to

---

[8] Senate Resolution 192; House Concurrent Resolution 25: Seventy-eighth Congress, first session.

other nations as well as to our own negotiators that such support in all probability will not be forthcoming unless certain conditions are met, or perhaps not at all.

James A. Robinson has reviewed twenty-two of the major foreign policy decisions since the middle 1930's. He found strong congressional involvement in sixteen, but predominant influence in only six of these. The most usual pattern involved executive originated legislation with relatively minor changes.[9]

Though the devices carry no formal authority, the mere holding of hearings or even speeches on the floor of either house may exert considerable influence in the highly sensitive field of international relations. Many hearings constitute a sharp post-audit of our foreign policy. Others indicate that Congress is interested in or concerned about a certain subject and would like to have the executive at least turn its attention to it—such, for example, as Atlantic Union or international cartels or the fundamental nature of our policy in Vietnam. Speeches, especially by influential members, are listened to outside the United States as well as, or perhaps even more than, within our own official circles. The price of coffee, nationalization in Great Britain, the plight of refugees, British conduct in Palestine, fraternization with Latin American dictators—these will serve as examples of fields in which speeches have been influential. Dangers obviously lurk in such unco-ordinated efforts, and they may easily complicate or even block carefully prepared negotiations by the State Department. It is especially worthy of note that in recent years Senator Fulbright, Chairman of the Foreign Relations Committee, has not hesitated to question a number of current executive policies. He believes that by doing so discussion is promoted. In the course of the debates thereby evoked, it became clear that in the Kennedy and Johnson administra-

---

[9] James A. Robinson, *Congress and Foreign Policy Making* (Homewood: Dorsey Press, 1962), chap. 2.

tions, unlike those of Truman and Eisenhower, the committee chairmen were not customarily consulted or at times even informed prior to important decisions.

Yet what Congress is struggling to do through all these instruments is to forge tools whereby it can, if not wrest the initiative from the executive, at least share it to the extent that it can influence policy sufficiently in the informal initial stages and thereby make its will felt affirmatively in the end results. In other instances monitoring or setting metes and bounds of executive action is the objective. Congress has learned this much at least from history: that our nation's foreign policy over the years has been seriously handicapped through failure of executive-legislative rapport. It is not willing to solve this problem through following the executive wherever it leads. It is rather seeking through usage to fill this gap (or remedy this defect, if defect it be) in our Constitution by positive, co-operative means. This was the meaning of much of the "great debate," or that part of it which centered upon the power of the President to send troops abroad in peacetime. The pledge of consultation on the part of President Eisenhower in this field was a powerful instrument in inducing Congress not to tie his hands. Yet there is, in the author's opinion, as much danger that the executive will disregard this move or mood on the part of Congress as that the latter will fail to co-operate, if co-operative participation is sought genuinely and sincerely on the part of the State Department as far back as the formative stage in those instances in which the time factor will permit.

At the risk of dating this writing unduly, the author would suggest that during much of the postwar period Congress has been most interested in finding ways of insisting upon certain conditions as the price of foreign economic and military aid. This is a highly delicate operation, national pride being what it is. Because of the conventions of diplomacy, the executive cannot make such conditions—at least openly—

without grave jeopardy to the objectives themselves through reactions of injured pride in the nations aided. Can Congress make such conditions, and, if so, how? Speeches and resolutions, even appropriations riders or preambles to acts, all are possible vehicles for conveying warnings. Embarrassing to our negotiations they may in fact be, but, on the other hand, they may contain just the element of irresponsibility necessary to remove their sting while they convey their meaning. If so, they could in fact strengthen our influence in the direction of such objectives as a western European federation, the arresting of socialist trends and the strengthening of private enterprise, the decartelizing of foreign industry, the lessening of trade barriers, the abolition of colonialism, the removal of communists from positions of influence, safeguards for American investors, curtailing of trade with the Soviet, a shift from neutralism, increased military preparedness. If Congress believes that conditions of this type are in fact essential to the success of a particular measure, who shall say it is out of its province so to declare?

Does Congress in fact know enough? Over the years certain of its members have been or have become specialists. Its committees have staffs of comparable ability, if not of comparable size, to those of the executive. It is less a prisoner of its past than is the executive. The frequency of committee meetings is noteworthy. In 1965 the House Foreign Affairs Committee met 189 times; the Senate Foreign Relations Committee, 125 times. Meetings of subcommittees should be added to these figures. Partisanship has grown less and less strong, especially in the Senate. These considerations and others would argue that, regardless of the implications of the Constitution as drawn and perhaps as intended, House and Senate alike need not hesitate to exercise initiative —save only they exercise it responsibly.

That such a sense of responsibility is in practice overriding is the unmistakable verdict of the decades from 1940 to

1960. Both the House Foreign Affairs and Senate Foreign Relations Committees have operated in bipartisan or non-partisan fashion. The Senate Committee in particular developed a deeply felt pride for many years in presenting a unanimous report in all its major recommendations, whether or not the President was of the same party as the Senate majority. Vandenberg boasted of forty-seven critical occasions in the Eightieth Congress. This practice survived serious strain—temptations to make partisan capital; slights, especially in the form of failures on the part of the executive to consult in advance before making important moves; issues deeply felt and controversial. Presidents normally had greater support from their own party, but it is also worth noting that those chairmen of the committee from the opposition party (when it was in control) were normally both able and willing to demand greater policy concessions than those of the administration's own party.[10] Such bipartisan support was not always extended to policies of the executive that did not require congressional endorsement, such as the anti-Chiang orientation. Nor has it been uniformly extended in the economic sphere. The International Trade Organization still awaited implementation for years after its drafting and was eventually deemed dead. In the early 1960's under the influence of Halleck's leadership, Republican vacancies on the House Committee were filled in general by members from the more isolationist anti-administration wing. This changed the character of the Committee, making its future orientation less certain. Yet, if the over-all story be viewed, the give-and-take between the branches of government has been remarkable, and partisan voices and action have been but minor elements in the total picture.

In this connection tribute must be paid to the efforts on

---

[10] Cf. Malcolm E. Jewell, *Senatorial Politics and Foreign Policy* (Lexington: University of Kentucky Press, 1964), p. 146. The entire book is an illuminating study of events and political forces in the Senate from 1947 through 1960.

the part of the State Department to keep Congress acquainted with the developing issues and to associate Congress with actual negotiations. Where this latter was a reality, as in the Bretton Woods agreements and the framing of the United Nations Charter, success of the undertakings usually followed. In regular briefings of the committees, often in executive sessions, in facilitating congressional visits to the locale of international issues, in naming congressmen as delegates to conferences—in these and other ways the Department has effected a congressional relation with international policy which has contributed to its texture and assured its implementation. Regrettably the practice of prior consultation, though not of executive session briefing, has apparently been abandoned. Consultations are especially important in new programs.

There are a few special aspects worthy of notice before concluding. For one thing, the House has assumed a new importance in this whole field. Its Foreign Affairs Committee, formerly regarded as a minor committee, finds membership on it highly coveted. The shift from emphasis on treaties to emphasis on programs and policy has had as its by-product an enormously enhanced House responsibility. The economic and the ideological have joined the political and military. Appropriations, ordinary laws, and joint resolutions all require bicameral action. For example, of the 260 international agreements in 1956, ninety-five per cent were under legislative enactments. Only five were treaties.

Moreover, the staffs of the two Committees and of the Legislative Reference Service, as well as the staffs of special committees in the foreign field, such as the Herter Committee and the Joint Committee on Foreign Economic Co-operation, have played an important though undetermined and largely unrecorded role in the total operations. In the congressional staff work preceding the adoption of the Marshall Plan, for example, some thirty experts in the employ of Congress in the three Committees and the Legislative Reference Service worked on all phases of the problem. Independently of, but in close touch with, experts in the executive branch, they insisted that the latter document their contentions and reconcile any discrepancies in their findings. Moreover, the congressional staffs made a number of studies of their own, some of which were the basis for congressionally instigated changes in the program. At all times, the staffs, like the Committees to which they were responsible, operated without thought of partisanship. In presenting E.C.A. on the floor of the Senate, Senator Vandenberg spoke of the staff work as constituting "the most complete studies and surveys I have ever seen in a congressional committee."

For the most part, the State Department and others in the executive co-operate with these congressional staffs in making available to them even the confidential information in the departmental files. Some reluctance is understandable, though not defensible in this regard, in the light of the long tradition of executive leadership and responsibility. Second only to the military, our State Department experts have expected to be listened to and not subjected to rival interpretations or advice. Back of this expectation lie not only greater access to confidential information but also a constitutional theory of great prestige. Members within Congress itself have not been lacking who have believed and who still believe that State Department research and analysis are adequate for the purpose and that Congress does not need its own staff aids. However, these members are distinctly in the minority. The difference today is that Congress can face the Department as its self-respecting equal, not merely constitutionally, but in its command of competence as well. In no small degree this is accounted for by staff facilities. That the possession of these potentially rival facilities by Congress has in fact coincided with the greatest assumption of national responsibility in history in the international field—an assumption which Congress has almost as often forced as agreed to on executive urging—is witness to the sense of high obligation in the presence of facts, which has pervaded both branches of our government. There have been differences between the two branches. In at least the most important instance, the China problem, the perspective of history may well show that Congress was apparently better served by its staff than the Secretary of State by his. If Congress is to continue, as it doubtless will, to play an affirmative role in international affairs and likewise to play its constitutional part as the indispensable implementer for the policies of the executive, then the availability of staffs of great competence to explore alternatives, to analyze executive presentations, to aid in the organization of hearings, to provide unbiased, thorough information quickly—this availability would seem to be a prerequisite for that success on the part of Congress which the importance of the issues demands.

Nor is the expertness, let alone the wisdom, confined to the staffs. There are members of both houses who have devoted many years of study to, or who have had many years of practical experience in, some area or problem in international relations. Their influence is very great. There are other members who between sessions have traveled abroad as serious investigators of a problem or problems about to face Congress. The months prior to Marshall Plan debate and action saw about two hundred members engaged in on-the-spot study of one or more aspects of foreign aid. Many of these members were briefed in advance, not only by the State Department, but also by their own staffs. One result was that during floor debate there was almost always at least one member who from firsthand knowledge could speak on a particular point raised. The end result was the attainment of consensus rather than settlement of a controversy by a roll call vote.

The high standard of education in our country reflects itself in this—that in this field of international relations the debates in Congress reach a standard of informed intelligence that has no parallel in our earlier history.

One more aspect deserves comment. Foreign policy is in fact made in many departments of the executive beside the State Department. It is made in Defense, in Commerce, in Agriculture, in the Central Intelligence Agency, in Justice, in Labor, in the cultural-relations program of the Library of Congress (an agency, but not in the executive), in many other agencies in at least a minor fashion. So also among the corresponding committees on Capitol Hill. The effect of the projection into the international sphere of our policies in trade, the military, territorial government, atomic energy, food supply and raw materials, cultural relations, immigration, shipping, labor standards, and many other spheres is to project international considerations to some extent into the deliberations of the majority of these congressional committees.[11] Problems of coordination and overview are serious in both branches. Nor is the picture complete without calling attention to the power of nationality groups, such for example as the Zionists, and the lobbyists for foreign powers in matters as diverse as sugar quotas and our China policy.

We are a world power. Our cultural leadership, our military strength, our political influence, to some extent even our economic power—these have not been of our own seeking. There probably never was a more reluctant world leader in all history than the United States. Yet this very reluctance makes us less feared and more readily followed. Other peoples have tended to personify us in the shape of the individual who happened to be our President at a given time. They have assumed that the voice of the President was necessarily the total voice of America. Yet these other peoples

---

[11] See Holbert N. Carroll, *The House of Representatives and Foreign Affairs,* rev. ed. (Boston: Little, Brown, 1966), for an illuminating exposition of this point.

that make up the world, free and regimented alike, need more than an understanding of our President: they need to understand the influence of our representative body, the Congress. They need to see Congress as a living symbol, to see that our Republic has Congress too among its institutions of leadership—incorporating not only the hesitations and cross purposes of its people but also their sense of responsibility and the agreement on objectives and instruments which these people's assembled representatives have produced following hard study and discussion.

CHAPTER FOURTEEN

Legislative Responsibilities in National Defense

THE authority of technical competence has no sphere more absolute than defense and warfare in a nuclear, chemical, and biological age. Weapon systems are out of date before they leave the drawing board. The possibility of mutual annihilation is already with us. The very capacity for inspection and control in the event of armament agreements may already be a fantasy, rendered obsolete by the minuscule character of lethal weapons or the ease and speed of future conversion and production. Moreover, there is also the problem that defense policy must be formulated and adopted, not only in a nuclear age, but also in an ideological age—an age in which hostile ideologies are in combat amid the revolutions of rising expectations, the revolts of color and class, and a population explosion of unprecedented magnitude.

How does, how should, Congress operate in defense policy in such a setting?

As in foreign policy, so also in defense the Constitution seems deliberately ambiguous and ambivalent. Overlapping functions were assigned to Congress and the executive. While the Constitution made the President commander in chief, it gave to Congress the power "to make rules for the government and regulation of the land and naval forces." No authority on constitutional law has been able to draw the line between the two. Congress must appropriate, but the executive may successfully plead national security in refusing to disclose ways in which substantial portions of the money appropriated is to be or has been spent.[1]

In this setting there have grown up images in the two branches, each of the other. To the professionals in the armed services, Congress has often appeared as a group of fumbling amateurs, interfering where it should not interfere, making it difficult for those who know the answers to put them into operation.

On the other hand, from the perspective of Congress, the defense establishment often appears to be a group of warring factions, protecting vested interests and personal empires, allergic to the latest scientific discoveries and habitually trying to handle rather than convince Congress as the representatives of the people.

Each sees itself as dedicated to the national interest, conscientious and hard working, trying to arrive at the best answers to overwhelmingly difficult problems in a world that at any time may crash around it.

There is an element of truth in all these images, and the thoughtful persons in each group will concede the truth of the favorable as well as the unfavorable side of the other. This is the setting in which Congress works out its role in the defense picture.

Of national security itself, Congress also has an image— a composite image which has grown gradually. There is, for example, the suspicion that "generals always fight the last war." Basically it was the mistake of the French General Staff between World Wars I and II that alerted Congress to this danger. The Maginot Line became a symbol carrying with it a warning against the vested interests and thought-patterns of earlier wars creating their blind spots in policies looking toward future wars. After this came Pearl Harbor, and from it

---

[1] See Max Kampelman, "Congressional Control *vs.* Executive Flexibility," *Public Administration Review,* Summer 1958, pp. 185–88.

an idea emerged of noncommunication between branches of what is now the Defense Department. To this was added an impression of danger of slackness or laxness. Yet as the war progressed, counteracting though not eradicating these unfavorable images there arose a growing confidence in the armed services leadership, in men such as Marshall, Nimitz, Eisenhower, and Bradley.

Congress must assume a large share of the responsibility for the drastic demobilization after the war—a demobilization reflecting the mood of the times. Yet as Congress views this error in retrospect, it does so with an intent never again to permit such weakening unless and until there are no centers of great strength remaining elsewhere in the world.

The Korean war contributed to the image. In the first place, it left some doubt as to whether we were really prepared for a limited war. Questions in this regard have figured ever since in committee hearings and executive sessions. The MacArthur hearings vindicated Congress' devotion to civilian supremacy, but they did another thing fully as important. This was to dramatize effectively that defense and foreign policy were and are a seamless web.

The expression, "a balance between the Armed Services," has of late acquired an unfortunate connotation. Unhappily one of its most vigorous recent uses coincided with a request for appropriations for the three branches of approximately the same amount, and hence entered the image as a connotation of a balancing of spending and size rather than of function.

These, then, are some facets of the composite image which Congress holds today, facets to be reckoned with as responsible for initial reactions, if not ultimate decisions, in the defense field. They suggest roles of acceleration, thorough review, search for obsolescence, reappraisal—but not hostility.

It is well before probing these roles more deeply to call attention again to certain general developments within Congress, to the setting in which defense decisions are made. First is the fact of specialization. In defense matters, Congress, for practical purposes, is the Armed Services Committees, the Atomic Energy Committee, the relevant appropriations subcommittees and perhaps the closely related committees in the field of foreign policy. In the second place, nonpartisanship has characterized these committees and Congress as a whole in defense matters. True, the party of the President has the responsibility of presenting the President's program, but not of supporting it. The party opposite to the President has the responsibility of criticizing the President's program, but not of opposing it. Presentation and criticism are basically party functions. Support and opposition are not. In the third place, the growth of competent congressional staffs, already discussed, has taken place in the defense field as elsewhere. A few such specialists may seem insignificant compared with the vast research and analysis personnel, and all the contractual research which goes to buttress it, in the executive branch. Yet when such specialists are added to the long years of committee service of the members themselves, it becomes possible for a committee to probe precisely, to bring together and analyze the voluminous unclassified material, to sense the architecture of the issues facing defense, and hence to review and analyze policy, if not to initiate it.

That there was for many years a downgrading or a deflection of activity of those organs in the executive branch supposedly devoted to long-range, coordinated planning is generally accepted. The National Security Council has become more of a bargaining forum than a planning agency. The Policy Planning Board of the State Department has been preoccupied with the succession of immediate crises. The Weapons Evaluation Board has been definitely downgraded. Till recently there was absolutely no center of planning for substantial disarmament and the necessary controls to ac-

191

company it. It seems that only in some of the congressional committees, notably in the Senate, did substantial research take place on long-range over-all foreign policy, disarmament, and the processes of defense and foreign-policy formation.

Of late there has been a marked change in the executive branch, a change in which congressional influence may well have played a part. The central functions of the Department of Defense have been upgraded, the Arms Control and Disarmament Agency has been established, the Space Council has been activated.

Can we then identify the congressional role or roles? A series of examples will be helpful. These examples are of defense policy decisions in which rightly or wrongly Congress believes it has been an important participant: [2] the B-52's, the RS-70's, the heavy tanks, the reversal of the decision to build non-nuclear submarines before the Nautilus was fully tested, small nuclear weapons, setting a numerical floor to the Army's personnel, retention of the Marine Corps in full strength, the acceleration of the missile program, resolution of the disputes between the Nike-Talos and Hercules-Bomarc, the knocking of heads together to develop a national space policy, the role of scientists, civilian control of atomic energy, a more operative unification of the armed services, the present reserves policy, retention of the National Guard, more adequate transport facilities for airborne troops, scales of military pay. This is not to argue one way or the other as to the wisdom of these or other decisions. It is rather to emphasize their importance, and the patent belief of Congress that it had a share, perhaps the decisive share, in them.

Do these and other similar episodes shed any light on the type of function, the role, that Congress performs?

It is clearly difficult for Congress to make affirmative policy decisions in opposition to a hostile executive. A few years ago it tried to do so by increasing the size of the Air Force, but

---

[2] Particulars of documentation for the most part cannot be disclosed. These were usually obtained in confidence.

the Bureau of the Budget impounded the extra money appropriated. The next year, on congressional insistence, the money was spent; but less was asked for the following year. Even though a forced change of policy may be difficult and perhaps unsuitable, such change by no means exhausts the possibility of congressional correctives.

For example, many of the instances cited were matters of acceleration of pace, especially in the adoption and implementing of the newer weapons systems. There are built-in dangers tending toward adherence to the status quo. There is the built-in danger of pressure from the contractor who has a vested interest in continued manufacture of an existing product. There may be a similar (though perhaps largely subconscious) vested interest on the part of those in the armed services who have committed the most recent years of their lives to the mastery of a particular weapons system. It has been suggested that the Strategic Air Command may belong in this category. In other words, quite apart from the seemingly unconscionable lead-time in development of a new weapons system, Congress feels that there is an additional danger of feet-dragging at various points, and hence regards it as one of its functions to accelerate important new developments.

There is, furthermore, the "review" function. In one sense, Congress plays something akin to the role played by Her Majesty's Loyal Opposition in the British system of government. Many even of the major decisions of the Joint Chiefs of Staff, by the time they reached the National Security Council or the President, were decisions in which the criticism and opposition that had attended their formulation had been filtered out. Only the pros and not the cons were presented to the President. Usually these decisions were sound—but not necessarily always so.

Hence, wherever there has been substantial and responsible opposition to a particular security policy, Congress believes it has the function from time to time of retracing the arguments. That is why by statute high-ranking members of the armed services are required on demand to speak freely their own minds on these subjects. This is frequently resented and is always risky. Yet Congress believes that the issues involved are too great, the national safety is too important, for Congress not to have the benefit of all possible thinking and information. So it regards it as a proper function, this role of going over the ground again to make sure that the original decision was in fact the correct one.

A third function is that of forcing the executive to make up its mind—as to choice of missiles, its attitude on reduction of armaments, a national space policy. This it does primarily through questioning in committee. In other words, when Congress sniffs a postponed decision, it will often, as Secretary McElroy once put it, "hold an administrator's feet to the fire."

A fourth function is that of reinforcing an executive branch decision. When staff work is well done in the executive and presented with candor, the executive has a right to expect congressional endorsement and the requisite appropriations. It normally receives these in the defense field, and with such endorsement goes a sense of the support of a united people. We have a united strength back of much of our national security policy today, because Congress has gone over the same ground and come up with substantially the same answers. This is a contribution in and of itself.

It is now clearly realized that the point of leverage lies in connection with innovations or major alterations in weapons systems. This led in 1959 to the requirement that all such changes be authorized specifically prior to appropriations. Aircraft, missiles, and naval vessels were listed in 1962 and in 1963, the research, development, and evaluation stages were added. This has resulted in greater and more intelligent focus in the hearings and inquiries, especially in the Senate Armed Services Committee.[3]

---

[3] For a detailed account of the background of this change, see Raymond A. Dawson, "Congressional Innovation and Intervention in Defense Policy," *American Political Science Review,* March 1962, pp. 42–57.

The total picture includes a number of less lovely elements.

There is an unconscionable waste of the time of officials high in the executive branch, wandering from committee to committee, often repeating substantially the same testimony. The congressional justification is found in the publicity involved—publicity, on the one hand, that assists the members of the committee in consolidating their electoral following, and, on the other hand, that airs the issues and informs the public. Whether and under what circumstances it is worth the price is discussible.

Moreover, congressmen are responsible to their districts and states. This gives them an undue or distorted concern as to the location of Navy bases, Army camps, airfields—not to mention the awarding of contracts to firms who are their constituents. It is often almost impossible to close down an installation without the consent of a particular committee. Secretary McNamara's efforts in this direction ended in a compromise. For a period the House Armed Services Committee was characterized as primarily a "committee on real estate." A public administrator quite naturally regards such matters as costly and dangerous intrusions into his administration.

Sometimes it seems as if it is Congress, rather than the executive, that holds on to the past too long. Most striking and most obviously contrary to the preponderance of military authority is the emphasis laid by Congress on the state-sponsored National Guard. It is not that a case cannot be made out for the Guard, even at its present strength; but there is a strong suspicion that it is the local loyalties of Congress rather than any expert military judgment that account for its devotion to this branch of the services.

What may be fairly said on balance? One school of thought believes that Congress not only does not, but also should not, play any significant role in defense policy. This doctrine rests upon an alleged executive monopoly of *expertise* and the existence of so much classified information, and also upon the record to date. It would grant a role to Congress in matters such as economic mobilization, selective service, re-enlistment incentives, veterans' legislation, and other instances in which co-operation of the civilian arm is important or is affected. To this school, the instances of decisively favorable interventions are outweighed by the complications and frustrations created through harmful "interference."

But those who hold this view have failed to take into account certain factors already mentioned. Chief among these is Congress' own *expertise,* including that which it can command from its own staff, the tips from within the executive branch of those who have been overruled, expert witnesses among military critics and retired military men of great distinction.

Moreover, it is not civilian "supremacy" that is the issue. This is conceded in principle by all concerned. Rather it is the frequent failure in the executive branch itself to structure into its procedures effective, responsible, even daring and unconventional criticism of a status quo or a continuous challenging of today's decision in the light of the drastically changing circumstances of tomorrow and the day after. Within the armed services themselves we must not expect too much in this regard. The reasons are inherent and obvious. They lie in a hierarchical system of organization with promotion too often dependent upon conformity, in interservice rivalries and jealousies, in supervision by civilian secretaries and assistant secretaries whose tenure averages but two or three years. The Office of the President is a possible location for such built-in criticism, and to some extent has been used as such, as witness the activities of the Bureau of the Budget and several *ad hoc* special commissions. But in the long run this is a function that must at least be supplemented by and often performed by Congress.

To accelerate the implementing of decisions already made, to review controversial decisions for their soundness, to force decisions in areas in which there have been none, or too many contradictory ones—these are the major elements in the role which an informed and patriotic Congress must play in a dangerous age. Such a role in national defense deserves the respect of all concerned; it should be welcomed by the armed services themselves. They can assist its performance best by that combination of candor and humility which first seeks to convince rather than bypass, and, failing to convince, re-examines its own record and decisions to see if perchance these may have been wrong. To quote Holbert Carroll, "Regardless of the depth of its involvement, whether it chooses to monitor, to attempt to govern, or, more commonly, to blend the two tendencies in varying proportions, the Congress participates significantly in the shaping of national security policies. No major legislature in the world can match the extent of its participation." [4]

---

[4] Holbert N. Carroll, "The Congress and National Security Policy," in David B. Truman, ed., *The Congress and America's Future* (Englewood Cliffs: Prentice-Hall, 1965), p. 152.

CHAPTER FIFTEEN

Policy Roles in Science

THE explosion of knowledge in the natural sciences has sent its reverberations throughout the Federal Government. As a matter of fact, most of the American expression of this explosion has been nurtured by the government itself. Research and development appropriations now range well in excess of $15,000,000,000 a year, and seem to be rising inexorably. Defense accounts for the greater part, but space research is not too far behind, and atomic energy and public health and medicine are of the billion dollar magnitude. More than forty agencies are seriously involved. Moreover, it could probably be documented that more than eighty per cent of all the scientists that ever existed in our own and other nations are still living. In other words, we are witnessing a quantum leap: combining the climax of an educational system, the inexorable urge of weaponry, man's insatiable curiosity, his not-to-be-denied desire to live longer and better.

In such a sphere, can Congress really function? What are its roles, if any?

Not that the problem is intrinsically new, or even different from what Congress has been grappling with for many decades—save only in the whirlwind speed of its development and the cascades of its specialized details. We must start with the members themselves in facing the congressional roles. Clearly, the presence of a score or so of scientists and engineers in membership [1] is utterly inadequate to assure competence in monitoring all the technical details of every agency

---

[1] Seventeen in the Eighty-ninth Congress were either scientifically educated or vocationally oriented toward science.

project. Nor should it be. Congress is not charged with the mastery of science, but of science *policy*.

Its role in science policy is the role of value judgments, of selection of objectives from among alternatives, of evaluation of results. Its role is also to provide or evaluate appropriate forms of organization and procedure, to ferret out vested interests, to balance or stimulate manpower, to look for secondary or derivative effects of decisions.

So new is this explosion in the scientific field that it is not possible to go beyond citing a few examples of congressional action. Congress as a whole probably still suffers from the same trauma which pervades the public at large, as it views something too great and awesome really to comprehend. It may well be that the combined power of the defense establishment, the industries dependent thereon, and the scientists, research corporations, and university personnel and equipment spawned by both will prove too much for Congress and President alike to control. In this connection it is significant that President Eisenhower made this danger the principal theme of his farewell message. He should know. Nor is the power structure confined to a defense orientation. Research in outer space has achieved a momentum and magnitude of its own, which up to the present time have swept aside criticism. The heart of the congressional role may well be in the fact that in all these matters Congress has considerably less vested interest than the bureaucracy. Therefore it may well be the more hopeful branch of government in dealing with matters when that day comes when the whole apparatus may have to be shrunk or at least redirected.

Turn first to the choice of objectives. With costs mounting as they are, disciplined value judgments concerning alternative uses of these billions are clearly within not only the prerogative but also the competence of Congress. The major choice is obvious. Sooner or later the Soviet Union and the United States, not to mention China and Western Europe, will have to choose between, for example, unlimited achievements in outer space on the one hand, or, alternatively, such programs as, military overkill capacity, grappling with the problems of an urbanized society, or full-bodied co-operation in raising the living standards of the "have nots" the world over. Will billions spent on reaching Mars be more valuable than similar billions in agricultural productivity or population limitation or oceanography or weather control—without even leaving the natural science area? A search for consensus in objectives challenges Congress' best efforts. Admittedly, thus far Congress has dealt mostly with the fringes, being inclined to leave to the Defense Department, for example, the choice of weaponry. Much congressional effort to date has even consisted in a certain "egging on" of science agencies to spend more—and faster—rather than less. The Air Force and the National Institutes of Health have been the favorite candidates for increases in appropriations.

Turn next to the evaluative role. Perhaps the major study of this sort has been of the National Science Foundation. This study is the product of the Subcommittee on Science, Research, and Development of the House Science and Astronautics Committee. In many respects it is a model of what can be done, given the will and intelligence. Its course is worth tracing. In late 1964, the Subcommittee called upon the Legislative Reference Service to make a factual study of the first fifteen years of the National Science Foundation. This was completed and published as a Committee Print (of 286 pages) in May 1965. After the members and staff of the Subcommittee had had the opportunity to familiarize themselves with the study, public hearings were held. These took place during June, July and August. More than forty top-level witnesses testified, most of whom were on Committee invitation. Additional statements and information were solicited. Executive sessions for review, analysis and evaluation were held during September and October, with the final report transmitted to the full Committee on December 30 of the same year. Legislation to carry out the Committee's recommendations was introduced in 1966, and as of present writing is still pending. During the entire process the professional staffs of the Committee and of the Legislative Reference Service worked closely with the Subcommittee, suggesting witnesses and questions, analyzing testimony and drafting reports according to instructions. Without going into details, the gist of the recommendations called for the Foundation to stake out for itself a far more significant role in leadership and coordination than it is at present playing. As perhaps the only non-operational agency it is peculiarly suited to assume responsibility for guidance toward adequate quality and quantity of scientific resources, and Congress is the appropriate medium to give it this mandate [2] following the evaluation.

The most usual congressional concern thus far, apart from appropriations, has been in the field of organization and procedure. This is not surprising, considering the number of executive agencies with important science reponsibilities. For example, congressional inquiry elicited the fact that no less than fourteen bureaus and agencies had some program related to the weather. Oceanography is among the most recent areas of interest, and here also numerous agencies are involved. Duplications, lack of coordination, and confusion may be expected in situations of this type, and the executive branch is often either unable or unwilling to do much about it, except under congressional prodding.

Among the top congressional achievements in the field of the organization of science must certainly be placed the National Aeronautics and Space Act of 1958.[3] Sputnik tra-

---

[2] The National Science Foundation. *Report of the Subcommittee on Science, Research, and Development of the House Committee on Science and Astronautics.* Eighty-ninth Congress, Serial M.

[3] The standard work on the legislative history of this Act is Alison Griffith: *The National Aeronautics and Space Act* (Washington: Public Affairs Press, 1962).

versed the heavens in September of 1957. Congress moved into action immediately, first to spur the executive and then to develop its own policy. Early in 1958 it delegated responsibility to two "blue ribbon" special committees, headed respectively by Lyndon Johnson, the majority leader of the Senate, and John McCormack, the majority leader of the House. The two Committees probably held over fifty sessions, and the end result was the Act setting up the National Aeronautics and Space Administration. Here, as with the aforementioned National Science Foundation inquiry, preliminary studies were made by the Legislative Reference Service, whose staff subsequently cooperated with Committee staffs in organizing the hearings and analyzing the data as they came in.

It is worthy of note that congressional initiative was primarily responsible for setting up the Office of Science and Technology in 1962 in the Office of the President. This gave a statutory base to what had previously been a matter of White House discretion and privilege. On the other hand, the reconciliation of conflicting interests in the formation of the Communications Satellite Corporation was largely undertaken in the executive branch prior to any submission to Congress.

The longest continued special relationship between Congress and the executive in science policy has been in the field of atomic energy. The organic act setting up the Atomic Energy Commission charged it with the responsibility of keeping the Joint Committee "fully and currently informed with respect to the Commission's activities." This went considerably beyond the usual provisions for congressional oversight, and notably so, inasmuch as classified information was clearly included. Why was this done? In large part it represented an attempt by Congress to fulfill what it regarded as its normal responsibilities. Clearly it would not be realistic for the entire Congress to share in this, in the light of the secrecy involved. What was not practicable for the entire body would be feasible for a smaller group, and the Joint Committee device was chosen.

Since the inception of the program, the Joint Committee and the Commission have worked together closely, though by no means always harmoniously. Differences of opinion arose concerning security precautions and the manufacturing of the hydrogen bomb—to mention two important matters. The Committee's views eventually prevailed, in the latter instance through President Truman's personal decision. Notably under the chairmanship of Senator McMahon, the Committee brought continuous and on the whole successful pressure for expediting the Commission's activities. In turn, the Committee assumed substantial responsibility for securing ample appropriations for the Commission's work, and in general identified itself with and rose to the defense of the latter.[4] Success appropriation-wise was especially noticeable in the Senate, on whose particular Subcommittee three members of the Joint Committee sat ex-officio.

Congress has always concerned itself with persons, and scientific manpower has been one of its most recent *foci* of attention. It has fostered its development with liberal funds, but its concern has not stopped here. Questions of in-breeding, of undue concentration in certain universities, of the danger that ideas from outside the "establishment" will not be given due consideration, have all fallen within its purview. The Government Operations Committees as well as the Science Committees have sponsored such investigations. These topics are all quite appropriate for congressional monitoring.

How have Congress and its Committees equipped themselves to deal with these esoteric subjects? The story follows

---

[4] For the full story of these relationships, see Morgan Thomas, *Atomic Energy and Congress* (Ann Arbor: University of Michigan Press, 1956) and Harold P. Green and Alan Rosenthal, *The Government of the Atom* (New York: Atherton, 1966).

similar lines, differing not too much from other legislative and investigative fields. The great majority of committees at least occasionally are faced with decisions requiring scientific data for intelligent consideration. Three Committees, the Senate Aeronautical and Space Sciences, the House Science and Astronautics, and the Joint Atomic Energy, are primarily science policy oriented. So too are the newly formed subcommittees of the two Government Operations Committees—the (House) Research and Technical Programs and the (Senate) Government Research. Committee staffs have been or have become competent in setting up hearings and analyzing material. The Legislative Reference Service added a senior specialist in science in 1958. In 1964 scientific activity in L.R.S. was raised quantitatively by congressional authorization and appropriation to the level of a division. A few of the subcommittees have perfected the panel technique in one form or another, whereby highly competent witnesses, perhaps the best the nation has, are consulted prior to policy decisions. Care is taken to include a cross-section of points of view. Committee prints and documents testify to the high order of the work done, including the capacity to state issues and basic data in language intelligible to members. Conscientious and usually non-partisan work on the part of the latter make of them specialists in this field in a fashion quite similar to the specialists among the members in other areas of more traditional concern.

As for the future, here also, as in foreign policy, defense, and economic planning, separation of powers and checks and balances would appear to be serving us well. Colossal and intricate though the tasks of formulating and executing science policy are, the presence of a legislative branch which must be convinced on the basis of facts and analysis will, in no small measure, make for that consensus in the nation as a whole which will assure sound foundations of support. Likewise the legislative presence as subsequent monitor may well be decisive in disciplining the vested interests that inevitably cluster around and nestle in aggregates of great power and money. That this monitor may also command as witnesses those in the electorate at large who may feel aggrieved by or profoundly doubtful of executive policies must be reckoned as a major asset in the process.

Thus equipped, we may look forward to an exciting future in "Science, the endless frontier."

CHAPTER SIXTEEN

Congress and Localism

ODAY Congress finds itself charged with greater responsibility to perform another role under the Constitution, one which in the past it had been assumed lay more within the orbit of responsibility of the Supreme Court. This is to safeguard states' rights—or rather the vitality of state action which is the operative reality behind the legalistic phrase, "states' rights." Closely related to this is the role played by Congress in seeing to it that state and local needs, interests, and peculiarities receive recognition in national measures and the administration thereof.

Our founding fathers thought they had built our federal structure truly and well. Nation and state, each in its sphere, were autonomous. To those who feared the encroachments of the larger unit, it was pointed out that to the nation were entrusted only certain strictly limited powers.

Now few of these powers were such, or originally such, that they touched directly the daily life of the ordinary individual. Hence the practice grew up of assuming that it was the responsibility of the states and the cities and the local units to provide regulations (if regulations were necessary) and services for all the ordinary, multifarious relations and aspects of everyday life—health, education, local business, most utilities, labor, the home and family, most public works, recreation, poor relief. So it continued for a hundred years more or less, though toward the end of the nineteenth century disquieting signs were noted.

Such a distribution of powers was to be safeguarded, not only by the Constitution itself and by Congress operating in observance thereof, but also by the Supreme Court, its living exponent and guardian.

But now the scene has changed radically. No longer is the Supreme Court the protector of local autonomy it once was. The importance of congressional restraint has correspondingly increased.[1] In some ways Congress is admirably suited to this role of state protector; in others it is not so congenial. At best it is ambivalent, especially in financial matters.

Before proceeding to a detailed consideration of this role of state protector, it is worth while briefly to recapitulate the values traditionally associated with state and local vitality so as to recapture some portion of the old sense of its importance in the event that the lure of a rampant centralization may have eroded our former faith. These traditional values were many. They included the opportunity to experiment, given the necessary prerequisites of taxable capacity and civic vitality. They included the facility offered to differentiate governmental activities in accordance with differences in population and environment. By developing functions in the smaller units, the size of the central establishment could be kept down, and the terrific managerial and political problems associated with big government were lessened accordingly, or at least became less acute than they otherwise would have been. Above all, local responsible experience was educational in the best sense of the word. Mistakes and successes were brought home to an electorate not too large to understand the manageable issues facing it. Responsible fiscal experience was thereby gained through learning the simple lesson that activities voted must be or at least ought to be paid for by taxes. This is a slender thread at best that limits what voters want to that which is practicable in terms of their own efforts; and the thread has already snapped in many nations and peoples who have gone far down along the treacherous path of insisting upon their wants and dodging the sacri-

---

[1] In the field of the common law, the Court has been more regardful of state divergences. See David Fellman, "Federation," *American Political Science Review*, December 1947, pp. 49–53.

fices involved. Some believe that we, too, are in this unhappy
state, but to the extent that we are not, surely a large share
of the credit for this belongs to the fact that we have been
educated to responsible political behavior in the school of local self-government.[2]

We venture to quote at this point from the *Report* of the
Intergovernmental Relations Commission:

> Experience amply justifies the view that our federal system, with the
> degree of flexibility that it permits, can be adapted to crises of the
> present and future as successfully as it has been to those of the past.
> As an instrument of positive government, it possesses—at least for a
> nation as large and diverse as ours—a clear advantage over a strongly
> centralized government. In helping to bolster the principle of consent;
> in facilitating wide participation in government; in furnishing training
> grounds for leaders; in maintaining the habit of local initiative; in pro-
> viding laboratories for research and experimentation in the art of gov-
> ernment; in fostering competition among lower levels of government;
> in serving as outlets for local grievances and for political aspirations—
> in all these and many other ways, the existence of many relatively inde-
> pendent and responsible governments strengthens rather than weakens
> our capacity for government. On the whole, therefore, the enduring
> values of our federal system fully warrant every effort to preserve and
> strengthen its essence.

But for local and state self-government to continue to possess the vitality necessary to fulfill this role, they must continue to have a zone of discretion and creative action in a
sufficiently large sector of governmental activity to be real, to
attract the interest, to enlist the participation, and to command
the loyalties of their citizens. Merely to act as agents of a
central government that has made all the significant decisions
is not enough, even though officials are still locally elected.

It is therefore of cardinal importance for us to realize that
as far as the field of statute law is concerned, we no longer
live under a genuine federal system constitutionally speaking.
The freedom and autonomy of the states have lost most of their

---

[2] Cf. Ernest S. Griffith, *The Modern Development of City Government in
the United Kingdom and the United States* (London: Oxford University
Press, H. Milford, 1927), chap. 11, for documentation of this paragraph.

assumed constitutional protection. What they do, the decisions they make, the laws they pass, are now largely on sufferance—protected not by the Supreme Court but by the restraint of Congress in not passing such laws as would wipe out the discretionary element in their still quite substantial remaining functions.

Let us look for a moment at recent Court decisions. The most important of these are a succession of cases under the commerce clause. *Swift and Company v. United States,*[3] *National Labor Relations Board v. Jones and Laughlin Steel Corporation,*[4] *United States v. Darby,*[5] *United States v. Wrightwood Dairy Company,*[6] *Wickard v. Filburn,*[7] *Alstate Construction Company v. Durkin,*[8] and *United States v. Employing Plasterers Association,*[9] *Radovich v. National Football League,*[10] *Atlanta v. United States,*[11] and *Katzenbach v. McClung* [12] should be especially noted. Under these and other cases the basis has been laid for central regulation of wages, hours, prices, working conditions, and business practices of *all* business enterprise (including even such matters as insurance [13] and the gathering of news,[14] professional sports, and public accommodations) as "affecting" interstate commerce and not merely the practices of those businesses engaged in such commerce. Thus at any time the national government apparently can, if it so desires, take over the regulation of all our economic life and drive the states and localities out of business in this regard.

---

[3] 196 U.S. 375 (1905).
[4] 301 U.S. 1 (1937).
[5] 312 U.S. 100 (1941).
[6] 315 U.S. 110 (1942).
[7] 317 U.S. 111 (1942).
[8] 345 U.S. 13 (1953).
[9] 347 U.S. 186 (1954).
[10] 352 U.S. 445 (1957).
[11] 379 U.S. 241 (1964).
[12] 379 U.S. 294 (1964).
[13] *U.S. v. South-Eastern Underwriters Association,* 322 U.S. 533 (1944).
[14] *Associated Press v. U.S.,* 326 U.S. 1 (1945).

In the generally costly area of public works, the states and cities find themselves hard pressed for revenue. While the property tax (or real estate tax) seems still to be peculiarly theirs, under its taxing power the national government is steadily encroaching upon one field of revenue after another of those that remain. On the one hand this lessens the capacity of the smaller units to undertake activities on their own initiative. On the other hand the fact that the federal government returns large sums as subsidies, under conditions set by it, lessens local discretion by the same act that it enlarges local resources. The effect is the same, even though it is frequently the locality beset by financial stringency rather than the federal government that presses for the subsidy legislation. Hence, in those proposals in which national standards are tied in with grants-in-aid, the average member of Congress calculates the fiscal effects on his district or state, and hostility to centralization is inevitably modified if the financial aspects appear advantageous.

Just as the economic sphere of state exclusiveness of action has yielded chiefly to new interpretations of the commerce clause, so in the social sphere state autonomy of late has more subtly but none the less surely been undermined by the spending power. Under the Social Security cases,[15] financial temptation (under the grants) was held not to be coercion and hence not forcing the states to abdicate their powers. The Court stated explicitly in *United States* v. *Butler* [16] that "the power of Congress to authorize expenditures of public moneys for public purposes is not limited by the direct grants of legislative power found in the Constitution." This had in fact been inferred as implicit from the very earliest days of the Republic. Grants-in-aid of such functions may be made conditional upon the performance by the states of the functions

---

[15] *Steward Machine Company* v. *Davis,* 301 U.S. 548 (1937); *Carmichael* v. *Coal and Coke Company,* 301 U.S. 495 (1937).
[16] 297 U.S. 1 (1939).

in question in accordance with the stipulations of the central agency.[17]   Apparently there is inherently no constitutional limit to the transfer of discretion through conditional grants-in-aid in matters such as education, health, libraries, relief of distress, recreation, or at some future time even police and fire protection and the courts, if Congress shall similarly appropriate and decree them to be matters of national concern.   It is perhaps gratuitous to point to other Court decisions under other clauses of the Constitution where the trend is in the same direction.   Regulation as conducive to efficient collection of taxes was upheld in *United States* v. *Doremus*.[18]   Equal and even identical educational facilities were required of the states for all races under the Fourteenth Amendment, the states not being allowed to substitute interstate co-operative provisions of such facilities.[19]   In its rulings on segregation the Court has now stipulated that this "separate but equal" doctrine is superseded, and states must move in the direction of an integrated school system.[20]   Then, too, the Court has consistently held that nonspecified powers presumably retained by the states are legitimate subjects of international negotiation.   No stop has yet been put to this use of treaty or international agreement to extend federal activity, though the Bricker amendment, had it been adopted, would seemingly have drastically curtailed such use.

This is not in any sense to hold up the Supreme Court as the villain in the play.   After all, these laws enlarging the sphere of the national government and lessening that of the states were passed by Congress in the first instance.   Emphasis is placed only upon the fact that of the original two safeguards of operative federalism, the attitude of the Court

---

[17] *Oklahoma* v. *U.S. Civil Service Commission,* 330 U.S. 127 (1947).

[18] 249 U.S. 86 (1919).

[19] Especially under *Missouri ex rel. Gaines* v. *Canada,* 305 U.S. 337 (1938); *Sipuel* v. *Board of Regents,* 332 U.S. 631 (1948); *Fisher* v. *Hurst, Chief Justice, et al.,* 333 U.S. 147 (1948); *Sweatt* v. *Painter,* 339 U.S. 629 (1950); *McLaurin* v. *Oklahoma State Regents,* 339 U.S. 637 (1950).

[20] *Brown* v. *Board of Education of Topeka,* 347 U.S. 483 (1954).

211

and the restraint of Congress, the latter has assumed a greatly enhanced importance.[21] A complete picture would also include the fact that in a whole series of decisions the Court has been instrumental in extending greatly the sphere of permissive state activity (but not autonomy) in the economic sphere through its more liberal interpretation of "due process" and other clauses which for many years restrained effective economic legislation.

One cannot look to the executive branch for any assurance of protection of state and local autonomy. Here and there a bureau or department chief may have a genuine conviction in the direction of local autonomy, and for a while his agency may show remarkable restraint in seeking additional power at the expense of the smaller units. Such a line of thinking has at times been not without its influence in the Department of Agriculture and the United States Office of Education, to mention but two examples. But in the long run the scales are inherently weighted otherwise. These bureaus and their clientele believe in the importance of their objectives. They see, or think they see, that these objectives would be more easily attained if power and discretion were transferred to them from the states and localities. If some lingering doubt exists regarding the constitutionality or even the wisdom of coercion in a given bureau's particular field, then the alternative of the conditional grant-in-aid offers itself. The state or locality may be persuaded—some would call it bribed—when it cannot be forced. Into the scales in many instances is thrown the importance attached in bureaucratic circles to size of staff and budget, to power for its own sake—very human, no doubt, but irrelevant to the real issue of local vitality and autonomy.

Finally the President himself is nationally elected. It is he

---

[21] But cf. Fellman, "Federation," *American Political Science Review,* December 1947, for the field of state interpretation of common law, in which the Supreme Court has of late shown more concern for the autonomy of the state courts.

in our system who has come to represent the national point of view. His campaigns are on this note. His emphasis is upon the unities, upon the goals that have the widest appeal. It is so easy to make a case for the point of view that we are one people, that the health and education and welfare of the people of Mississippi are of importance to New York and the nation. Yet as the author wrote in another connection:

> Any legislative act but concerns a number of individuals, and must rest for its ultimate sanction upon their will. Initially, or at any given instant, progress may be given the appearance of acceleration by central mandate—yet if the various human beings concerned or the various communities involved are not convinced, further and still further mandates must be the rule—until the government becomes a kind of central dictatorship, and the local life is gone.
>
> Each step taken by individual or local initiative means individual or local growth in consciousness and knowledge. Initially, the way is slower; ultimately, the results justify. It is easy, but it is also dangerous, to dictate reform or change in advance of individual or local willingness. It is difficult, but the gain becomes the greater, to raise a whole people to a conviction for progress. . . .[22]

If we regard our nation as in one sense the sum of its several parts, then a strong case can be made out that, from this perspective, Congress is more "national" than a Washington-centered agency in the executive branch. Surely both viewpoints are needed in arriving at an ultimate consensus.

The economic and social forces are for the most part on the side of centralization. Business and labor are organized on a national scale, and from a practical standpoint the furtherance of their interests or the regulation of their conduct to be really effective must more and more frequently be on a scale commensurate with the problems involved. Transportation and communication are nation-wide. The great river basins usually know no state boundaries. Population is increasingly mobile, and the local and state loyalties are lessened

---

[22] Ernest S. Griffith, *The Modern Development of City Government in the United Kingdom and the United States* (London: Oxford University Press, H. Milford, 1927), II, 598.

thereby. The schools of Oklahoma educate the future workers of California. We have been through two world wars and for all practical purposes, except large-scale shooting, are in the middle of a third. These experiences intensify our national outlook. Finally, many factors vital to our individual welfare must now be settled at the international level, and only the nation can negotiate.

All these things have been said before, either with approval of the trends or with regretful resignation.

Yet there is still very great state and local vitality. While widening the bounds of permissive federal action, the Supreme Court has also widened the bounds of state action. State and local activities continue to mount, even in the unsubsidized and uncontrolled sectors. State expenditures were $2,734,-000,000 in 1932. In 1953 they were $14,677,000,000; in 1958, $23,536,000,000; in 1963, almost $40,000,000,000. If the problem of an inadequate revenue base could be solved —and it can, if the will is there—much of the argument for centralization because of inadequate local resources would disappear. However, the trend toward federal grants-in-aid of state and local activity has now increased so much both quantitatively and functionally that it may be too late. Between 1946 and 1963 such grants increased from $847,000,-000 to $8,600,000,000. Fifty-seven of the eighty programs were newly added.

The organizations of both of the major political parties are predominantly state and local, even though more and more of the major issues are becoming national. The deeper effects of this on Congress will be considered presently, but at this point it is sufficient to note that party organization is on the side of localism.

Most important of all for our present consideration is the fact that Congress is locally minded and apparently still believes in our federal system. If there are values in this system it would seem that it is to Congress and not to the restraints of the Supreme Court or the initiative of the President that one must largely look for their preservation. It is to Congress also that one must largely look for recognition of the state and local viewpoint when national legislation is framed and passed. A permanent Advisory Commission on Intergovernmental Relations, established in 1959, may be expected to keep the issues alive.

This localism of Congress is under severe criticism. Certainly the majority of the political scientists would appear to desire a change in the direction of greater congressional emphasis upon the national viewpoint. Spokesmen of Congress have for the most part been inarticulate on the subject, probably in many instances not realizing what the larger issues at stake really were.

Why, then, has Congress shown on the one hand a greater watchfulness over local interests and on the other more resistance to the national approach in the handling of problems and also more devotion to state and local vitality and freedom than has the executive branch? The reasons are many.

In the first place, members owe little or nothing to their party nationally for their election. In closely contested states or districts in presidential election years, and sometimes in the mid-term elections, national headquarters will provide modest funds in aid of a local campaign. Speakers of national reputation may also be detailed to help, but often as much or more for the presidential or gubernatorial candidate as for the congressional. In general, members wage their own campaigns, primarily aided by the local or state organizations.

In the second place, subject to the direct primary, the member is the nominee and frequently the product of the state or local party organization. In the case of the Senate, perhaps ninety per cent had already held a public office, most usually that of governor, representative, or member of a state legislature. Intervention by the President or by national headquarters in behalf of one of the contestants for the nomi-

215

nation may even be a liability, so strongly does the local tradition rule.

In the primary and the general election alike, locally important issues figure largely. Those issues on which the district or state (because of regional economic factors) are substantially united are taken for granted by all candidates. If the locally favored position on one of these issues happens to be contrary to that of the national platform or the President, if of the same party, the candidate ordinarily explicitly dissociates himself from the national viewpoint on the particular issue. The presence of the direct primary tends to render ineffective attempts at national conformity, if contrary to local views. The net result in any event is a sensitivity to or sharing of the dominant local viewpoint on issues deemed locally important.

Moreover, all the time the member is in Congress his constituents and his local party organization maintain a steady stream of letters, telegrams, telephone calls, conferences, and visits to the end that he shall not forget what is important to his state or district. Visits home from time to time strengthen the same mood.

Curious anomalies follow therefrom. In 1948 Iowa elected a solid Republican House delegation but the state went for Truman. It is as if the people said, "We like the President's national program as a whole, but we want our own people there to see that our local interests are safeguarded by those who have proved that they understand us and are one of us." Within the President's own party are large numbers of senators and representatives who differ with him on many of the issues on which he made his chief campaign. Here again local considerations are dominant.

How concretely does Congress give expression to this localism? It evidences itself first in an emphasis on local interests in national legislation and the administration thereof and, secondly, in a reluctance to increase centralization.

The most obvious expression of the first is through securing for their particular state or district the maximum number of public improvements. This is a paradox, for it is national action and national money that are involved in local construction—but the motivation is primarily local. New post offices, veterans' or armed services' hospitals, public roads, grants for new schools or slum clearance, defense establishments of one sort or another, and, above all, great water-resource projects whose magnitude dwarfs the earlier examples—these are cases in point. Many, perhaps most, of these are justified, and our nation as well as the locality is the better for them. Pure logic might frequently have dictated their location elsewhere, perhaps concentrating more of the projects in a few places— but the values of diffusion are not inconsiderable and the localism of Congress must take credit for their realization. In some instances, national planning might well have overlooked certain worthy local projects, though this is conjectural. The other side of the picture, the wastes and politics involved, is well known and has been documented. At this point our interest lies in observing the phenomenon rather than in passing judgment on it.

Then, too, in those instances in which there is actual federal pressure or control, local and state governments can and frequently do obtain adaptations or modifications through intervention by their congressmen. Few are the laws in which administrative discretion is nonexistent.

Of a similar nature, though confined to the President's party, is the patronage element in federal personnel. Apart from its use to strengthen the members' own political standing, there are two more general usages worth noting. By the so-called "courtesy of the Senate," the senior (and sometimes the junior) senator of the President's party is consulted in regard to nominations of persons (civilians) from his state who require senatorial confirmation. If the duties of the position lie wholly within his state, he is customarily allowed to name the person to fill the post. This applies chiefly to judicial appointments and postmasters, but with the growth of government other nominees outside the classified service and the military are increasing in number. The practice is defended on the theory that the senator knows his own state better than the President. An effect is to strengthen the state party organization, irrespective of the effect on the party nationally.

Within the classified service which comprises the great mass of government workers, localism took a different form. This was the imposition by statute of an apportionment provision for employees in Washington whereby such employees were to be divided among legal residents of the states in accordance with the state populations. For a number of years an attempt, not wholly successful, has been made to give effect to this provision. This of course was founded upon Congress' regard for state equality. It was defended on the ground that there were values in such a distribution—values of fair play, of widespread interest in and responsibility for government.

More pervading and fundamental, more far-reaching for good or evil, is the localism associated legislatively with regional economic interests. An obvious instance was the conflict between the oleomargarine-cotton interests and the butter-dairy interests. When Congress wrote the details of tariff acts, it was each man for his own state or district. The St. Lawrence Seaway pitted the Great Lakes States against the Atlantic seaboard. The West as a whole has a vital interest in irrigation and the equalization of power resources. With the increasing industrialization of the South, there has been a growing protectionist sentiment in this traditionally free-trade area. The Tennessee Valley Authority enjoys almost unanimous support of the members from its area, regardless of party or general economic orientation. The power of the silver bloc is widely known. Thus, in part, this economic regionalism reflects itself in the form of seeking greater and greater federal expenditures in the area, in part in promoting legislation deemed favorable to its economy. In either case the end result may be good or it may be bad, but at least it makes sure that attention will be given to each area. None will be overlooked, though the effort may be more successful in the case of those areas whose representatives belong to the majority party.[23]

Another widespread manifestation of this localism is the all-pervading rural-urban cleavage. Up until the reapportionments following the 1960 census, there was no doubt that Congress, and especially the Senate, was more inclined toward the rural than toward the urban viewpoint when the two were in conflict. Rural areas were in fact overrepresented in both the Senate and the House. Represented in the Senate are twelve states under 1,000,000 with a population predominantly rural and only one, or possibly two, if Nevada is so treated, under 1,000,000 that are urban. In the House, on the basis of the 1940 census, the 235 districts with no city above 100,000 within their boundaries averaged 283,000 each; the 71 districts which had both a city above 100,000 and considerable rural areas averaged 318,000 each; the 122 urban averaged 331,000 each.[24] A sampling of 115 of these districts based on the 1950 census shows a widening spread. The averages are 318,000; 357,000; and 385,000 respectively. This was compounded by the relatively safe nature of many rural seats, with the result that the committee chairmanships and their attendant power are still predominantly rural. James MacGregor Burns points out that in a recent Congress the half of the congressional districts that were the more rural furnished seventy-four per cent of these chairmanships including a disproportionate number of the more

---

[23] For a sophisticated discussion of congressional-constituent relations in this regard see Lewis A. Dexter, "The Representative and His District," in Robert L. Peabody and Nelson W. Polsby, *New Perspectives on the House of Representatives* (Chicago: Rand-McNally, 1963), chap. 1. Patterns of response of members differ widely, on the basis of a number of variables.

[24] Figures for districts, 1940 census; for cities and states, 1950 census. Members elected "at large" have been omitted.

219

important ones.[25] However, by 1966 the discrepancies in population of the various districts had begun to disappear in the light of the Supreme Court reapportionment decisions and state uses of the 1960 census, and what remained was a time lag between censuses and reapportionments, largely penalizing suburban areas. The committee chairmanships remained disproportionately rural.

The masses of the great cities may be the major factor in electing the President, and he may reflect this in his conduct, but they count for less in Congress, where their voting power is felt by only a minority of the membership. Representatives from the so-called working-class districts in the House vote overwhelmingly for a particular point of view, and in an urban state like Rhode Island the same viewpoint is reflected in its senatorial elections. However, in the great majority of states and in a substantial majority of the districts, the combination of rural, suburban, and middle-class urban voters still outweighs the often very considerable labor element. The suburban and middle class cannot hope to win without the rural, and so at least until recently the rural tended to call the tune on matters which it deems important. Among such matters was its preference for local rather than central handling of problems. An exception is, of course, in those matters in which rural economic prosperity is better served by national handling. Even then, local agricultural committees and the role of the land-grant colleges are retained and the county agent takes on a local coloration. Rural co-operatives run much of rural electrification; rural co-operatives are favored in marketing.

But the localism of Congress expresses itself not only in a watchfulness over local and regional interests but also—and this is more to the point in any consideration of the future of federalism—in many instances of reluctance to increase the

---

[25] In Sec. 2 of Joseph S. Clark, ed., *Congressional Reform* (New York: Crowell, 1965), p. 65.

extent of centralization if there is any other feasible way to meet a given problem. In federal aid to education, for example, recent bills usually provided explicitly that the grants to the states were to have no strings tied to them involving central controls. Until recently these measures failed of passage because some members felt the grant to be an entering wedge which later on would grow into a national system of schools—and Congress was not yet ready, even if the Court and executive were, to amend the Constitution by indirection in this fashion. The emphasis until recently upon federal aid to school building programs instead of to educational systems as a whole was in part an expression of distrust of the results of long-continued federal subsidies. The most recent versions of rent control allowed state and local autonomy as regards whether or not to apply such control. Under congressional insistence state governors retain a limited veto over certain antipoverty programs. State unemployment-insurance systems still rule in spite of the desire on the part of the Bureau of Employment Security that they be nationalized. Proposals for river-valley authorities either explicitly provide for retention of existing state and local powers or include regionally constituted advisory or policy boards or both. Interstate compacts are highly favored as a device if at all practicable. The retention of local initiative, autonomy, and discretion could and would go even further with Congress if Congress realized more clearly that a large part of the situation which seems to call for action on a national scale is accounted for by the inequalities in taxable capacity and the absence of sources of local revenue—this latter in part because of the pre-emption of so many revenues by the federal government. With such a realization might come a solution whereby certain revenues (such as the cigarette tax or telephone tax) would be transferred back to the states or equalizing grants-in-aid could be given without strings attached. The Commission on Intergovernmental Relations saw a development

221

of this type as important in reinforcing state autonomy.

In 1959 Congress largely on its own initiative created a permanent Advisory Committee on Intergovernmental Relations. This is a mixed legislative-executive-federal-state-local bipartisan committee, whose orientation is toward co-operative action. It has also favored general rather than functional agencies. It has sought to strengthen the effectiveness of the state and local units. Much of its effectiveness is traceable to its congressional members and the Subcommittees on Intergovernmental Relations that they represent.[26]

Congress instinctively and articulately opposes a large bureaucracy. In part it does this because it desires economy, in part because it senses that bureaucracy with its command of facts and acquaintance with problems is a formidable rival in the maturing of legislation—an area which Congress regards as largely its own under the Constitution. In part, however, it is because it knows from experience in the United States as well as in other countries that such a bureaucracy becomes an increasingly powerful force in the direction of the centralized state. Consequently, for many years to come Congress may be expected to drag at the wheels of the onward march of big government and centralization—even though it may in practice prove impotent to reverse the trend.

The implications of this situation for party solidarity and discipline may also be noted at this point. So long as members are locally nominated and locally elected, just so long must they pay attention to local and regional interests. Here is a serious obstacle to party solidarity, for the member or senator who puts party ahead of district or home state on a matter which the district or state regards as vital will probably not survive the next primary—not to mention the next election. There would accordingly be a danger either that parties would become more sectional and regional than they

---

[26] Cf. Neil S. Wright, "The Advisory Committee on Intergovernmental Relations," *Public Administration Review*, September 1965, pp. 193–202.

now are or that they would completely surrender to all groups, regardless of contradictions, and without the very considerable corrective which is now supplied by independent voting.

In conclusion, let it not be thought that there are not values, great values, attendant upon the national viewpoint in contradistinction to the local. All that is claimed here is that *both* are of value, and decisions ought to be made with a full awareness of both aspects and without the scales unduly weighted in either direction. It is the author's contention that this purpose is best served if, as the founders of the Republic originally intended, both a national and a state and local viewpoint are woven into the fabric of our government—and the action taken represents a compromise between the two viewpoints. The President, or the executive, represents wholeheartedly the national viewpoint. Is it not therefore all the more important that those elements in our government which by conviction sustain the values of local autonomy shall not be whittled down or eroded by so altering our structure, whether of party organization or of government itself, that this function is no longer effectively performed? Much of the genius of our Constitution lies in the way it allows no one center of power, no one group or point of view to ride roughshod over others, but rather fosters government by consensus, which encourages united action on the things on which there is unity but allows for diversity in other matters. In the total picture the values of decentralization would seem to be essential to the strength of the nation—a part of our belief that operative pluralism is a major pillar and expression of the democratic way.

CHAPTER SEVENTEEN

Political Parties and Congress

O F ALL the subjects of contemporary controversy concerning Congress, probably
none is more difficult to resolve than the role to be played
by party. It enters into, if it does not pervade, most of the
other questions. It is the principal factor in the organization
of Congress. It is both a solvent and an irritant in legislative-
executive relations. It restlessly snipes at unanimity in foreign
policy. The dispersiveness of our society with its insistent
pressure groups finds party one of the mediums for attaining
these group ends. Its local roots reinforce the localism of
Congress. Its looseness and vagueness are the despair of
those whose minds run to comprehensive and integrated programs.

While the broader implications of party must necessarily
be brought into review in order to understand its congressional impact, our chief concern lies with the place of party
in the congressional scene. What role do these two loose
confederations of state and local organizations, whose elements at times seem to have little else in common but their
name and their presidential candidate, play in Congress?

Historically viewed, the story of the past fifty years is undoubtedly one of increasing weakness or even of disintegra-
tion as regards the hold of party on Congress. Emphatically
we do not have integrated party government in this country
now, whatever we may have had in the past. During most
of the nineteenth century party discipline and solidarity had
been part of the congressional picture. The binding party
caucus was a vital factor. By 1900, in the House the Speaker

224

had come to be in a position to punish, and did punish, any member of his party who had the temerity to break seriously with the party line. Except that the President tended at times to be more liberal or more nationally minded than those of his party in Congress, there was for the most part agreement between him and them on most major issues. At any one time the great issues were very few in number, thus allowing a member to follow his party without too frequent a strain on his intellect or conscience. Today the issues are many and do not divide themselves neatly into alternative programs.[1]

Political behavior in the nineteenth century was less rational than it is today. Party names were symbols to conjure with or be fought over. Torchlight parades, songs, and slogans worked up the kind of enthusiasms and loyalties that discounted reflective thought. The party with the greater enthusiasm might well be more likely to win than the one with the better argument. Today we are really a better educated and more sophisticated people and at least like to think that reason and argument, and not loyalty to symbols, are what sway us.

As disciplinarian and unifier, the party in Congress has fallen upon evil days; as an influence and organizer it is still one of the principal factors in arriving at decisions.[2]

In the first place, on it lies the responsibility for organization. In effect it elects the Speaker of the House and the President Pro Tem of the Senate. It determines the membership of committees. Seniority within a committee modifies party control, and even the party leadership is reluctant to transfer a member from one committee to another without his consent. Thus a member with even a modest length of ser-

---

[1] For an excellent summary of the historical trends in party discipline, see Clarence Berdahl, "The Workings of Party Discipline," reprinted in Theodore Lowi, ed., *Legislative Politics, U. S. A.* (Boston: Little, Brown, 1962), pp. 113–32.

[2] For the best study of the contemporary leadership structure and operation, see Ralph K. Huitt, "Democratic Party Leadership in the Senate," *American Political Science Review,* June 1961, pp. 334 ff.

vice is rarely punished for being out of step with the majority of his party or with the President, if of his party, or with his party platform. In other words, party strength determines the number of its members on a committee, but once the initial choice is made, continuity or seniority of service largely determines retention of such membership, if the member so desires. On the other hand, party regularity is most certainly a factor in a member obtaining his transfer, should he so desire it, to a committee of greater importance or of more interest to him.

Moreover, it is in the inner circles of the majority party that the legislative schedule is chiefly determined. This is somewhat less important than might appear, because of the tendency of Congress to stay later in the year in order to clear up all the important or urgent items on the docket. Traditions of seniority and tenure have at times made certain of the Democratic members of the Rules Committee of the House somewhat out of tune with the larger portion of their party colleagues, with the result that there has been something of a cleavage between the actions of the Committee and the wishes of the core leadership of the party. When it comes to voting on measures, party leadership is influential rather than coercive. It argues and pleads rather than threatens. Yet in both parties there are very many members who vote "with the party," especially if the issue involved is not one to which they have given any very serious scrutiny. Party loyalty is less certain on major issues with a high degree of visibility. It is difficult to single this out as a factor, especially as so many of these members would doubtless have voted the same way had there been no party lead at all. Perhaps the best summary would be to say that the leadership faces the problem of building majorities, even across party lines. This involves conferences and concessions, more than the exercise of power.

The effect of party on legislation is thus extremely difficult

226

to appraise.[3]   As regards members of the President's party, there is (even apart from coincidence of views) a natural desire to support him and to close ranks against the opposition.[4] At the very least he can count on his party in Congress to present his program, though not necessarily to support it in its entirety.   Certainly under Lincoln, Franklin Roosevelt, and many other presidents, the weapon of loss of patronage and the prospect of a reward in the shape of a future job were used to induce party conformity in support of the President's wishes.   Under Roosevelt, at least, this often built up resentment and, as time went on, probably lost votes as well as gained them.

The opposition party tends to function as much as a critic as a dissenter.   In other words, when in a minority its members frequently endorse the objectives of a bill, vote for it in final form, but press for amendments on the way.   Sometimes the motion to recommit is used as a peg on which to hang amendments or even an alternative proposal.   This is especially useful if the House faces a measure under a "closed rule" with the consequent denial of opportunity to offer amendments from the floor.   Yet it is unusual for the minority to propose a major alternative for meeting the problem in question; rarely does it deny the existence of the problem or deny that its solution lies in governmental action. Even where many of the opposition hold one or the other of these latter positions, still others go along with the major portion of the bill—albeit usually united in criticism of certain portions of it.   This criticism is an important function, though

---

[3] For a thorough study of the period 1961–63 among the House Democrats, see Lewis A. Froman, Jr., and Randall B. Ripley, "Conditions for Party Leadership," *American Political Science Review*, March 1965, pp. 52–63.

[4] This is brought out empirically in David Truman, *The Congressional Party* (New York: Wiley, 1959), chap. 8.   For the best analysis of party leadership in the House as a whole see Richard F. Fenno, Jr., "Internal Distribution of Influence: The House," in David S. Truman, *The Congress and America's Future* (Englewood Cliffs: Prentice-Hall, 1965), pp. 61–70.

not the dramatic function which an alternative party program would be.

Where the opposition party is in the majority, its function as critic often tends in the direction of submission of alternative measures for meeting problems identified by the President. Certainly during the Eisenhower administration, the Democratic majority made a strong attempt to be constructive, and at the same time to suggest identifiable differences between itself and the President. However, in general it sought action more than issues, and did not court the veto for the sake of an issue. After the election of Ford as minority leader on the House side, a similar policy of presenting alternatives appeared more frequently.

Far more than is commonly realized, Congress is at heart bipartisan or nonpartisan. So much has been made of the bipartisan foreign policy that it is not appreciated in how many other fields a similar approach is followed. Even among the members of the all-important Appropriations Committees, there is a relative uniformity of approach, and such differences as there are are frequently not along party lines at all. Usually the minority will single out one or two items in a bill in order to make an issue of them, but, as for the measure as a whole, there is a remarkable absence of partisanship in the executive sessions.

Turning to the substantive committees and measures, House Interstate and Foreign Commerce has prided itself for many years on its tradition of nonpartisanship. So also have both of the Judiciary Committees in much of their agenda. The 1950 revision of the Social Security Act was completely nonpartisan in both Ways and Means and Finance. In two-thirds to three-quarters of the committees, nonpartisanship in executive sessions has been the rule. Differences of opinion there usually are, but not on partisan lines. Probably in most of the other committees large portions of the legislation before a committee are approached without reference to party.

The occasional measures singled out for partisan controversy usually make the headlines, but this should not obscure the fact that the bulk of the consideration of foreign affairs, housing, national defense, civil service, governmental reorganization, education, health, reciprocal trade, social security, immigration quotas, water-resource projects, water and air pollution, atomic energy, transportation, taxation, agriculture, combating subversives, conservation, and civil rights are not partisan at all. Controversial they may be in many of their aspects, but the controversy is not partisan. Only in labor relations, agriculture, public power, and some aspects of the President's antipoverty program does strong partisanship figure—and even here there are substantial minorities of each party supporting the position taken by the party leadership of the opposite party. These minorities consist on the Democratic side of members from the South, and on the Republican side of many from urban areas.

Closer examination of votes on major measures [5] will reveal the looseness of party ties and the extent to which lines are crossed.

During the entire Eighty-first Congress votes on party lines were virtually nonexistent on final passage of measures. An occasional amendment, such as the vote in the Senate to include a "peril point" proviso in the Reciprocal Trade Agreements Extension, might be carried or defeated on virtually 100 per cent party voting. Such amendments were occasionally offered by the Republican minority (and supported by most or virtually all of them) in order to dramatize a particular position. A good example was the alternative proposal of the Republicans to the excess-profits tax. Motions to recommit were likely to be more partisan than votes on final passage, and it may be urged with some cogency that these motions to recommit often represented a more critical roll call than the

---

[5] For a more sophisticated and thorough study of roll calls in this particular Congress, see David Truman, *Congressional Party.*

229

ones on final passage. Of the Acts as passed, only the vote on the International Claims Settlement Act in the House and the Senate vote on the Conference Report on Increased Borrowing Power for the Commodity Credit Corporation (of even the moderately important measures) divided on party lines. All other major measures were passed or defeated in both sessions in both houses by either a majority of both parties or a majority of one party plus ten per cent or more of the other party.

The subjects on which a majority of both parties agreed on final roll call included:

HOUSE

Extension of Reciprocal Trade Agreements Act
Hawaii statehood
Army Air Force Act of 1949
Executive Pay Act
Repeal of tax on oleomargarine
Reorganization of executive branch
Antipoll-Tax Bill
Extension of European recovery program
China Aid Act
Expansion of Air Force
Voluntary F.E.P.C.
Amending the National Bank Act and the Bretton Woods Agreement Act

Veterans' Pensions (H.R. 4617)
Internal Security (H.R. 4703)
Agricultural Act of 1949
Increase of minimum wage
Social Security Act (H.R. 6000)
Spanish War Veterans
Extension of selective service
Housing Act of 1950
General Appropriations Act
Foreign economic assistance
Reduction in excise taxes
Federal Aid Highway Act (1950)
Defense Production Act
Subversive-activities control

SENATE

Executive Pay Act
Investigation of gambling and racketeering
Federal aid to education
Increase of minimum wage
National Housing Act of 1949
Extension of European recovery program (1949) (1950)

Liberalization of Displaced Persons Act
Foreign Aid Appropriation, 1950
Columbia River Basin Projects (defeated)
Flood control, and rivers and harbors
Social Security Act

Korean aid
Mutual Defense Assistance Act
Defense Production Act
Extension of rent control
Repeal of tax on oleomargarine
Codification of the Articles of
  War
Increase in borrowing power for
  Commodity Credit Corporation
Extension of selective service
Reduction of federal employees'
  annual and sick leave
  (defeated)
Aid for Spain
Internal Security Act

The subjects on which a majority of one party and from ten to forty-nine per cent of the other party concurred furnish a somewhat shorter list. These represent party splits, usually both ways. Relatively few of these measures in the Senate had under twenty-five per cent of one party voting with the majority of the other party. Between ten and twenty-five per cent was more frequent in the House. The principal subjects falling in this category were:

HOUSE

Basing point pricing legalization
National Minerals Act
Korean aid
Alaska statehood
Export control
Amending the Natural Gas Act
Housing and rent control (1949)
  (1950)
Wood Labor Bill
Veterans' Pensions (H.R. 2681)
Increasing the postal rates
National Science Foundation
Flood control, and rivers and
  harbors
Mutual Defense Assistance Act
Prohibition of filling ninety per
  cent of vacancies in agencies

SENATE

Labor Relations Act of 1949
Bridge Canyon dam
Basing point pricing legalization
Extension of rent control
Point Four program
Extension of Reciprocal Trade
  Agreements Act
Amending the Natural Gas Act
Cloture on F.E.P. Act
Stabilization of agricultural prices
Five per cent blanket reduction of
  appropriations
Authority to appoint General
  Marshall Secretary of Defense

It is interesting to note two votes by way of illustration of how the two major clusters of issues—the domestic economic and the foreign assistance—cut across party lines. The Mu-

231

tual Defense Assistance Act passed the Senate 51 to 24. The 51 votes were 36 Democratic, 15 Republican; the 24 negative votes were 10 Democratic, 14 Republican. The Housing and Rent Act of 1950 passed the House 200 to 163. The 200 votes were 170 Democratic, 30 Republican; the 163 negative votes were 45 Democratic, 118 Republican.

Without going into so much detail, it is clear that the first session of the Eighty-fourth Congress was, if anything, even more nonpartisan. Again directing our attention to the roll calls on important measures, the majority of both parties were on the same side in forty-seven instances in the Senate, forty in the House. Those in which a substantial portion (a median of about thirty-eight per cent) of one party joined a majority of the other numbered seventeen in the Senate, thirteen in the House. In only four instances in the Senate and one in the House was a measure carried or defeated on substantially partisan lines. When the teller and viva-voce votes are added (the great majority of which were overwhelming with both parties), the picture is impressive.

In the Eighty-sixth Congress, Charles Halleck succeeded Joseph Martin as Minority (Republican) Leader. There is little doubt that in part his election was an expression of a desire for more vigorous party leadership. His coming altered the picture from what it was during the time that Martin and Rayburn would often work together to get things done. In more than half (97) of the 180 roll calls a majority of the Democrats were on one side of the issue and most Republicans on the other. Partisanship in roll calls increased. By the Eighty-seventh Congress the Republican House members came largely from sociologically conservative districts. The reduced numbers that accompanied this gave a stronger partisan tone percentage-wise than in those Congresses in which their liberal wing was larger.[6] The increased use of

---

[6] Lewis A. Froman, Jr., "Interparty Constituency Differences and Congressional Voting Behavior," *American Political Science Review,* March 1963, pp. 57–61.

the Party Conference and Policy Committee strengthened this, to such an extent that the negativism thereby expressed created so much discontent among party members that Halleck was replaced by Gerald Ford in the Eighty-eighth Congress. In the first term of the Eighty-ninth Congress the majority of both parties were on opposite sides on the repeal of the "right to work" clause, urban redevelopment, reapportionment, establishment of the Department of Housing and Urban Development, loans to depressed areas, agriculture, the retention of the governor's veto in poverty programs, rivers and harbors, the Arts and Humanities Foundation. The houses split in this regard on medicare, foreign aid, highway beautification, and sugar quotas. In other fields the majorities of both parties were on the same side.

In spite of this increase in partisanship, the long-range factors point in the other direction, with the Republican realization that their future in Congress lies in success in urban areas.

Contrasts between various Congresses as regards degree of party influence and solidarity suggest the presence of a number of important variables. Certainly the personality of the congressional leaders and of the President, the majority or minority status of a party, whether or not the two branches are in control of the same party, the type of issue, the attitudes of particular committee chairmen, all play important roles. Parties are essentially mediators in seeking a consensus, rather than ideological rivals.

There have always been numerous predominantly partisan divisions on amendments or motions to recommit. Particularly in the case of amendments, personalities often figured heavily. These amendments or motions were in many instances the means chosen for the minority party to perform the function of criticism of detail; they fell far short of opposition.

The fact is that there is a certain premium placed on independence, especially if a member's own state or district agrees with his dissent. "Party loyalty" has sunk far down the scale as a plus symbol of value, and independence, "unbossed," "thinking for myself," have correspondingly gained in prestige. Party loyalty contains within itself certain connotations of being a puppet, a nonrational implication which is a liability. This has gone along with the steady increase in split voting and independence among the electorate at large, the despair of the party organizers, but one of the chief factors making it necessary to nominate better candidates in large sections of our country than used to rule when the voters would swallow almost anything, if it bore the correct label.

The desirability of strengthening party ties and party discipline has received unexpected support of late from among the political scientists. After many decades in which a large portion of their writing and teaching in this field was devoted to exposing the corruption, the irrational character, the susceptibility to special interests of the party organizations, probably a majority of the political science profession are now advocating the strengthening of party organizations, the development of party discipline, the insistence upon party solidarity in Congress. They would play down independence in voting and substitute therefor the rational contribution of the educated man within party circles. It must be admitted that these scholars have made a powerful case for their *volte-face*.

Entering into this line of thought is certainly an admiration for the workings of party government in Great Britain. It all seems so smooth and orderly. Programs are advanced and fought over. Her Majesty's Loyal Opposition criticizes and carries the debate and its alternatives to the hustings. Platforms mean what they say. An election really decides something. Despairing of ever amending our own Constitution so as to introduce the parliamentary system, this line of reasoning seems to imply going as far as possible without such amendment. Chief reliance is placed in this regard upon strengthening the party machinery and clarifying its responsibility.

It is all very logical—unless one goes behind the scenes in England and finds such things as a bureaucracy maturing almost all legislation and increasing by leaps and bounds; the two parties outbidding each other with promises of governmental largesse, so as to attract marginal groups; a division of the nation along class lines; the sacrifice of independence of thought and action on the part of the individual member; the pressing home of such a drastic measure as the nationalization of steel, though a majority of the voters supported candidates opposed to it at the preceding election. Nor is there any real assurance that parliamentary or a near approach to parliamentary government would develop British usages in the American setting. Geographic, sociological, economic conditions all differ drastically.

Moreover, probably a majority of our intellectuals tend to think in terms of "left" and "right," "radical" and "reactionary," and probably a disproportionate number of the more articulate belong to the liberal left. There is nothing reprehensible about their so believing, but, when they speak of "program" in the sense of a party program, they normally mean further governmental intervention in behalf of the common man. Here again there is nothing reprehensible. The nub of the matter, however, is this: if they had their way, the United States would be divided into two parties, one "left" and one "right." In other words, in so far as party divisions came to be logical they would become nationally divisive instead of basically unifying as they tend to be today—and we would be a step nearer class cleavage if not class warfare. Our present habit of advancing by substantial consensus, stressing pragmatic rather than ideological considerations, of waging our political campaigns largely emphasizing the unities and not the divisions, they would replace, if not with the Continental brand of politics, at least with the British. This may

235

or may not be desirable. That is a matter of opinion. But at least the total picture should be better understood than it now is, before steps are taken in this direction. The Goldwater campaign was almost certainly an exception.

Certain proposals akin to this viewpoint were brought together in what was certainly a masterly and challenging *Report* of the American Political Science Association's Committee on Political Parties.[7] It is not the place here to cover the entire report. With much of it—the emphasis upon research and statistics, the broadening of the base of popular participation in party activities and policy formulation, the continuity of consideration of issues by the party leaders and membership, the democratization of the national convention —few would disagree, and very practical suggestions were made to attain these ends. It is rather the over-all objectives, and the congressional application and implication of these objectives, that are seriously questioned.

The case presented is powerful. Platforms democratically arrived at should be contracts with the voter which are binding upon members of Congress. They should be explicit. They should incorporate a comprehensive and integrated program. A party council should be formed with state as well as national representatives and should include the President and congressional leaders. Within Congress the President's party should strengthen its intercommunication with the executive, and the President should share policy decisions with the congressional leaders of his party. Both parties should form stronger policy committees entrusted with the mission of carrying out the party policy as incorporated in the party platform. On matters not therein included, the party organization should strive to work out with the members a course of action in general harmony with party principles. There

---

[7] *American Political Science Review,* Supp., September 1950. For an exposition of a theory of parties which lies between this *Report* and the viewpoint expressed in this work, see Clinton Rossiter, *Parties and Politics in America* (Ithaca: Cornell University Press, 1960).

is an implication that the seniority rule of committee chairmanships should be modified at least to the extent that only loyal party members should be allowed to be chairmen. Loyalty is defined as agreement with the party platform and program. Penalties—such as deprivation of committee or even party membership—should be imposed upon recalcitrant members. Caucuses should be more frequent and binding if matters of principle and program are involved. The party leadership in Congress should be given greater responsibility in the national party organization, including the national convention. The national organization should exercise a measure of control over state and local party organization, including active intervention in behalf of candidates for Congress in the primaries who are pledged to the national platform. By these and other measures, party responsibility would be established, our two-party system would function more effectively, the voters would be confronted with real alternatives, the hold of the special interests would allegedly be lessened.

A powerful case, indeed, and so important that it deserves the closest examination and the most searching analysis.

The first argument that might be noted against it—an argument decisive, if true—is that it may not be possible to put into practice. It may well founder on the rock of regional interests. If by party program there is meant anything more than giving everybody at least something—in other words, if there are to be teeth in the platform and especially if it is to represent an "integrated" program, it will run smack up against certain regional realities. For example, civil liberties. Can either party pledge its candidates to this in concrete terms and as generally understood and even yet carry a southern primary? Or take private power. Would a party opposing public power do anything other than commit political suicide in the West? Or take the Taft-Hartley or Landrum-Griffin repeal: for or against, large sections of the country would

237

be lost by any party categorically committing all its candidates to one side or the other. Strengthening the United Nations, extending foreign aid—these at present both would promise. As for agriculture, would either party dare *not* promise the farmer an approach to parity—and might not an opponent of such a privileged position well carry a primary in an urban area smarting under the high cost of the necessities of life? There are other issues, similar in character, to which decisive importance is attached in certain parts of the nation—the price of silver, the Upper Colorado program, the Pick-Sloan plan, urban renewal, certain tariffs and quotas, antigambling or gambling, and others somewhat less intensely felt. Surely, enough examples have been given to indicate grave doubt as regards whether the direct primary would allow "national party discipline" to work in practice.

Moreover, to support such nationally imposed viewpoints would be an invitation to many state and local party organizations to commit political suicide by renouncing indefinitely any chance of electing local candidates. Assume, as seems likely, that the liberal wing of the Democratic party succeeded in incorporating the civil-rights program into those planks to which candidates must pledge allegiance in order to use the party label and that the Republicans did the same. Would a third party capture the South or would its party organizations do just what they now do—defy or disregard the national party platform? In one case, the two-party system breaks down; in the other, "national discipline" proves impracticable. To read these members out of positions of influence in Congress would almost certainly bring about a coalition in Congress for organization purposes which would effectively hamstring what party responsibility now exists.

Nor would such probable refusal on the part of local organizations to commit hara-kiri be confined to the South.[8]

---

[8] See Ira Ralph Telford, "Types of Primary and Party Responsibility," *American Political Science Review*, March 1965, pp. 117 f., for reinforcing evidence.

The probabilities are that elsewhere the same phenomenon would show itself, even without reinforcement from the direct primary. If the example of England is pointed to, it should be borne in mind that the situation there is quite different. The weapon of dissolution is a powerful disciplinary factor. Local government has no appreciable party spoils, and local organizations are relatively weak. Moreover, the regional one-sidedness which it is predicted national party discipline would bring in the United States has in fact shown itself in very many constituencies in Great Britain, notably the rural counties and the working-class areas of the cities. The cleavage is a cleavage along class lines and is divisive.

Moreover, the American Political Science Association *Report* attaches great importance to unified "programs" in contradistinction to the vagueness of present party platforms, or at least to the inattention now paid to them both before and after an election. Is this really practicable? Is there really any basic unity of approach possible that could in fact obtain a majority in support of the same definite positions on the great controversial issues of the present day? Look more closely at these issues. They certainly include the desires of the trade-unions to be free to act uninhibited by the restraints of government, the desires of agriculture to have a privileged position in the price structure, civil liberties, bigness and monopolistic tendencies in business, international co-operation, the nature and extent of national defense, the nature and extent of foreign aid, public housing, foreign trade, federal aid to education, combating subversive elements at home, health insurance, taxing-spending-deficit financing, anti-poverty—to mention some of the principal issues. What possible common denominator can be found that would run through all of these and command a majority without forcing a subordinating of conscience and judgment considerably greater than now obtains? The "left-right" cleavage comes the nearest to fitting the actualities. But this division is not meaningful in connection with the issues of international relations, agriculture, national defense—not to mention others. There are too many issues and too many possible positions on each issue to make a program binding without sacrifices. Integration of the various separate policies raises still more difficult problems, the solution of which may well antagonize the groups with mass support upon which so much depends. The present system of majority voting in Congress, with its permutations and combinations of bipartisanship and cross-voting, comes much nearer meeting the realities than would two parties irrevocably committed to rival programs.

In addition to the primary question regarding whether these proposals and objectives would in fact be practicable, there is the equally important question of their advisability, assuming they could be made to work. What values in the present system would be surrendered or impaired, and for what?

At the present time we have in the presidential years two platforms which of late have rarely shown substantial differences. Nineteen sixty-four was clearly the exception. Till then such differences as existed were usually accounted for by concrete actions of the party or President in power, or by differences between the records of the parties in Congress. Individual planks typically incorporate two or more impeccable principles which in their concrete application come into conflict and require compromise. This gives the party the best of both worlds. It attracts support from rival groups, each of which reads its own emphasis into the wording, and then leaves its leaders and members in Congress free to work out what they deem to be appropriate solutions, without violating their pledges. A few minor planks—home rule for the District of Columbia, statehood for Alaska and Hawaii—were unequivocal enough, but the "pressure of other business" may interfere with the carrying out of these pledges. In any event, candidates for Congress feel quite free to contract out of one or more planks, if they so desire. Whatever the concrete position a candidate takes on the various issues, he goes to Congress with the confidence a man feels who has the electorate behind him.

One of the results of this convenient vagueness in the party platforms is that an attempt is made to appeal to all groups in our national life. Only straw men are denounced. Class appeals are conspicuously lacking. Racial appeals are for greater recognition of minority groups and not, except among some elements in the South, for their curbing. Because of the breadth of appeal, the net result is that our national campaigns are essentially unifying. We have, as it were, a "government by consensus." No one group or region can have its way unless it can carry with it substantial fractions from each of the other great groups or regions. The very looseness in platform-framing lays the groundwork for this. It is possible in the end that even the minority-rights program of the Negro may seek and find a middle ground as at least a temporary stage which will command a measure of support even in the South, and the tradition and practice of government by consensus will again be demonstrated and vindicated. We have seen that there is a strong possibility that attempts at nationally imposed party programs may actually result in more, rather than less, sectional cleavage than occurs at present. There is also a strong possibility that it may bring about a labor party fighting on class lines.[9] If either or both of these should result, our national campaigns and two-party system would be divisive rather than unifying and government by consensus would be replaced by government by class.

Alternatively or concurrently, there is a strong probability that parties with programs whose support is made the test of party membership would come to embrace the special groups more than ever. By and large, the most probable form this would take would be labor versus the middle class and busi-

---

[9] The *Report* rejects this possibility (pp. 20–21, 95–96), though this author does not find convincing the reasoning therein.

ness, with each side bidding for agriculture, the veteran, the civil service, the aged, and the Negro vote. It is urged by the advocates of nationally responsible and unified parties that thereby the special interests (or at least the lesser ones, numerically speaking) would find themselves less powerful whereas the greater groups, numerically speaking (meaning chiefly labor and agriculture), would operate in the inner councils of the party, and this experience would cause them to curb those portions of their demands which would not be in accord with the national interest or not in harmony with an integrated national program. It is, of course, possible that this would be so. In general, in situations of great national emergency, labor parties have in fact been able to curb the demands of their own memberships somewhat in Great Britain, Australia, New Zealand, and the Scandinavian countries. But there are limits, and the long-run behavior of the labor parties in the nations mentioned has not been so reassuring. Mention has already been made of the weakened strands of responsible fiscal behavior with the lessened reliance upon state and local action, and parties with a strengthened national emphasis might well find themselves in a political position in which fiscal irresponsibility came to be a condition for political survival.

In other words, there is at least an equal chance that, instead of nationally imposed party programs lessening the power of the pressure groups, they would in fact increase such power. Programs as contemplated in the Association's *Report* are a series of integrated policies; programs likely to emerge in practice if the *Report's* proposals are adopted are a series of unintegrated promises to special groups (much as at present) but without the saving grace of independence on the part of many members of Congress at the time of decision. The parties in search of votes might well embrace the special groups more than ever, with this additional and highly important further difference. They would in the new setting be able to coerce their members in Congress to go "down the line" for the pledges made to the special groups. No longer could coalitions of independents drawn from both parties block, as they frequently now do block, the extremes of treasury raids or special legislation crassly favoring a special interest at public expense. The party would, it is true, have a "program," but it would in all probability still be a dispersive one and one which would lack the restraints now put upon it by independent voting. It might also seriously impair the tradition of government by consensus. The present system of allowing members of a party to contract out of portions of a party platform and to interpret its ambiguities in accordance with either their own judgment or the wishes of their constituents may well be more in the public interest. This is not to deny the frequent contemporary examples of such contracting out also under pressure of special interests, though these frequently cancel each other out.

Nor are the values associated with independence lightly to be discarded. They may sacrifice the smoothness of operation and superficial logic of the monolithic party in the parliamentary system, but they do introduce a much wider variety of considerations into debate and decision. The result may be an illogical conglomerate compared to the type of general legislation that is matured in the civil service and that vests this same civil service with subsequent greater discretion, which is typical of the British system.[10]   But then also our legislation may be closer to the popular will, less full of bureaucratic blind spots, more thoroughly aired in hearings and debate. Who shall say? These are generalities whose only significance is to indicate the doubtful nature of the verdict.

---

[10] The *Report* believes that a more responsible party government and program would lessen the existing influence of the bureaus with special-interest clientele and strengthen the influence of the party in Congress and the bureaus with an over-all viewpoint. The author pins more faith upon the development of independence in Congress based upon fact finding and research.

One thing seems certain. The type of individual attracted to Congress in a setting in which he is committed in advance to follow his party would be different from many now in Congress. There would be little or no room left for independence of judgment.[11] The premium would be upon party loyalty. In our churches, schools, and colleges we have long emphasized the importance of rational decisions, of weighing the pros and cons of issues, of that integrity of character which requires that an individual express and vote his convictions, of independence (albeit coupled with a willingness to compromise, if thereby half a loaf is obtainable). Are we now to reverse all this and still hope to obtain many men of the same high caliber that so many in Congress are today? Will the opportunity for greater participation in formulating the party program in fact be a real substitute for the present opportunity to cast the final vote on each separate item, if this opportunity to participate requires as a pre-condition a virtual pledge to go down the line for what the majority in the party decide, regardless of one's own convictions? These questions should at least be asked, though their answers lie in the field of conjecture. The opportunity to participate in formulation of party policy should certainly be increased, but this does not or need not imply a blind commitment to the end result as a condition of party preferment or even membership.

There are two other values of independence already mentioned in the course of earlier considerations. The independent on a given issue is in a position to criticize and vote against a special interest; the disciplined party man cannot do this if the desires of the special interests have been incorporated into his party's program. The opportunity to urge his views in the councils of the party is a poor substitute for the sacrifice of his freedom at the time of the final, respon-

---

[11] Here as in so many other matters the *Report* reaches different conclusions (pp. 70, 72). The reader must compare the argument therein presented with the present argument and draw his own conclusions.

sible decision. It was our earlier contention that the social and economic structures of our districts and states are such that in connection with legislation sponsored by every substantial group—save possibly the veterans and (in a few decades) the aged—there are a very considerable number of members not under obligations to any particular group who can afford to speak out in behalf of the more general interest as they see it. If the party (or both parties) is committed to a group's program, this can no longer be done without risk of party discipline.

Similarly and more subtly, the values associated with the localism of Congress would seemingly be eroded in the face of binding national-party programs. It would not be necessary to postulate the rise to a dominant influence of the bureaucracy, as in England, to foresee this outcome, for Congress has expert staffs of its own. It is only that the strengthening of party responsibility as visualized by its advocates calls for a lessened role to be played by the state and local organizations and also for the greater influence on party programs of nation-wide groups with large memberships. Both of these are centralizing factors. Government by consensus applies not only to the great groups but also to agreement among the regions and to the equilibrium between the states and the nation—that is, to the federal element in our Constitution. National party strength would move in the direction of seriously impairing these latter two.

We have in our Congress a government by shifting majorities, and not by party. In this type of government the individual's views have far greater play; and conscience, intelligence, and local concerns can be much more influential than would be practicable in a parliamentary system, in which party discipline is virtually a prerequisite to stability in government. Only separation of powers makes individualized voting possible, for the executive does not depend upon the legislature to retain its office.

245

What do people vote for when they vote for a representative or senator? To a very considerable extent they vote their confidence in the man. By this they bear witness to their appreciation of the complexity and multiplicity of issues and their belief that integrity and ability matter. Would a party program be a substitute? To some extent they vote on issues, generally one or two that seem to them important and on which the two opposing candidates offer a genuine choice. If a particular issue at a given time is emotionally charged, a candidate's stand on this particular issue may be decisive. Such an issue was prohibition; such an issue is civil rights.[12] Moreover, the party in its selection of its candidates obviously takes into account their views on issues. There are advantages in widening the base of issues to be considered, and a party program would tend in this direction, though at the expense of discrimination and selection. Many people vote a party label. This would be unchanged. Others vote in return for favors rendered. Perhaps this element would be lessened, perhaps not.

The search for means of combating the power of the special interests and narrow sectionalism, and of securing the better integration of the several issues, is essentially sound. The solution offered, of greater party responsibility, even if it were to be effective in these matters (of which there is grave doubt), by no means exhausts the list of things that might be done. We have spoken of congressional staff aids largely in terms of their usefulness as a corrective vis-à-vis the executive. They are equally important in equipping Congress to deal correctly and intelligently with the recommendations of the special interests. It is trite to say that the ultimate answer to problems of this sort lies in the area of education and civic responsibility and integrity, but it happens to be true. As the knowledge of the nature of public affairs spreads, as the level

---

12 Cf. Warren E. Miller and Donald Stokes, "Constituency Influence in Congress," *American Political Science Review*, March 1963, pp. 45–56.

of education moves ever higher, members and voters alike come to appreciate the secondary and often harmful effects of some of the seemingly plausible demands of the special interests. They come to appreciate the need for an inner harmony or compatibility in a legislative program, over against the dispersiveness which has prevailed in the past. Civic responsibility and integrity are more subtle things, less easy to teach, part rather of the mores of a people, the sphere of their religion. To the extent that they become influential they will tend to curb the selfishness of groups, to give courage to those who would fight against this selfishness, to lessen coerced or blind party loyalty and increase the responsible behavior of the individual member.

This approach and the values placed on independence must not be carried too far. The existing party mechanism fulfills functions too important to be scrapped or reduced to a farce. It is still the best mechanism we have for selecting and electing candidates. It singles out certain issues from time to time for public discussion. It forces the successful party candidate for President to present a program and the majority party in Congress to assume some responsibility for presenting for discussion and possible enactment either this program or alternatives thereto if the party in control of Congress is not the same as that of the President. It assures an opposition that will criticize the President's proposals in their detail, even though it may support the objective and main provisions of many of them. By so much, it creates a reasonably effective mechanism to get things both discussed and accomplished—and without either the class bitterness or sacrifice of individual independence of thought which characterizes many other countries. Proposals to democratize party platform making and to utilize its machinery for more research and discussion at all levels are all to the good. These would increase the value of its contribution without impairing those values of our political and governmental structure

247

that lie elsewhere than in party. Let the parties remain administrative rivals, but one should think long and hard before urging that they espouse rival ideologies. The genius of Congress lies not so much in the expression of the politics of conflict as of the politics of consensus.

CHAPTER EIGHTEEN

Congress and the Education of the Public

THE political education of the public is one of the recognized functions of Congress. How it performs it and ways whereby it may be better performed have been the subject of some research and more writing. While there is relatively little to add to what has been said elsewhere, an incomplete picture of Congress would result if no mention were made of it.

The channels for such education are many. More frequently than not such political education is a by-product rather than the chief end of congressional behavior. The chief ends remain: to put through a policy or program, to solve a problem, and to be re-elected. The education of the electorate is chiefly valued as it contributes to one of these, but regardless of whether or not it is consciously sought, it nevertheless takes place continuously.

Campaigns to be elected begin the process of voter education, even though on occasion it may seem that a candidate strives to confuse an issue rather than to clarify it. On the other hand, members frequently call upon each other to speak in one's district. This is usually, but not always, partisan, but in any event it does add to the political ferment and often enlightenment as well.

Floor debate and discussion customarily attract the best press. The really great debates—on foreign policy, on taxation, on national defense, on labor relations—attract widespread attention in all the principal media of communication. Even though sessions of Congress are at present

249

neither filmed, broadcast, nor televised, there are follow-ups by commentators or members themselves through all these media that project the floor debate into other settings and obtain considerably wider attention than if the press were the sole reliance. Whatever may be said for and against the bringing of members of the Cabinet onto the floors of Congress for questioning, at least it may be safely predicted that there would be widespread press and other coverage, with at least a modest increase in political education thereby.

Second only to the publicity attending floor debate is that accorded the committee hearings. The aggregate publicity of the latter almost certainly exceeds the former. Here the possibilities and variations are innumerable. Television is the most recent and most spectacular innovation. Criticism has frequently been voiced of the amount of time often required of key administrators to appear before not one committee but several. On the other hand, there is no doubt that the public-education function of Congress is thereby considerably better performed, for press and other coverage of the subject matter at issue is assured by such means. Criticism has also been voiced that this outside coverage is largely confined to the spectacular and that the solid substance of many hearings is correspondingly overlooked, that this premium on the spectacular tempts Congress to distort the nature and purpose of the hearings. Insofar as they are designed to be solidly informative to Congress on the substance of the issues involved, the point may be well taken. Insofar as the public's attention is thereby attracted to an issue of which it was previously unaware and is induced to discuss that issue, however superficially, there may still be some gain. These defects, if defects they be, lie as much with the press and the public who demand such dramatization as the price of interest, as they do with Congress.

To the serious student, the records of the hearings are mines of information. Here are set out in detail, and subjected to cross-examination, many of the basic data relating to the nature of our economy, the underlying factors in foreign relations, the future of our resources, the strategy of national defense, the problems in labor relations, and many another field of importance and interest. If even after such study the details still do not reach the general public, they are sufficiently used to be influential as background for much of our current writing—editorial, economic, and other. On the other hand, a number of the committees deliberately plan some of their hearings with the education of the public in mind and choose subjects and witnesses accordingly.

Due credit must also be given to the publications of Congress. In addition to the record of floor debate, there are the transcripts of the hearings and the published committee reports. A wealth of miscellaneous and fugitive, but often thoroughly important, material exists among the mass of inserts printed in the Appendix of the *Congressional Record.* Then from time to time Congress or one of its committees or one of its staff agencies publishes some important study. Among the best-known in recent years probably are the publications of the Temporary National Economic Committee, the Senate Foreign Relations Committee's *A Decade of American Foreign Policy, Trends in Economic Growth: A Comparison of the Western Powers and the Soviet Bloc,* issued by the Committee on the Economic Report; and the studies of the organization of national security policy by the Jackson subcommittee of the Senate Committee on Governmental Operations. With the growth of professional staffs, this type of educational document is likely to increase, both in quality and in number. Many members make it a point to see that certain of these reports reach appropriate constituents.

Finally, as an educational instrument there should certainly be included the various ways in which a member reports to his constituents. By radio and television, by press release and letter, by speeches and multiplication of personal con-

251

tacts, members seem more and more to be associating their constituents with the problems that face Congress.[1] A large majority report regularly by radio or television or newsletter or all three. Sometimes these vehicles of communication pose problems; at other times they explain the member's stand on a particular issue; at other times they invite constituent reaction. As the level of education of the electorate steadily rises, and as media such as television make such communication more and more easy, we may expect this personalizing of political education steadily to increase. It helps the member on all counts: it builds up support for measures he believes in, it enables him better to understand the viewpoint of his district, it makes it possible for him to perform the public service of spreading the knowledge of public affairs, and it helps him get re-elected by becoming better and more favorably known.

Political education is almost necessarily selective as regards the type of issue lending itself to the process. Highly technical subjects receive little publicity, however important. Noncontroversial subjects seldom spark much public interest. Subjects whose importance is confined to one group receive coverage by and for that group but are given little general attention. It is in the areas of great controversy or of general familiarity that most publicity is concentrated. Differences between the President and Congress always are newsworthy. The cross-questioning of a man in whom there is widespread popular interest receives attention—whether the man is Secretary McNamara, Alger Hiss, Walter Reuther, or Bishop Oxnam. Crime, subversive activities, universal military training, radioactive fall-out are subjects with which people generally regard themselves as familiar. Hence they, too, are newsworthy. In other words, the political education re-

---

[1] This seems especially to be true of Republican members from the closely contested districts with electorates of above average educational levels.

sulting from congressional activity is not only selective, it tends to be disproportionate and distorted. Nevertheless, in the aggregate, it is quantitatively very considerable, and on balance one of the greatest assets we have in our functioning democracy.

As a by-product, even the normal congressional activity often makes a particular member himself newsworthy, especially in the Senate. This personal visibility in turn can be and is used for the further education of the electorate. Congress as a body may suffer, as Holcombe has put it, from "exhibiting its indecisions in public." Individual members may so conduct themselves as to draw ridicule as well as publicity. All this is part of the game. It should never be forgotten that the major part of the constructive work of Congress is done in committee and not on the floor.

There is high hope that this particular function of Congress of political education will continue to be performed, as it has been of late, with increasing responsibility, intelligence, and effectiveness. It lies near the heart of the democratic way.

CHAPTER NINETEEN

Congress in a Crisis

THUS far the picture of Congress has been highly favorable as regards both function and behavior. However, many of the underlying assumptions have been those of a more or less leisurely age during which issues may mature and solutions for problems may obtain a broad base of consensus prior to adoption. But this is not the kind of age in which we now live. Its tempo is rapid. It moves from one crisis to another. It seems to require correspondingly prompt action on the part of government, in the international field because of existing tensions, in the domestic field because of a sensitive and interlocking economy. Moreover, the issues are of very great importance, not only to contemporary society but to future generations. Can government in general and Congress in particular muster the sustained high-level thinking and conduct that the great responsibilities involved seem to require?

In part, it is our Constitution with its checks and balances, its separation of powers, that is on trial over against the parliamentary type, or in comparison with the probable results if it should be amended materially. In part, the issue is more far-reaching, involving the success or failure of representative institutions in a struggle with totalitarianism for the strength and loyalty of their supporters, and the success or failure of a free economy over against the communist order.

This second issue is partly a matter of what is known and what is concealed, so that impressions may be misleading. The revelations of the inefficiencies, lost motion, internal friction, and other errors of the dictatorships of Italy, Germany, and Japan are now a matter of record, exposed so that he who wishes may read and ponder. They apparently are at least

254

equal to the errors made by the democracies and may well exceed them by an appreciable margin. The gains, if any, from being able to move without having to reckon with opposition or criticism are seemingly outweighed by the losses resulting from not having the benefit of such criticism. This is obviously an oversimplification but contains an important truth. On the other hand, reports from the Soviet Union and communist China are mixed in character. Some carry the same story of inefficiency and waste through terror, lack of incentive, cynicism, suspicion, and espionage. Yet, however inefficiently these dictatorships may in fact have administered their societies, it is important to remember that they give the appearance of effectiveness, both to their own people and to others. They can cover up their mistakes and liquidate their critics. On the other hand the extent of Soviet and even of Chinese success has in a number of respects been noteworthy, and we would be fooling ourselves if we disregarded the substantial achievements in the fields of rate of growth, capital formation, and scientific progress. In this connection it is therefore all the more important that democracies and especially our own democratic republic shall be so effective that he who runs may read; that these democracies shall in fact rise to the great demands of the age.

Criticism of our Constitution from those who uphold democratic values concerns largely the relationships between Congress and the President. Especially does this criticism center upon the risks involved or revealed in a crisis situation. Without more power in the hands of the President or, as regards Congress, without more strict party discipline and stronger party leadership relating itself to the program of the President or party, it is alleged that Congress cannot or will not act with the necessary speed.

A still more acute situation, it is held, arises when the majority of Congress and the President belong to different parties. Under such a situation it is assumed or at least feared that a deadlock will ensue, as has happened before in our history. This contains the danger of blocking all action, no matter how serious the situation, or at least the danger of prolonged delays. At best, it is assumed that politics in the bad sense will more or less dominate such a situation and the legislative output will be quite other than the high occasion of the critical hour should have evoked.

As regards a remedy for this latter event, a simple amendment raising the term of members of the House to four years to correspond to that of the President is usually among the measures advocated.[1] It has been pointed out that until recently the divergence in party control has customarily been almost wholly associated with mid-term elections.

Those who propose fairly drastic alterations in the actual relationships between the President and Congress ordinarily have been greatly influenced in their thinking by the deadlock following the First World War. To this deadlock the two-thirds rule governing treaty ratification undoubtedly contributed. Yet so also did partisanship, so that one wonders whether measures strengthening party discipline and loyalty might not operate in reverse, especially in the field of treaty ratification with its two-thirds requirement. In periods calling for a sustained high purpose, more may be gained by muting partisanship than by invoking its disciplines.

Moreover, the alleged extent of ineptitude and delay in congressional dealings with crises has unconsciously been seriously overstated through the type of news coverage given to congressional debate and activity. The press tends to exaggerate the crises and to create a public attitude of impatience, which leaves the impression that any congressional delay, whether procedural or deliberative, is prima-facie evidence of inability to act quickly. Even the Senate filibuster which greeted Kennedy's proposed civil rights measure de-

---

[1] However, this would probably increase the number of rival candidates a senator whose election fell in an off year would have to face. House members with senatorial ambitions could compete with immunity as regards their House seats, unless the constitutional amendment provided otherwise.

layed its enactment only a few months, while Kennedy himself had waited two years after his pledge to propose it. Similar impressions of great controversy and intransigent partisanship are given by the nature of items chosen for reporting, when the realities may be quite otherwise.

There have been some very significant changes since 1920, changes which have revealed themselves in the record of Congress before, during, and after the Second World War.

In the first place, as Corwin has shown,[2] the emergency powers apparently permitted the President under the Constitution have been greatly enlarged, allowing for immediate action on his part, with Congress called upon later to endorse or reject such action.

In the second place, Congress itself, and particularly the House, is better organized and more "streamlined," especially since the Legislative Reorganization Act.

In behavior as distinct from organization, we have already noted the lessening of partisanship and the growth in consideration of legislation on a bipartisan or nonpartisan basis. This lends itself to high-level action commensurate with the importance of the problems to be dealt with. Watchdog committees such as the Truman Committee during the war have not uncommonly matched the occasion with their mood.

Actually, Congress is more and more shifting to reliance on research rather than controversy as the basis for decisions on issues and problems. The more facts that can be agreed upon, the less the remaining orbit for partisan or other controversy. The education of the electorate has increased and so has that of Congress. It could probably be demonstrated that Congress is today at an all-time high in the ability and sense of public service and integrity of its membership.

All in all, we seem to have learned something of a lesson. It was the Eightieth Congress, in control of the opposition party, that voted the President the most substantial program

2 Edward S. Corwin, *The President: Office and Powers*, 4th ed. rev. (New York: New York University Press, 1957), pp. 147–58, *et passim*.

of international co-operation that has ever been voted any administration. Here is no paralysis, no deadlock, no jockeying for partisan advantage with great issues at a great moment. The Eighty-first Congress in turn quickly granted the President emergency powers in the economic and defense crisis—in fact more powers than he had asked for. Here also was not delay, or dragging, or failure to respond to need. The Eighty-fourth Congress, again one controlled by the opposition party, moved rapidly and responsibly. The only arguments seemed to be concerned with which party most co-operated with the President, or whether Congress improved upon his program. In the Eighty-sixth Congress, it was Congress itself which sought acceleration and re-appraisal in space, defense, foreign aid, and foreign policy generally—over against an apparently improvising and lagging executive.[3]

There is still a danger of future deadlocks, of undue and even disastrous delays, and this should be borne in mind. Yet the factors that made the difference in congressional-presidential relations after the Second World War as compared with those following the First World War were not fundamentally accidents, such as differences in the personalities involved, though these played some part. The real differences are to be found in social trends, which are not likely to be reversed—unless indeed partisanship by some means or other finds itself strengthened. In the latter event a unified party behind the President might be able to move faster. There is no assurance that it would move more skillfully or with the large measure of consensus in a united nation which the present operation and usages of our Constitution appear to bring. The very change in the types of personality involved, so far as this has been a factor in the differences, may itself be one of the many effects of the larger horizons of the present age.

---

[3] For a particularly striking case study of this see Alison Griffith, *The National Aeronautics and Space Act* (Washington: Public Affairs Press, 1962).

CHAPTER TWENTY

Congress and the
Years Ahead

THE time has come to bring together the various strands in our thinking. Of what sort is this government of ours, and what is the place of Congress in the over-all setting? [1] Certainly we can no longer speak or write of our government, as Woodrow Wilson did late in the last century, as congressional government. Nor can we speak of it as presidential, though during the period 1933–1945 there was certainly a temptation so to do—based upon the rapid ascendancy of presidential activity and leadership during these years, an ascendancy that has ebbed and flowed in the years thereafter. What we are dealing with today is, in all probability, not so much a swing of the pendulum back to Congress, much less a change in the personality of the President, as it is rather the development of new usages, a new equilibrium within the framework and behind the façade of the Constitution. The coordinate and independent positions assigned to the executive and legislative branches have set the metes and bounds of this new equilibrium, and the nature of contemporary society has determined its major contours.

Let us summarize briefly our argument hitherto. The formal constitutional powers and position of Congress have changed but little, by either amendment or judicial interpretation. An exception is in the expansion allowed to the President in emergency situations, though much of this expansion was present in embryo in the powers exercised by

[1] In this connection see also the excellent analytical study by Roland Young, *The American Congress* (New York: Harper, 1958).

259

President Lincoln. The internal organization of Congress has changed measurably in the direction of clarity and fluidity, the latter most noticeable in the diffusion of leadership which allows considerably more scope than formerly for the individual member. The center of the stage is occupied by legislative-executive relations. These are an intricate pattern of conflict, compromise, and co-operation. On balance, each branch possesses under the Constitution a formidable set of powers with which it can force the other to take its point of view into account and hence assure responsible behavior. The nature of contemporary society with its premium upon leadership and rapid, informed action has given the executive an advantage in those informal factors which are frequently decisive in a power struggle. But Congress has restored the equilibrium somewhat by adding professional staffs of its own, thus equipping itself in technical terms to meet the executive on a basis of parity, even in the matter of initiating or maturing alternative policies. Special importance also attaches itself to the appropriating process, which is developing uses more or less extraneous to its original concept—disciplinary uses and uses in over-all fiscal policy and political economy. Various co-operative devices making for better executive-legislative relations are appearing, notably in the multiplication of informal contacts, some of which have become regularized. For the most part these are still in the experimental stage. The unifying factor of party government is less effective than formerly.

A dispersive society reflects itself in pressure groups, each with its own program. Such programs tend to be incorporated in bureaus in the administrative structure of government, where the bureaus continue their active intervention in behalf of their clientele, with a semifreedom from even presidential control. In Congress these dispersive elements are influential in committee memberships and elsewhere, but there are also elements of independence in Congress that curb and filter their excesses considerably. Looseness of party discipline permits this independence. The further problem of an integrated, over-all program—either of legislation or of beneficial inaction—is not yet solved. The Joint Economic Committee seems to be the most hopeful avenue for seeking a solution, but its possibilities are a long way from realization. Now that the Supreme Court has accepted nationalism, the task of safeguarding our federal system has fallen into the lap of Congress. An inherent localism in its viewpoint makes it possible for it to do much in preserving state and local vitality and autonomy and in attending to local interests. Thus Congress is seemingly instrumental in the direction of attaining a reasonably satisfactory equilibrium between the pressure groups and the general interest and between what should be done by the nation and what should be left to the states and localities.

Proposals to strengthen the role of party discipline run up against the probability that this would weaken the very real independence of thought that has developed in Congress in opposition to the special interests and most certainly would accelerate the trend toward centralization that threatens our local self-government.

Congress performs an important function in educating the electorate. It is utilizing new media to perform this function, as well as the time-honored methods of the hearings, reports, and floor debate. The hearings in particular have attained new stature as educators.

Congress has demonstrated its capacity to act quickly in a crisis and to sustain a mood of high purpose in an age of major problems.

In all the foregoing the importance of person-to-person relationships must not be underrated. When acquaintance ripens into mutual confidence, a situation influencing policy almost invariably occurs.

As for its future development and program, it is not necessary to speak in detail. Books have been written on the merits and defects of Congress and the several remedies that are prolifically suggested for the latter. Here let me speak in more general terms.

In the first place, there should be further experiment in the give-and-take of executive-legislative relations. Initiative in policy matters may appropriately be taken by either branch inasmuch as the measures originally suggested by each must be responsibly defended and justified before the other, else they will not become law. In international relations, a special case, the resolution furnishes an appropriate medium whereby Congress may initiate, correct, support, or guide the executive in those critical formative stages prior to matters hardening into a treaty or agreement. In fields in which Congress wishes to experiment before it commits itself semi-irrevocably in detail, the "legislative veto" and measures with terminal dates have already offered hopeful lines of approach to co-operative and continuous action in such matters as plans for executive reorganization. These practices deserve extension.

The dominant position occupied by the pressure groups requires that their tremendous vitality be in fact channeled into the course of the public interest, that their conflicts be constructively resolved, that the over-all economy be kept functioning at an increasingly high level, that the fiscal policy of the government be kept under control. This would seem to call for a more influential position to be accorded to congressional instruments which are charged with the over-all view, such as the Joint Economic Committee. It also calls for constantly more and better staff work throughout congressional activity, designed to uncover the secondary and long-run effects of legislative proposals and to buttress the increasingly large group of members who are seeking to understand such effects prior to debate and voting.

Because of the vast number of issues, and the impossibility

of finding common denominators for party loyalty except by sacrifice of a member's discrimination and by compromise, the present trend toward independence and cross-voting should be encouraged. It is in accord with the rational and ethical elements in our culture; it allows more accurate representation for the states and districts; it promotes government by majority; it promotes intelligent criticism. Procedurally, rules governing the filibuster in the Senate should be modified, so that ultimately the Senate can work its will.

These proposals may seem to some to constitute a very modest program. No constitutional amendment is involved, no very drastic break with current congressional usage. They are advanced in this fashion in part because they lie squarely within the orbit of the proved genius of our Constitution and because they express some of the best strands in our contemporary culture.

We are suspicious of concentrations of unrestrained power, but we also profoundly believe in and have a genius for multiplying the areas of creative and spontaneous action. We seek the success of our economy in equilibriums between the great forces therein operating and not in the triumph of any one of them—in an equilibrium between capital and labor, between producer and consumer, between buyer and seller, between farmer and city man, between independent and chain store, between big and little business.

So also in our government. We seek its success also in equilibriums and balance—between legislature and executive, between state and nation, between party loyalty and independence, between the vitality of the special interests and the over-all viewpoint of the public interest, between a sound nationalism and world responsibilities, between radical and conservative viewpoints, between regionalism and the national view. We would not force or coerce any group or section to the breaking point. We would rather wait for some measure of support from within all major groups or sections before instituting important changes. We are equally suspicious of a too-dominating President and of a Congress which is purely obstructionist. We rebel at the very thought of class warfare. We do not want our parties on class lines. We give great scope to individuals, but we would hold them responsible.

It is highly probable that today no major measure can be passed or major change instituted unless at least a substantial fraction of each of our three major groups—business, agriculture, labor—supports it. Curiously, and unintentionally, each of these groups incorporates its strongest veto power in a particular institution. The over-representation in the Senate of the smaller agricultural states, together with senators from other states with substantial rural populations, guarantees that no important legislation hostile to agriculture can ever pass. Similar guarantees against punitive legislation for business are found in the House of Representatives, in which members from growing suburban districts unite with the conservative representatives of the rural areas and small towns and villages of the East, Middle West and South to give this body a more conservative economic tinge. On his part the President, through his power of veto, may be counted upon to safeguard the position of organized labor against any serious attack, for it is he who is chosen under an electoral system which requires substantial support from the large industrialized states as a condition of success.

Thus the genius of our government expresses itself in a kind of government by common consent.[2] Our Constitution contained within it the principle of equilibrium but left to usage the great flexibility which alone would make this prin-

---

[2] This is akin to the thesis developed in Herbert Agar, *The Price of Union* (Boston: Houghton Mifflin, 1950). See also the eloquent emphasis placed by James Burnham on what he calls "intermediary institutions" in assuming, not plebicitory majorities, but concurrent majorities, as the hallmark of constitutional government. James Burnham, *Congress and the American Tradition* (Chicago: Regnery, 1959), pp. 313–16 *et passim*.

ciple work. It contained within itself in its checks and balances the principle of responsible, official behavior, but it left scope for creative leadership. We can move rapidly in a crisis, but we can also move surely step by step in those great tidal developments in legislation that the age of technology and power seems to demand. These then mark the role and responsibility of Congress in the years ahead: to safeguard the great constitutional principles of a responsible executive and a representative legislature, to preserve and foster the vitality of our states and localities and of the freely functioning economic groups to which we owe our unmatched prosperity, to intervene in the national and world interest when the occasion demands, to operate with independence at that high level of governmental action, rationally and ethically, which our education and our religious faith have made an integral part of the American way. By so doing, Congress will have fought a good fight; it will have kept the faith.

Index

Index of Cases